LETTERS

FROM A

DOUGHBOY

LETTERS
FROM A
DOUGHBOY

THE WARTIME EXPERIENCES OF

ROBERT DOAN TRUESDELL

IN WORLD WAR I

Katherine Truesdell Schumacher

RIT | RIT Press

Letters from a Doughboy: The Wartime Experiences of Robert Doan Truesdell in World War I
Copyright © 2019. Rochester Institute of Technology
and Katherine Truesdell Schumacher.

Published and distributed by:
RIT Press
90 Lomb Memorial Drive
Rochester, New York 14623-5604
http://ritpress.rit.edu

Printed in the U.S.A.
Designed by Marnie Soom
Typeset in Franklin Gothic, Century Old Style, and Bodoni
Printed and bound by More Vang, Alexandria, VA

Cover image: Private Truesdell in front of his tent at Camp Wadsworth.
Title page image: Panorama view of Camp Wadsworth (see page 116).

ISBN 978-1-939125-61-3 (print)
ISBN 978-1-939125-70-5 (ebook)

Library of Congress Cataloging-in-Publication Data

Names: Truesdell, Robert Doan, 1894-1973, author. | Schumacher, Katherine
    Truesdell, editor, writer of added commentary.
Title: Letters from a doughboy : the wartime experiences of Robert Doan
    Truesdell in World War I / Katherine Truesdell Schumacher.
Description: Rochester, New York : RIT Press, [2019] | Includes
    bibliographical references and index.
Identifiers: LCCN 2019012245| ISBN 9781939125613 (soft cover : alk. paper) |
    ISBN 9781939125705 (ebook)
Subjects: LCSH: Truesdell, Robert Doan, 1894-1973—Correspondence. | World
    War, 1914-1918—Personal narratives, American. | United States. Army.
    American Expeditionary Forces—Biography. | Soldiers—United
    States—Correspondence. | Soldiers—United States—Biography.
Classification: LCC D570.9 .T74 2019 | DDC 940.4/1273092 [B] —dc23
LC record available at https://lccn.loc.gov/2019012245

Dedicated to the memory of my father
Robert Doan Truesdell

and also dedicated to
his grandchildren
Sara and Alec

and to
his great-grandchildren
Conor
Isabel
and
Robert

CONTENTS

ACKNOWLEDGMENTS

I am grateful to numerous people who have helped to make this book a reality. First, I want to thank Jim Gandy, Assistant Librarian, and Courtney T. Burns, Chief Curator, of the New York State Military Museum for their help at a time when I was in the initial stages of my research. At a later point, during a tour of World War I sites in France, Great War historian Mitchell Yockelson offered historical context to the places my husband and I visited, as well as helpful advice. During that visit to France, I also benefited from the information provided by Jeffrey Hays, Superintendent, and Stéphane Bonnouvrier, Cemetery Associate, at the Somme American Cemetery. They explained the troop movements of the 27th Division on September 29, 1918, when the division attacked the Hindenburg Line. In Rochester, New York, where I live, I am grateful to Stephen L. Nash, Librarian, Science and History Division, Central Library of Rochester and Monroe County. He made an essential connection for me by referring me to Rochester City Historian Christine Ridarsky, whose careful reading of the manuscript and valuable recommendations resulted in a far stronger submission to the publisher. I am particularly grateful to her. Thanks also go to Daniel Cody, a well-known Rochester professor and WWI historian, who also read the manuscript and encouraged me to move toward publication. I am further grateful to Dr. James Winebrake, Dean of the College of Liberal Arts at Rochester Institute of Technology, for suggesting that I might want to submit my work to the RIT Press. Others at RIT who have been especially helpful include

Elizabeth Torgerson-Lamark, Visual Resource Producer, and Wendy Way, Circulation Services and Outreach Librarian. I am certainly indebted to Dr. Bruce Austin, Director, and Molly Cort, Managing Editor, of the RIT Press. They, along with the anonymous reader whom they engaged, provided very helpful recommendations for strengthening the manuscript. I greatly appreciate their courtesy and professionalism. And finally, I want to thank my husband, Jon L. Schumacher. His steady support and encouragement are deeply appreciated beyond measure.

PROLOGUE

M any Americans today seem to know very little about World War I, a global conflagration fought 100 years ago. The Civil War and World War II are more likely to draw the attention of those who are interested in American military history, but occasionally we might see old photographs in sepia shades that show the dismal realities of trench life, hear about the staggering numbers of soldiers who lost their lives, or read about World War I generals who, more often than not, are remembered for squandering their soldiers' lives. It is these experiences that tend to remind us of the great tragedy of the First World War. The war was indeed global; more than 20 countries on five continents played a part in the conflict. Those who fought in and survived the Great War, as it was initially known, are long gone, but occasionally a soldier's account of his wartime service is newly discovered, and it is that kind of discovery which has produced this addition to wartime remembrances. In his years after the war, Robert Truesdell almost never spoke of his war experience, but he left a record of his service in more than 100 letters written to his parents, beginning with his regiment's arrival at Camp Wadsworth in South Carolina, continuing through his service in France and Belgium, and ending with his participation in the 27th Division's victory parade in New York City following his return from France after the Armistice. Many years after his death, his daughter, Katherine Truesdell Schumacher, discovered the letters, which had been kept, along with his last uniform, gas mask, and other personal items from WWI, in an old trunk in the attic. The letters represent a great mix of reflections and information. Some of the subjects pertain to matters of only family and local interest. Other subjects reflect the experiences and observations of a young man who has heretofore not traveled at all widely but who sees not only the South in the United States but the killing fields of Belgium and France and the great cities of Paris and London as well. Of course the letters written abroad, like all letters sent by soldiers, were subject to censorship, a policy meant to avoid releasing information that could be useful to the enemy.

Although Robert Truesdell's letters are often longer and perhaps more detailed than those of many other soldiers, they nonetheless tend to be typical of soldiers' correspondence during the war. Historian and literary critic Paul Fussell notes that letters written by British soldiers, especially when they were censored after troops went abroad, tended to follow a pattern: The writer says he is well and hopes the recipient is also well; he comments on the weather; he expresses thanks for what-ever the recipient has sent him—letters or perhaps parcels with such things as socks, caps, or cigarettes; and he sends his regards to those at home.[1] It is quite likely that letters written by American soldiers were similar. Certain phrases that soldiers used 100 years ago may seem quaint now. For example, British soldiers seemed to favor describing themselves as feeling "in the pink," whereas Robert Truesdell often reassures his parents that he is "finer than silk" or "fit as a fiddle." Fussell also refers to the claim that wartime letters became "a kind of literature of their own."[2] In general, while soldiers occasionally described with candor some difficult or dangerous aspect of their training or front-line experience, they usually seem to have been solicitous of the feelings of those at home. It was probably better to assure families and friends on the home front that a positive attitude prevailed.

Infantrymen who fought in World War I, such as Robert Truesdell, were known as "doughboys." Although there has never been entire agreement about the origin of the term, one explanation is that infan-trymen stationed in the American Southwest became so covered with dirt and dust after a long march that cavalrymen said the foot soldiers looked like adobe, a building material common in that part of the U.S. Usage of the word "adobe" in reference to the soldiers gradually turned "adobe" into "doughboy." Another explanation is that the buttons on soldiers' uniforms looked like lumps of dough and thus the soldiers themselves began to be called doughboys.[3] In any case, like the British "Tommy" and French "poilu," the informal term "doughboy" was the way that American infantrymen referred to themselves—rather than "Sammy," referring to Uncle Sam, and "Yank," which were also terms sometimes applied to the American soldier.

Robert D. Truesdell was born in 1894 in Binghamton, New York, and grew up there. After graduating from high school, he went to work for his father's company, Newell and Truesdell Co., Importers and Wholesale Grocers. He began as a salesman and traveled to numerous small towns in a widespread area around Binghamton to take orders for products sold by "New and True." He continued to live at home with his father Edwin S. Truesdell, Sr., stepmother Lilian Root Truesdell, and sister Edith (Ede), who supported the war effort on the homefront. He also had an older brother, Edwin, Jr. (Ed), who saw service in the army as well, although never abroad. As a young man with an outgoing and affable personality, Robert (Bob) apparently had an active social life and a comfortable existence. When the United States declared war on Germany in 1917, he was about to celebrate his 23rd birthday. He registered, as required, but soon enlisted in the 1st New York Infantry Regiment of the National Guard, and, as of July 15, 1917, became one of the many thousands of American young men about to experience an entirely different existence.

Now as we mark the passing of 100 years since the Great War, readers may find a young doughboy's correspondence, so well preserved, to be of some historical interest. The reader will undoubtedly come across occasional errors in grammar, punctuation, spelling or other mechanics, but the letters have intentionally been left in their original form.

Letters from a Doughboy with accompanying commentary placing the letters in historical context is intended to be a useful resource to those particularly interested in learning more about the day-to-day doughboy experience. Much of the contextual material touches on Pvt.

Truesdell's own experiences; other times the historical context is broader, reflecting a "bigger picture" of the war. Thus, the commentary occasionally includes references to military actions in farflung parts of the world as a reminder of the worldwide nature of the war. Whether one is studying the American soldier's life during the Great War in a classroom setting or simply hoping to extend his or her knowledge of World War I from the point of view of an infantryman, these letters and commentary will provide added information to the interested reader.

Notes

1   Fussell, *The Great War and Modern Memory*, 182–183.
2   Ibid., 182.
3   Yockelson, *Borrowed Soldiers: Americans under British Command, 1918*, 241.

THE WAR YEARS LEADING TO
AMERICAN INVOLVEMENT

As an American citizen, Robert Truesdell didn't become a soldier until a point shortly after the United States declared war on Germany on April 6, 1917, but he surely must have been aware of the months-long battles and appalling losses seen not only on the Western Front but on the Eastern and Italian fronts as well as in various places around the globe. He was also probably aware of the unprecedented use of unrestricted submarine warfare, lethal poison gas, and deadly machine guns, as well as airplanes designed for reconnaissance and bombing, and if he didn't know about tanks, he would soon learn about their use, as he writes in one of his letters. We do know from his letters, when he asks for newspapers to be sent to him, that he was accustomed to following the news, so he probably had read about the way the war began and progressed. And as he read those accounts, he may have wondered, just as we do now 100 years later, how the world found itself engaged in such savage warfare.

Over the years, historians have indeed studied the conditions that led to the outbreak of war and cite various possible explanations, such as the arms race, militarism, imperialism, nationalism, revenge, Social Darwinism, the ambitions of rising nations, the fears of weakened nations, and the formation of alliances in which nations agreed to come to the assistance of their allies in wartime.[1] Two main alliances existed in Europe in the early 20th century: Britain, France, and Russia formed the Triple Entente, and with the subsequent addition of Italy, the alliance became known as the Allied Powers; Germany, Austria-Hungary, and Italy formed the Triple Alliance, but Italy quickly dropped out of the Triple Alliance at the beginning of the war. Germany and Austria-Hungary, later joined by Bulgaria and Turkey, became the Central Powers.[2] In addition, domestic pressures, including growing labor movements, revolutionary movements, class conflict, and the struggle for women's suffrage have been cited as conditions leading to World War I.[3]

It was against the backdrop of these conditions that Archduke Franz Ferdinand, heir to the throne of Austria-Hungary, and his wife were assassinated during a formal visit to Sarajevo, Bosnia, on June 28, 1914. The assassin Gavrilo Princip, a young Bosnian Serb, was a member of Young Bosnia, a radical patriotic organization influenced by the deeply secret Serb nationalist group known as the Black Hand.[4] Although no blame for the assassination could be traced to the official Serb government, Austria-Hungary nonetheless blamed Serbia and, after seeking support from its ally Germany, sent an ultimatum to Serbia. The Serbs accepted almost all of the conditions of the ultimatum—but not all, with the result that Austria-Hungary declared war on Serbia on July 28, 1914.[5]

This declaration of war quickly led to hostilities beyond the Balkans. Russia, which considered Serbia its "little brother," ordered general mobilization. Germany, in support of Austria-Hungary, soon declared war on Russia. Since Russia and France were allies and since Germany did not want to fight a two-front war—east and west Germany put into effect its war plan known as the Schlieffen Plan, which called for invading France through neutral Belgium, fighting a swift victorious war in France—a war that would take about six weeks—and then turning its might on Russia. Despite Belgium's confirming its neutrality, Germany invaded the smaller country on its way to France.[6] In turn, Britain, an ally of France and Russia and supporter of the neutral Belgium, declared war on Germany. Austria-Hungary, further drawn into the web, declared war on Russia.[7]

Belgium put up a stronger defense than expected, but facing truly formidable German forces, Brussels soon fell.[8] The small but highly skilled British army, having initiated its landing in France and rushing to defend Belgium, was forced to fall back. The way was then open for the Germans to enter France.[9]

Meanwhile, the French sent five armies, still in 19th-century uniforms of blue jackets and red trousers, to Alsace and Lorraine, provinces that had been lost to Germany in the Franco-Prussian War of 1870–1871 and for which France had sought revenge and recovery of the lost territory. Despite fighting with élan, an important part of French military doctrine, the French faced a disaster. In just a few days, the French army had suffered horrendous losses—more than 200,000 casualties, including 75,000 who had been killed. Bravery had not been able to overcome machine guns.[10]

With weakened supply lines, the Germans wheeled inward, moving northeast of Paris toward the Marne River. It was here that the French and British made a broad counterattack in early to mid-September. During this First Battle of the Marne, the military governor of Paris famously transported infantry troops to the front in taxis; the Germans, forced to retreat northward, fell back to positions north of the Aisne River.[11] With deadlock on the Aisne eastward, the enemies tried, throughout the fall months, to outflank each other to the west and north and ended up establishing lines of trenches, which introduced static warfare that lasted until 1918.[12] The trench lines stretched from the North Sea to Switzerland, a distance of more than 400 miles.[13] The Belgians held the top 40 miles—north of Ypres, the British held the next 90 miles, and, to the south, the French held the rest.[14] Both sides experienced enormous loss of life when they clashed in late October and early November in the First Battle of Ypres, and while it was supposedly considered an Allied victory, in reality neither side made any progress and stalemate settled in.[15] Christmas 1914 became memorable when an unofficial truce in Flanders brought British and German soldiers together to celebrate in No Man's Land. Such fraternization was quickly squelched.[16]

British casualties in 1914 were so heavy—around 90,000[17]—that Britain was forced to compensate by drawing several divisions from overseas garrisons, and Lord Horatio Kitchener, Secretary of State for War, began a program of military expansion with a call for 100,000 volunteers to form "New Armies."[18] The United States, when it later entered the war in 1917, had to take similar action by building a large fighting force to supplement its small army.

Horrendous casualties occurred on the Eastern Front as well. The Russians suffered an enormous defeat in the Battle of Tannenberg in the late summer of 1914. They lost nearly 100,000 men (killed, wounded, taken prisoner)—and their commander shot himself.[19] The Germans' Tannenberg success made their commander, General Paul von Hindenburg, a national hero, and the military reputation of his chief of staff, Erich Ludendorff, quickly expanded. The Austro-Hungarians meanwhile faced more tenacious Serbian forces than they had expected and suffered 230,000 casualties against a Serbian loss of 170,000.[20] Losses on this scale were clearly a horrific development in warfare.

Early in the war, Britain began its blockade of German ports to limit imports and exports. In time the blockade became, in part, a reason that food supplies drastically declined in Germany.[21] In the spring of 1915, Allied troops landed at Gallipoli in an attempt to attack the Ottoman army; the months-long battle, lasting until January 1916, was a dismal failure. The most successful part of that venture was its well-managed evacuation of troops, but when that whole sad story ended, there had been half a million Allied casualties, mainly British, approximately twice those of the Turks.[22]

Also in the early months of 1915, the Germans declared unrestricted submarine warfare and in May sank the passenger liner *Lusitania* off the coast of Ireland; 1,201 lives, including 128 American citizens, were lost. President Woodrow Wilson soon lodged a protest against the German policy of unconditional submarine warfare with the result that Germany agreed to warn passenger ships of an impending U-boat attack.[23] Besides the introduction of submarine warfare, the Germans introduced gas as a weapon of war on the Western Front in April during the Second Battle of Ypres; despite the ensuing panic, the British Expeditionary Force (BEF) was finally able to halt the German onslaught.[24] Gas warfare, on both sides, continued throughout the war. Also in the spring, the BEF made an attempt to reduce the large

German salient in northeast France. After initial British success, the Germans made a counterattack and recaptured the lost ground. The British, including troops from India, suffered 11,200 casualties, and the Germans lost about the same number.[25] Two months later, in May, the British tried again and made some initial gains, but success again turned into disaster.[26] About the same time, German airships began to make raids on London; these raids continued throughout the year and into 1916.[27] World War I was entering a new terrifying era in warfare as the very nature of warfare was changing.

In the fall, both the French and British attempted attacks on the broad German salient in northeast France—but with little success. High casualty rates continued, and with counteroffensives following the offensives, the lines remained much the same. Consequently, the British commanding general Sir John French was relieved of his command and replaced by Sir Douglas Haig, who retained his position for the rest of the war.[28] Overall, like the previous year, 1915 ended in stalemate.

In 1916, two prolonged battles took place: Verdun and the Somme. In February Germany attacked Verdun, a heavily fortified city in eastern France. The Germans were correct in thinking that France would defend Verdun, one of the last cities to fall in the Franco-Prussian War of 1871, at great cost.[29] The intent was indeed "to bleed France white," not necessarily to capture territory.[30] Despite the fall of Fort Douaumont, the centerpiece of the Verdun fortifications, the German commitment to the offensive diminished during the summer. Douaumont was recaptured by the French in late October, and the battle finally came to a close in mid-December.[31] In the end, Germany as well as France paid a great price—French casualties numbered 460,000, and German casualties were 300,000.[32]

Although, during the previous year, the French and British had begun to plan an attack on the Germans in the area of the Somme during the summer of 1916, it became particularly important to the French to draw the German army away from Verdun. Thus, the British, with French support, attacked the Germans on the Somme on July 1.[33] The Battle of the Somme, actually a series of battles, lasted until

November 18 when it was formally closed down.[34] Perhaps the Somme is most notably, and most sadly, remembered because of the tragedy of the first day, when more than 19,000 British soldiers were killed. By the time the battle ended, the casualties numbered more than 400,000 British soldiers, 200,000 French soldiers, and 650,000 German soldiers.[35] The numbers of losses were staggering.

Meanwhile, early in 1916, Russia lost 100,000 soldiers in a poorly managed offensive with no gains,[36] and later in the year, a new offensive, while considered a victory, left the poorly equipped Russian army in a state of plunging morale[37] that would lead to revolution and the abdication of Tsar Nicholas II the following year. Allied success was elusive in the Middle East as well. The British, who had conducted an offensive aimed at reaching Baghdad but who had been besieged in Kut al-Amara, were forced to capitulate and wouldn't be able to recapture the town and reach Baghdad until the following year.[38] The British claimed victory, however, in the Battle of Jutland, the only major naval battle of World War I; the Germans also claimed victory, but the German High Seas Fleet returned to port, where it stayed for the rest of the war.[39]

The year 1916 also saw the appointment of Generals Paul von Hindenburg and Erich Ludendorff, the latter taking the rank of first quartermaster general,[40] to command the German army on the Western Front. With their armies severely depleted as a result of the Verdun and Somme battles, Hindenburg and Ludendorff decided to form a new defensive position, later known as the Hindenburg Line, a line between Arras and St. Quentin that would strengthen the German front.[41] France also saw a military reshuffle. General Joseph Joffre, considered "stale," was named Marshal of France because of his devoted military service and was replaced by General Robert Nivelle, who became the commander of the French armies on the Western Front.[42] Both the Allies and Central Powers were hoping that a change in leadership would help to break the stalemate.

In the Middle East during the fall of 1916, another change took place. Thomas Edward Lawrence, a British Army captain, met with the Arab leaders who wanted to be free of the Turks. "Lawrence of Arabia" was successful in uniting the Arab tribes, but his success was "manipulated by the British and French, not to liberate the Arabs from the Turks, but to carve up Arab lands into largely artificial states to suit their own strategic and commercial interests."[43]

Meanwhile, after Francisco "Pancho" Villa attacked Columbus, New Mexico, in March 1916 and killed 18 American citizens,[44] General John Pershing was sent with a United States Army expedition force in pursuit of Villa.[45] American troops were never successful in capturing Villa, and, following mediation between the United States and Mexico, Pershing and his troops were withdrawn.[46] During the latter months of 1916, President Wilson successfully campaigned on a platform of neutrality for re-election in November but was unsuccessful thereafter when he tried, with continuing stalemate on the Western Front, to initiate mediation among the warring nations by asking them to state their peace terms.[47]

However, in early 1917, none of the belligerents were interested in a negotiated peace. Both sides sought a clear-cut victory. Anything less would have been viewed as a betrayal of those who had lost their lives in the national cause.[48] Germany forged on and, despite the risk of angering the United States, resumed unconditional submarine warfare on February 1, 1917. This indeed caused the United States to break off diplomatic relations with Germany within two days.[49] Shortly thereafter, Britain passed along to the U.S. a decoded telegram, known as the Zimmermann Telegram, which Britain's intelligence service had intercepted. The telegram was a message from Germany to Mexico, in which Germany offered Mexico a deal: upon victory, Mexico would regain New Mexico, Texas, and Arizona in return for declaring war on the United States. The contents of the Zimmermann Telegram were soon made public, causing American public opinion to shift more solidly in favor of the Allies.[50] President Wilson was now finally convinced that he must ask Congress for a declaration of war against Germany. The Senate and House quickly supported him, with the result that the United States declared war on Imperial Germany on April 6, 1917.[51]

On the Western Front, the British persevered in the spring with offensives south of Ypres, where they made modest gains.[52] After several weeks, they continued their offensive by opening what became known as the Battle of Passchendaele (Third Battle of Ypres).[53] The French, under Gen. Nivelle, also began an offensive in spring 1917. The offensive, in Champagne, proved to be a tragic fiasco. French casualties numbered 187,000 against German losses of 168,000. Nivelle was soon replaced by General Henri-Philippe Pétain, who then had to repair the damages in morale resulting from a mutinous army.[54] Stalemate continued; neither side was reaching the victory it sought.

Back in the United States, Gen. Pershing was appointed commander of the American Expeditionary Forces (A.E.F.), and shortly thereafter, President Wilson signed the Selective Service Act, which authorized wartime conscription. The first national draft registration day took place on June 5, 1917.[55] Conscription was necessary because the Regular Army was small: 5,791 officers and 121,707 enlisted men. The National Guard could strengthen those numbers, but Guard units added only 110,000 officers and men. Consequently, some 24 million men, ages 21 to 30, registered.[56] From that registration, draftees would be selected for the National Army to supplement the Regular Army (professional soldiers) and National Guard (state militia). Regular Army divisions had numbers 1-25, National Guard divisions were numbered 26-75 (although only about half of those numbers were actually used), and the National Army received numbers over 75.[57] The American 1st Division arrived in France in late June; other divisions that followed by the end of the year included the 2nd (half Regular Army and half Marines), the 26th (New England National Guard), and the 42nd ("Rainbow Division").[58] Upon arrival in France, these divisions, as well as other divisions arriving later, underwent further intensive training.[59]

Robert Truesdell enlisted June 24 in the 1st Infantry Regiment of the New York State National Guard. Assigned to the Headquarters Company of the 1st Infantry Regiment, he and other members of the local units of the New York State National Guard were mustered at the State Armory in Binghamton on July 15, 1917. After drilling for a few weeks at the armory (Pvt. Truesdell tells us that he left Binghamton on August 18), the local units were sent to Van Cortlandt Park, New York City, for further training. The upstate soldiers spent a little more than a month getting used to camp life, hiking, and learning regimental maneuvers in the park. On September 25, the regiment boarded trains at Pennsylvania Station in New York City and began a rail journey to Camp Wadsworth near Spartanburg, South Carolina. Two days later, the regiment arrived at the newly established training camp and detrained from their Pullman sleepers in a steady rain. Plodding "through a sea of soft, oozy mud for about three miles," they reached their campsite in an area that was still partially forested. The men then began a regimen of clearing land and digging up stumps, undertaking regular camp duties, and drilling under the direction of their officers, Captain Floyd McLean and Lieutenants Harry Darling and Morris Knapp.[60]

Camp Wadsworth, designated for training the New York State National Guard 27th Division, was one of many new training camps that had to be quickly established in order to train young civilians to be soldiers. The new camps were usually named for American military heroes.[61] Camp Wadsworth was named in honor of James Wadsworth, a former U.S. Senator and Union Army officer who had been killed in the Civil War.[62] Typically, National Guard regiments were sent to the warmer sections of the country, where canvas tents, each accommodating a squad of 10 or 11 men, were used as shelters for the troops as opposed to the more permanent barracks housing Regular and National Army regiments.[63]

Robert Truesdell indicates in his first letter that he, along with others in his regiment, had a comfortable train trip in Pullman cars from New York City to Camp Wadsworth. However, the chaotic arrival at the camp abruptly ended any sense of comfort, and it is at this point that he begins the account of his experiences as a doughboy.

Notes

1   MacMillan, *The Road to 1914: The War That Ended Peace*, xxv–xxvi.
2   Matloff, *World War I: A Concise Military History of "The War to End All Wars" and The Road to the War*, 55.
3   MacMillan, *The Road to 1914: The War That Ended Peace*, xxvi.

4   Meyer, *A World Undone: The Story of the Great War 1914–1918*, 6.

5   Persico, *Eleventh Month, Eleventh Day, Eleventh Hour*, 18–19.

6   Ibid., 21–22.

7   Ibid., 23.

8   Morgan, *The Concise History of WWI*, 16–17.

9   Ibid., 23.

10   Stevens, *The Great War Explained*, 13.

11   Simkins, Jukes, and Hickey, *The First World War: The War to End All Wars*, 52–53.

12   Morgan, *The Concise History of WWI*, 27.

13   Yorke, *The Trench: Life and Death on the Western Front 1914–1918*, 15.

14   Fussell, *The Great War and Modern Memory*, 36.

15   Morgan, *The Concise History of WWI*, 27.

16   Meyer, *A World Undone: The Story of the Great War 1914–1918*, 237.

17   Simkins, Jukes, and Hickey, *The First World War: The War to End All Wars*, 62.

18   Ibid.

19   Grant, *World War I: The Definitive Visual History*, 64–65.

20   Persico, *Eleventh Month, Eleventh Day, Eleventh Hour*, 42.

21   Stone, *World War One*, 67–68.

22   Ibid., 73.

23   Ibid,, 120.

24   Simkins, Jukes, and Hickey, *The First World War: The War to End All Wars*, 67–68.

25   Morgan, *The Concise History of WWI*, 28.

26   Fussell, *The Great War and Modern Memory*, 10.

27   Simkins, Jukes, and Hickey, *The First World War: The War to End All Wars*, 108.

28   Stevens, *The Great War Explained*, 39–40.

29   Keene, *World War I: The American Soldier Experience*, 12.

30   Stevens, *The Great War Explained*, 45.

31   Ibid., 55–56.

32 Matloff, *World War I: A Concise Military History of "The War to End All Wars" and The Road to the War*, 66.

33 Morgan, *The Concise History of WWI*, 38.

34 Stevens, *The Great War Explained*, 89.

35 Keene, *World War I: The American Soldier Experience*, 12.

36 Stone, *World War One*, 97–98.

37 Meyer, *A World Undone: The Story of the Great War 1914–1918*, 426–427.

38 Morgan, *The Concise History of WWI*, 93.

39 Persico, *Eleventh Month, Eleventh Day, Eleventh Hour*, 88.

40 Simkins, Jukes, and Hickey, *The First World War: The War to End All Wars*, 21.

41 Meyer, *A World Undone: The Story of the Great War 1914–1918*, 491–492.

42 Persico, *Eleventh Month, Eleventh Day, Eleventh Hour*, 123.

43 Ibid., 120.

44 Lacey, *Pershing*, 77.

45 Ibid., 79.

46 Ibid., 81–82.

47 Grant, *World War I: The Definitive Visual History*, 214.

48 Simkins, Jukes, and Hickey, *The First World War: The War to End All Wars*, 116.

49 Keene, *World War I: The American Soldier Experience*, xii.

50 Ibid., 10.

51 Ibid., 10–11.

52 Morgan, *The Concise History of WWI, 47–48.*

53 Stone, *World War One*, 138–139.

54 Morgan, *The Concise History of WWI*, 51–52.

55 Keene, *World War I: The American Soldier Experience*, xii–xiii.

56 Yockelson, *Borrowed Soldiers: Americans under British Command, 1918*, 3–4.

57 Ibid., 21.

58 Lacey, *Pershing*, 125–126.

59 Hart, *The Great War: A Combat History of the First World War*, 412.

60 Seward, *Binghamton and Broome County, New York, A History, Vol. I*, 575.

61 Van Ells, *America and World War I: A Traveler's Guide*, 50.

62 Yockelson, *Borrowed Soldiers: Americans under British Command, 1918*, 22.

63 Ibid., 21–22.

THE LETTERS WITH COMMENTARY

TRAINING AT CAMP WADSWORTH IN THE FALL AND EARLY WINTER OF 1917

The New Yorkers' arrival at Camp Wadsworth was confusing and disheartening. The circumstances were made more difficult by the heavy rain and deep mud, and beyond that, general disorganization seemed to pervade the movement from the siding where the men detrained to the actual campsite. In addition to the dismal weather, many of the men's feelings were probably influenced by the fact that they had not often been far from home and were beginning to feel homesick. Private Truesdell claims he is not homesick, but the very fact that he mentions it suggests that he really misses the familiar scenes of hometown Binghamton. Fortunately, he knew a number of Binghamton men who were also starting their training at Wadsworth. Whether he was a close friend of any of these men before he enlisted is unknown, but clearly he enjoys getting together with several of the "Binghamton boys" whenever possible. Names such as Ford (Tod) Mulford, Bill Bloomer, Bud Sheak, Russ Tuttle, Carlton (Clevey) Cleveland, Lem Larrabee, Dave Murray, and Bob Harris appear in Pvt. Truesdell's letters with some frequency. These bonds of friendship cause the men to feel concern when they hear a rumor that they may be split up and shifted to other units.

In his first letter, Pvt. Truesdell alludes to a rumor that some or all of the men in the 1st New York Infantry Regiment might be shifted to the 7th New York Regiment or vice versa. In fact, as Gerald Jacobson explains in *History of the 107th Infantry U.S.A.,* "an order changing the designation of the Seventh New York Infantry to the 107th Infantry, U.S.A., and assigning the regiment with the 108th Infantry to the 54th Infantry Brigade was issued from the Division Headquarters on October 1. By the same order, the designation of the division was changed from the 6th to the 27th."[1] The men of the 1st New York Infantry Regiment may not have been aware that the 7th New York would become the 107th U.S.A., but in any case, it soon becomes obvious that changing to a different regiment is disturbing to young men who thought they would be staying together throughout their war service. Nonetheless, William Seward reports in his history of Binghamton, New York that the 1st New York Regiment received orders that it would be split, "most of the men going to join the 7th New York, which was to be known as the 107th U.S. Infantry while detachments were to be sent to the 102nd U.S. Engineers and the 106th Field Artillery. Captain McLean and a few non-commissioned officers were to remain under the Command of Colonel Boyer, to form the First Pioneer Infantry."[2]

Perhaps the men of the 1st New York Regiment were concerned about changing to the 7th New York Regiment, known as the "Silk Stocking Regiment," because they thought that the men of the 7th came from a different, more affluent background. As Stephen Harris writes, the 7th was made up of "society boys many of them; silk stocking soldiers from uptown Manhattan or the wealthier suburbs of New York" while soldiers in the 1st New York, known as "appleknockers,"[3] came from a variety of small upstate cities and towns, as follows: Company A, Utica; B, Utica; C, Watertown; D, Ogdensburg; E, Newburgh; F, Walton; G, Oneonta; H, Binghamton; I, Middletown; K, Malone; L, Newburgh; M, Mohawk; Machine Gun, Utica; Headquarters Company, Binghamton; and Regimental Headquarters, Binghamton.[4] No doubt it was also difficult for many of the members of the "Silk Stocking Regiment" to accept the "appleknockers" from upstate.

In any case, around the middle of October 1917, some 1,600 men from the 1st New York Infantry, 320 men from the 12th New York Infantry, and a few men from the 10th New York Infantry were transferred to the 107th Infantry. The increased number of men in the 107th, now numbering 3,699, meant that the regiment was close to full war strength. Most of the men went to a company with a designation like that of their original company.[5]

According to Seward's history regarding the change of most of the 1st Infantry Regiment men to the 7th (107th), Col. Boyer told the men that "if they served under their new officers as they had him, there was no doubt but the enemy would be kept on the run. 'The Seventh Regiment has every reason to be proud of the type of men which they are receiving from the Old First,' he said."[6]

These various changes in part reflected an overhaul of the Army's structure. American divisions were large, approximately 28,000 men, twice the size of the Allies' divisions. An American "square" division had two infantry brigades; each brigade had two regiments.[7] The commanding officer of the 27th Division was 42-year-old Major Gen. John F. O'Ryan, the youngest commander of a division in the United States Army.[8] Just at the time that the 27th Division was being reorganized, Gen. O'Ryan received orders to leave for France. He joined five other divisional commanders and began an extensive tour of both British and French front lines[9] before returning to Camp Wadsworth in late November.[10]

One part of the Army's reorganization plan was the reduction of the need for cavalry units. Although Pvt. Truesdell mentions in one of his letters that there is a cavalry unit at Camp Wadsworth, by the time the U.S. entered the war, cavalry units were not being used very often. As the war progressed, both the Allies and Central Powers realized that cavalry was impractical in combat involving barbed wire and machine guns. Units of cavalry were replaced mostly by tanks.[11] However, large numbers of horses and mules were still necessary for transport and hauling.

For the first weeks at Camp Wadsworth, the men underwent a training program concentrating on disciplinary drill and physical exercise. By late October 1917, instructors from the French and British armies began to arrive. The French officers were predominately artillery specialists; the British officers provided training primarily in gas warfare and bayonet drill.[12] As Trevor Yorke explains,

Perhaps the most feared weapon when it was first introduced by the Germans was poison gas. There was chlorine gas which caused the tissue in the lungs to burn and soldiers to fall to the ground convulsing, choking and eventually dying. Phosgene was even more deadly, accounting for most gas-related fatalities during the war. The most notorious was mustard gas which, although it rarely killed, rendered soldiers incapacitated with horrific blisters on the skin, internal bleeding and the removal of the lining of the tubes leading to the mouth and nose.[13]

Regarding bayonet drill, according to the *History of Company "E", 107th Infantry 54th Brigade, 27th Division U.S.A., (National Guard, New York), 1917-1919*, bayonet instruction was a major part of the training schedule. With bayonets, the men practiced "leaping in and out of trenches, thrusting at the dummies, executing butt swings and strikes."[14]

In early October, Pvt. Truesdell tells us that he has had signal practice, an area of army work to which he was subsequently assigned and in which he remained for the duration of the war. One of the few times that Robert Truesdell spoke of his war experiences in later years was in connection to repairing disconnected lines, an extremely dangerous job that was one of the responsibilities of signalmen on the front lines. In *History of the 107th Infantry U.S.A.*, Jacobson notes that each squad was to be trained in a particular form of warfare and was assigned to one of the various classes specializing in some form of army tactics. The expectation was that when the regiment became engaged in actual warfare, each squad of every company would carry out its specialized work and each man within the squad would perform a particular job.[15]

One of the early tasks undertaken by the military at Camp Wadsworth was digging trenches. Although trenches were not a new technique for defense, in World War I trench warfare had become synonymous with the Western Front. The trenches at Camp Wadsworth, which wove through the hills, valleys, and woods near the camp, were laid out by the engineers, but the actual digging was done, with pick and shovel, by the infantry of the entire division. Pvt. Truesdell writes that "the trenches are laid out exactly as they are in France....They are being dug seven to nine feet in depth and three feet wide." Three lines of trenches were dug—frontline, support, and reserve—and altogether the lines totaled about eight miles. After the trench system was completed in mid-November, each battalion was assigned to occupy the trenches for 24 hours; a later tour of duty would last 72 hours.[16] The men had to begin learning the proper procedures for relieving the previous battalion, performing stand-to and stand-down, organizing patrols, and simulating all the work that had to be done in the trenches of France.[17]

It is unlikely that Pvt.Truesdell and the other soldiers-in-training were familiar with the realities of trench life that lay ahead. Soldiers in the trenches certainly faced periods of terrifying danger, but they also experienced times of extreme boredom.[18] Those who had trench duty learned that there was a good deal of variation in trench construction from place to place. For example, in the Somme area where the soil was chalky and likely to crumble after a rain, trench walls were usually lined with timber or sandbags.[19] On the enemy side of the trench, the men built a parapet of earth or sandbags; the parapet was two or three feet above ground. On the "friendly" side of the trench, a corresponding parados was built one or two feet high. Out in No Man's Land, the neutral space between the enemies' front lines, barbed wire entanglements were placed far enough in front of the trench to keep the enemy from being able to throw grenades into the trench.[20] In contrast, in Flanders where the water table was high, timber and sandbags were used to build upward above the sides of shallow trenches. As trench lines developed, a formalized pattern began to take shape. Front-line trenches or fire trenches facing the enemy sometimes followed the natural contours of the land; other times they were dug with bays so that any infiltrating enemy could be contained. Saps—narrow trenches extending from the front-line trench—ended in No Man's Land, where one or two soldiers were supposed, if possible, to listen to and observe the enemy. Behind the fire line (perhaps as much as several hundred yards) was the support trench, usually with dugouts carved out of the trench wall. Dugouts were places where a few men could rest or where signaling could take place. Duckboards, a slatted wood flooring, usually covered the trench floor. Behind the support trench (around another several hundred yards) was the reserve trench. Communication trenches connected the trenches with the rear; these trenches were used for troop movement to and from the rear and for the delivery of ammunition and supplies. Soldiers typically served in a rotation from the fire trench to the support trench to a reserve trench and then to a period of rest before repeating the cycle.[21]

Each morning, an hour before sunrise, troops in the fire trench were ordered to "stand to." They checked that their rifles were fully loaded, fixed bayonets, and climbed up to the fire step, cut from the front wall of the trench two to three feet above the trench floor. This practice was followed because offensives usually began at dawn. Thereafter, the cleaning and inspection of rifles took place, followed by breakfast, during which, in some places, a breakfast truce was observed by both sides so that the men could eat in peace and quiet. The day continued with trench wall and floor repair and various other jobs, but the days were often very boring. Soldiers sometimes used this time for sleeping or writing letters home. Around dusk, "stand to" was repeated, and then other assignments were made.[22] Such assignments might include bringing rations forward, repairing barbed wire entanglements, or being sent out into No Man's Land on a patrol.[23] Soldiers had to face not only enemy attacks but also the dangers, right in their own trenches, resulting from large numbers of rats, which spread disease and contaminated food. The soldiers used any method they could think of to get rid of them. Lice were another hazard to anyone serving in a trench. Lice were almost impossible to get rid of and were found to be the cause of trench fever. Trench foot, resulting from standing in wet trenches, was still another hazard. And finally, beside these horrible conditions in the trenches, soldiers experienced the awful smells associated with trench life: the stench of bodies long unwashed, the foul odor of rotting corpses, and the disgusting stink of latrines.[24] These were the conditions that the men digging trenches at Camp Wadsworth would later face in Europe.

When the opportunity arose, the soldiers at Camp Wadsworth went to nearby Spartanburg to get a good meal, do some errands, or enjoy some entertainment. The men might have an occasional meal at the Cleveland Hotel, the Finch Hotel, or a local restaurant in Spartanburg or enjoy an evening of entertainment at a vaudeville or moving picture house. They also were sometimes invited to the homes of townspeople[25] for a greatly prized home-cooked dinner. Pvt. Truesdell writes about such an experience in one of his letters.

However, going to and from Spartanburg was not always smooth. On October 17, about 300 soldiers were on their way to the Cleveland Hotel for a dance. They were on the interurban that ran from the camp's northern border to town when the interurban was hit from behind by a work train.[26] As Pvt.Truesdell reports, several men were killed and "scores of others were injured, many seriously."

Relations between Camp Wadsworth and segregated Spartanburg proved difficult. Pvt. Truesdell writes that the 15th New York Infantry, composed of African Americans, has just left Camp Wadsworth, a result of several incidents of racial tension in Spartanburg. While the residents of Spartanburg received white soldiers from New York State very hospitably, they resented the presence of black soldiers when the latter wanted to enter a store or hotel or use the sidewalk, which Southerners reserved for white people only.[27] After several examples of heated confrontations resulting in near violence, the Army sent the 15th to a different location.

Meanwhile in Europe, the fall months for the Allies were grim. The Italians, fighting on the side of the Allies since May 1915, were routed in late October by the Austrians in the Battle of Caporetto. British and French divisions were hurriedly sent to Italy to shore up the Italians.[28] The Austrians and Germans, far from railheads and supplies, finally called off their offensive on December 2.[29] Also in the fall of 1917, the British Army was mired in the costly Third Battle of Ypres, or Passchendaele. British "Tommies" experienced untold misery until the operation came to a close on November 6 following the capture of the village of Passchendaele. After this "victory," Gen. Douglas Haig called off the offensive. British casualties sustained in Third Ypres are estimated between 200,000 and 448,000 against German casualties ranging from 217,000 to 410,000.[30]

Despite the tragedy of Passchendaele, the British persevered with another offensive, this time near Cambrai. The attack began on November 20, and with heavy support from tanks, aerial reconnaissance, and more advanced use of artillery, the British "won an immediate success, with a considerable advance and a large capture of prisoners and guns. In England, the church bells were rung." However, the British advanced beyond their supply lines, the Germans counterattacked, and Haig had no reserves, so the offensive ground to a halt.[31] Although the Battle of Cambrai did not meet British expectations, it did indicate the growing effectiveness of tanks. Following a short but intense artillery attack, the infantry and tanks moved forward under a creeping barrage and made a significant initial advance before the German counterattack.[32] These tactics would bode well for the future.

The news of the success that the British initially experienced when they attacked the German front with tanks near Cambrai was greeted with great joy not only in England, but apparently also reached the soldiers at Camp Wadsworth. In his letter of November 29, when Pvt. Truesdell mentions the "great drive" made by the British the previous week, he is probably referring to the attack at Cambrai. However, he seems unaware that in subsequent days the British had not made continued progress and that the offensive had died away.

Further, the news from the Eastern Front was disappointing. On November 7, 1917, the Russian Provisional Government, which had seized power the previous March, was overthrown by the Bolsheviks.[33] The following month, the Bolshevik Russian government signed an armistice with Germany, releasing 33 German divisions on the Eastern Front to be transferred to the Western Front. In contrast, the Allies faced serious shortages in manpower. They looked to America for help, but American soldiers were not yet sufficiently trained in great numbers. There were only 130,000 troops in France at the beginning of December 1917, and all American divisions needed three months of further training on arrival.[34]While the Allies did experience success on the Palestinian Front in the Middle East with Gen. Sir Edmund Allenby's capture of Jerusalem from the Turks in December,[35] on the Western Front, Gen. Henri-Philippe Pétain, who had replaced Gen. Robert Nivelle following the latter's disastrous offensive at the Chemins des Dames in Champagne in April, chose to remain on the defensive until American forces would arrive in force. Following widespread mutinies in the French Army in the spring, Gen. Pétain concentrated during the summer and fall months on restoring tranquility in the Army by addressing just grievances and avoiding reckless offensives.[36]

Back at Camp Wadsworth, winter arrived with a vengeance. Ice, sleet, and snow made living in canvas tents dangerously cold for the men. Further, the Quartermaster Corps had not provided warm uniforms. Because of the clothing shortage, the soldiers were in especially desperate need of warm underwear. It can be no surprise that there was widespread illness at Wadsworth in December.[37]

By the end of the year, as Pvt. Truesdell tells us, the Headquarters Company of the 107th Regiment has finally been divided into its specialty platoons (Signals, Trench Mortar, One Pounder Cannon, and Pioneers, plus an Intelligence Section, Orderlies, and Band) and that he has been assigned to the Signal Platoon. Signals included a variety of communication methods: semaphore (holding flags in certain positions to send a message), signal lamps (worked only from forward positions to rear positions to avoid the enemy seeing the message), carrier pigeons, and field telephone (wires ran along the sides of trenches or below ground).[38]

The first letters that Pvt. Truesdell wrote home were postmarked "Spartansburg, S.C." By about the middle of October, the postmark had been changed to the correct spelling, "Spartanburg, S.C."

Letter postmarked Spartansburg, S.C., Oct. 1, 1917, 1 PM

N.B.—All is pessism in 1st part of letter—Much more cheerful towards the latter part—so don't worry.

Sept. 29—Sat. A.M.

Dear Folks,

Well, if you were to ask me what my first impression of Camp Wadsworth is, I'd tell you that it is the wetest, forlornest, most God-forsaken place I ever landed in. Rain from the time we landed here, red mud some places a foot deep, mud, rain, mud, rain—and that's all except confusion everywhere. I haven't had all my clothes off since the last time I slept in Van Cortlandt Park—last Monday night [September 24]. It certainly is a terrible comedown to land in such a place after traveling so comfortably in Pullman cars. I'm giving you all my passa-mism first and later will give you the better side of things.

Our first section arrived at the detraining siding—just an ordinary switch about 1 o'clock Thursday P.M. [September 27] about 2½ miles from our camping site. As we got off, it started to rain in torrents, the roads were very muddy. I was detailed to take charge of the Colonel's car after it was unloaded. I supposed it would be unloaded at the same place we detrained, so I stayed behind—the rest of the Company walked on to the camp. I afterwards found out there is a special switch nearer the camp for unloading freight & baggage, so leaving my blanket roll & saddle bags with the officers luggage that came out of their Pullman and which was waiting to be taken over to camp by a truck, and all of which was being thoroughly soaked by a hard rain, I started over to the freight switch in the mud & rain. I waited around until nearly six and found that the Colonel's car wouldn't be unloaded till the next day. So I caught a ride over to our camp—a distance of about 1½ or 2 miles. Our baggage was finally placed on the switch about seven o'clock that night and so after supper, the whole company had to fall to and get it over to our quarters. I was detailed to go over to the cars and help load on to the white trucks of the Quartermasters Corps, a company of which is here to help the different regiments get their baggage to their quarters. All this time there was very heavy rainfall and every place you touched was covered with mud. We finished getting over our baggage to quarters about 11 o'clock and everything and everybody was soaked. The whole company had to sleep in the mess shack that night as we had no tents up and it was pretty uncomfortable—on the hard floor and dirt everywhere. Yesterday I was on orderly duty at Hdqtrs. Also went over to the frt switch and got the Colonel's car which had been unloaded and drove around a little. As orderly I went over to Division Hdqtrs with Capt. Davis. Most of our tents were put up yesterday by men not on orderly duty so last night we could sleep in them on cots although there were regular rivers running thru them. This AM (Sat.) some of our squad are getting lumber to make a floor in our tent. There are big piles of lumber around left by the contractors after building the wooden shacks [semi-permanent structures housing utilities]. I am guarding our pile we have picked out and the other boys have gone over to see if they can get a niggar with a wagon to take it over to our tent—about ¾ mile.[39]

Sunday Evening [Sept. 30, 1917]

Just as I wrote the last sentence above, I discovered a coon who would take our lumber over for a quarter, so I helped him load it on and we went over. We got the frame up for our floor and got our cots in so we could sleep inside. It cleared up last night and has been fine today. Everything and everybody is drying out. Today we most finished our floor and are fairly well settled. I am feeling well except a little cough which I am doctoring and which is getting better. Our camp lies as below:

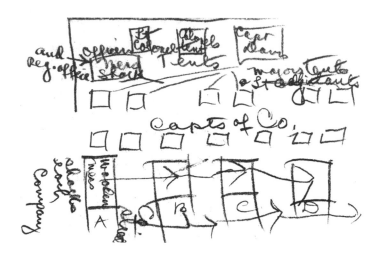

At end of each company street is a wooden shower bath building. We are in tents. Will have electric lights in tents soon. Have them now in mess shack.

Have heard rumors of our regiment being put in 7th, also of 7th being put in our [1st] regiment. No definite orders or news as yet.

Rec'd letters from Mother & Father tonight.

Haven't seen a thing of express package as yet.

It has dried off considerably today and is going to be fine after we get settled if it don't rain too much.

Monday A.M. [Oct. 1, 1917]

Tried to finish this letter last night but was too sleepy.

Took a shower-bath last night. <u>Awful</u> cold but made me feel finer than silk. Put on clean clothes and I'm good as new this A.M. Am on orderly duty and am taking a minute to finish this letter during a quiet spell. May take officers down to Spartanburg this A.M. in car. Hope so. Like to see what it looks like. Will write again soon.

Love to all,
Bob

Beautiful and clear this A.M., also last night. <u>Cold</u>.

Letter postmarked Spartansburg, S.C., Oct. 3, 1917, 1 PM

[Tuesday], Oct. 2, 1917

Dear Folks,

My address is –

Hdqtrs Co. 1st NY Inf.
Camp Wadsworth
Spartanburg, S.C.

Was over to the 1st Ambulance Co. last night and saw young
Partridge. Jim Ivory's brother was over here to see me today, from there.

Have had several letters and postcards in answer to my postals
sent to my customers.

There are about 30,000 men here which include the 1st, 2nd, 3rd, 12th,
23rd, 71st, 74th, 7th Regiments—also 14th, 1st Cavalry, 22nd Engineers,
1,2,3,4 Field Hospitals, 1,2,3,4 Ambulance Co.s, Supply Train, Military
Police, Field Bakery and Hqtrs Troop.

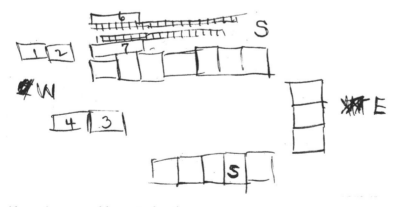

Above is general layout of entire camp.

1 is Division Q.M. Corps
2—Military Police
3—Division Hdqtrs
4—P.O. [and] Telegraph Office

5—1st Regiment
6 + 7—Warehouses on R.R.
switches near which we
unloaded our baggage.

Of course this is very crude. I don't know just where other regiments are located as yet. The ground is fairly level. Quite a bit of timber a good deal of which is being cut out as the regiments take possession.

I rec'd a card today from Amer. Xpress Co. NY City saying they had pckg. for me there. I have written them to send it to me here.

Please don't be bashful about sending me any eats (cake, candy, etc.) as they will be more than appreciated and letters and newspapers.

The weather has been fine the last two days. Nights cold, not much "south" about them. It is quite cool this evening and I am hurrying to finish this and get to bed. I am in our mess shack writing.

No news about changing regiments. Everybody feeling better with better weather and all working hard to clean up and fix up our street.

We will [have] electric lights in our tents, soon.

Haven't started on our regular schedule yet as we are still getting settled. Will tell you of it in next letter. Rec'd Mother's and Father's letters yesterday. Fine. Feeling fine. Lots of love from

Bob

Letter postmarked Spartansburg, S.C., Oct. 5, 1917, 1 PM

Thurs. P.M. [October 4, 1917]

Dear Folks,

Rec'd Father's letters today asking for my address. He has it. It was on his letter. I presume you have rec'd my other letters in which I gave my correct address.

The weather is fine. Days warm, in fact, hot during the noon time. Evenings, particularly toward morning, quite cold.

Our company being smaller than the other companies takes longer to straighten up its street and also we had a poorer street, more uneven. We are most thru — cutting down trees, chopping out stumps, raking [and] burning leaves etc.

We have our tent fixed up fairly well, now and are pretty

comfortable. We aren't going to do too much until we find out whether we change into the 7th or not. No news as yet.

Bud Sheak's sister, Mary, who teaches in Ashville, N.C. was here to see Bud the other day. Had a nice visit with her.

I'd very much like to receive a box containing some homemade fudge and a pckg. of seeded raisins. You don't know how I crave something sweet. Our feed is even plainer down here as we can't buy fried cakes [and] other things like we could at Van Cortlandt Park. I think the thing I miss the most in the line of food here is the fresh milk we used to get every morning for our cereal in Van C. Park.

I was on kitchen police duty yesterday. Dirty work.

Our program for the day is as follows—

Reveille	6 AM	You will notice that we are down for 8
Mess Call	6:35	hours of drill every day except Sunday
Fatigue	7:00	of course. Some drill. We do have Wed.
Stable Call	7:05	[&] Sat. afternoons off too.
Drill	7:30	
Recall	11:30	
Mess	12:00	Rec'd Ed's letter this AM.[40] Glad to hear
Drill	1:00 PM	from him. Come again.
Recall	5:00	
Guard Mount	4:00	
Retreat	5:45	Clevey tells me his father wrote him that
Mess	6:00	Martha Cutler was married in Bing.
Tattoo	9:00	recently. Who, and what all about it?
Call to quarters	10:45	
Taps	11:00	

Wrote the 1st part of this letter just before retreat—am now finishing it after supper in the mess shack. Have been down to the ambulance [&] Field Hospital Post Exchange with Bob Harris and Tuttle. Had three bananas, ice cream cone, bottle sarsp. pop, box choc. fingers, a little sack of salted peanuts and am now smoking a Franklin cigar. Gosh, it seems as tho I can't get enough sweet stuff and I have to let loose once in a while. Lots of Bing. cigars here, Franklins, Red Dots, Mr. Rals etc. It's about 15 or 20 minutes walk down to the canteen, so it takes about an hour to go down and back.

Am able to buy NY Tribune here for 3 cents, sometimes 4 cents, usually everyday although I don't always get it. Haven't had a chance to read much, but after we get settled will probably have more time.

Before we are able to apply for a pass to go down to Spartanburg, we must have a qualification card. In order to get that, we have to pass an examination in regard to traffic regulations of the camp, General Orders, attitude toward civilians, have to wear your clothing properly and to act soldierly, etc. Our first 8 days, during which it is absolutely compulsory we stay in camp, end tomorrow, and I am going to study up and take my examination, so I can get down town once in a while.

Everybody in our squad is well. A fellow, Max Constable, in the other squad, fell out of line yesterday morning, plunk. Had a touch of heart trouble. Came around all right.

Fred Jones, one of our men, (in the other squad) —I think Father met him, has gone home of an indefinite furlough. He is the one who was so sick in Bing before we left. He isn't well yet. He will probably come in the store or call up. Said he would.

Everybody write me all the letters they want to. I enjoy getting them. I'm not homesick understand but look forward to each mail. I appreciate Father's many little notes.

Well, I'll stop and read my NY Tribune a few minutes before going to bed. Love to all. I'd like to be at 100 Murray [Pvt. Truesdell's home address in Binghamton] for a few hours and see you all.

Saying that, makes me think of these Southern people—the way they talk. Very interesting to listen to. The [blacks] are funny as can be.

Good night—more next time. I'm falling asleep over this letter.

Bob

Letter postmarked Spartansburg, S.C., Oct. 6, 1917, 1 PM

Friday Evening, Oct. 5, 1917

Dear Folks,

Father's letter came this A.M. and Mother's tonight.

I am feeling first class, cough most gone. Took a shower bath this P.M., shave and put on clean clothes, certainly feel fine.

Some Sanitary Detachment and band fellows have just gone by, parading in a mock funeral. Got a fellow on a cot covered with a sheet, band fellows playing a funeral march. Crazy bunch.

Getting down to our regular schedule. Had wigwag semaphore signal practice this AM. This P.M. Capt. Davis took us on an 8 or 9 mile hike. Didn't bother me much.

I'm hearing a little music as I write. The Supply Co. next door have an Edison and they're playing it.

I hope you'll send me some cookies and cake. They'll look awfully good.

Am on orderly duty at Hdqtrs tomorrow. They're taking turns with the orderlies about driving the car.

Good looking new store [Newell and Truesdell Co.] envelope Father sent me.

How about insurance premium? Did Father pay it OK? Any other bills coming in for me? How do I stand at the bank with my note? Will send some money home as we have pay day for Sept. Ought to be getting our pay soon.

It seems pretty sure that the 1st will go into the 7th. That is, part of it. It now looks as tho the Hdqtrs Co. would stay here from what everybody thinks. It's pretty sure that part of the 1st will stay and I wouldn't be surprised if we staid. The regiment will then be recruited up with Nat. Army men. We have several R.[egular] officers attached to our regiment, temporarily.

I hear Florence Ford is married.

Well, I guess you have all the news for tonight. Will write soon again. Love to all.

> Bob

Drinking water tastes rummy down here. Soft, I guess. It's wet but don't give much satisfact[ion].

Letter postmarked Spartansburg, S.C., Oct. 7, 1917, 5 PM

> Saturday P.M. [Oct. 6, 1917]

Dear Folks,

Am on orderly duty today and have a few spare moments so will write.

I enclose a map of the camp that shows you about how we lie.

We are supposed to have Wed. and Sat. P.M.s off. I was on kitchen police Wed. and am on orderly duty today. Tomorrow (Sunday) what do [you] suppose we do? Going to dig trenches all day. The whole regiment is going to, the Mounted Orderly Section of the Hdqtrs Co. included. After the regiment digs theirs, they are going to be occupied day and night by a battalion. Don't know whether the Mounted Orderlies have to live in theirs or not. We've got to dig anyway.

Took Major Seymour to Spartanburg this A.M. Have been around Hdqtrs all this P.M.

I was thinking this P.M. about that conserve or jam Mother made this summer. Do a can up very carefully and send it to me — a large can. My squad will eat it and enjoy it immensely. Have Ed wrap it very carefully so it won't break. Our squad sits together at mess and we divide up on eats we get.

Have no news on changes as yet.

Feel well. Cough almost gone. The other boys in our squad are now troubled a bit with coughs and colds. I was a little ahead of them. Nothing serious with any of them.

Haven't received any Republicans [Binghamton newspapers] as yet. Probably will soon.

By the way—in sending me any packages, send them by parcel post as the Express Co. doesn't deliver here in camp.

I can't tell you how much I appreciate all the letters I get. Please continue to send as many as possible. I'm really not homesick but I enjoy getting news from home.

Don't forget to send some eats! I don't seem to be very bashful about asking, do I?

With love to all. Remember me to all the neighbors. How are the Griffiths?

When it rains, the roads are very muddy, and when the sun shines, they are knee-[high] with dust. I just happened to think of this, so I'll jot it down.

More next time.

                                                  Bob

Hdqtrs Co. 1st NY Inf.
Camp Wadsworth
Spartanburg, S.C.

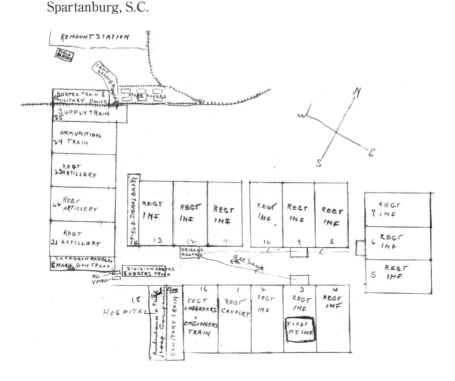

Each plot is numbered. We are on Plot #3. The 14th Inf. are in Plot #4. The 74th are on Plot #2. The 12th is in Plot #9. Don't know the rest.

The ground is quite uneven and fairly well wooded although the timber is being partially cut out as the regiments come in. The 1st Cavalry is on Plot #1. 22nd Engineers on Plot #16. Squadron A on Plot #20. Our Ambulance Co. is on Plot #17.

Letter postmarked Spartansburg, S.C., Oct. 8, 1917, 5 PM

Camp Wadsworth
Sunday Evening [Oct. 7, 1917]

Dear Folks,

Please excuse the looks of this paper but I'm pretty low and so I'll use it up.

I just started to sit down and write when fire call sounded and when that sounds everybody has to drop everything and fall in at the head of their street. Guess there wasn't much of a fire. We couldn't see anything. We had to get up the other morning at four o'clock, get dressed and fall in when the fire call sounded. It's a bugle call, you know. It's all right during the day time but I hate to hear it in the night. When there's a fire, each bugler in the regiment takes it up and each regiment all over the camp takes it up so the whole division by companies is formed at the head of the streets to fight the fire if necessary. There was a fire in the field bakery the other morning when we had to crawl out.

Rec'd Ede's letter this P.M. [Ede refers to his sister, Edith.] Also Mother's. Also one from Bill Hones. I can't tell you how much I appreciated the eats Ede sent. I rec'd. them in the same mail this P.M. I tell you they didn't last long.

Went to bed last night about 8:30 after writing a short note to Miss Hoag as I knew we would have a strenuous day today digging trenches. Such a nice quiet restful Sunday. I haven't realized it was Sunday, at all, except that we didn't have to get up until 7 o'clock. Breakfast at 7:30, after which stable call and then the whole regiment fell in at 8:15 to go dig trenches. It is about a mile away. The trenches are laid out exactly as they are in France—four or five rows in zig-zag lines with rest places, places for trench guns, etc. They are being dug seven to nine feet in depth and three feet wide. Our job (the Mounted Orderlies) was to dig a rest place, same depth as the trench already dug—about eight feet long and three feet wide—picture below.

The ground is fairly easy to dig in—no rocks and pretty soft. Used picks and shovels. Didn't mind it all. The walk over and back—four miles in all—thru very dusty roads was the worst part of it. We worked till 11:30 and from 1 till 4 o'clock. After we came back this P.M., I took a good shower and now I feel fine.

This noon we had apple pie for dinner. One of the men got up at 4:30 this A.M. and baked them. Made them from dried apples. They were pretty good pies and they tasted hunky dory. A regular treat.

Oh, I was going to say, after we all had a bath, I opened Ede's box and passed those good cup cakes around our squad and after digging trenches all day, they certainly came in grand and glorious. Then we dug into those peanuts and finished those. Honestly you can't realize how good they were. It makes me feel awfully bad to think those 24 never got to me. It just makes my mouth water. Ede's box came in good shape. I'll mention that, too.

About that little cap I wanted Ede to knit me—never mind it just now. I'll see if I can buy one in Spartanburg first. All I mean is a little knitted "skating cap" to wear at night and when I am loafing around in my tent.

I'll have to admit I forgot about Ed's birthday. Many happy returns of the day, Ed.

Those are good pictures Mother sent me. I'll keep them in my pocket book. We have no news of our expected change in the regiment as yet.

More about the trenches, as I happen to think of it. Each regiment takes a turn digging them for a day. We will dig some more in about ten days. When they are finished, each regiment will occupy them for a certain length of time. They say we will be in them for a couple of weeks, when they are done.

It was a great mail for me this P.M. Three letters and Ede's package. Well, this is all for tonight. It is now 10:30 and I am going to bed. With love to all of you—including Grandma and Aunt Sarah, and the Newells.

Bob

Letter postmarked Spartanburg, S.C., Oct. 12, 1917, 1 PM

Thursday A.M. [Oct. 11, 1917]

Dear Folks,

I have a few minutes before drill so I'll start a letter.

Tuesday I was on orderly duty at Hdqtrs. Very rainy and cold. Didn't do much driving with the Hdqtrs car. Cleared off Tuesday night and was nice and clear yesterday, warming up, some today. It doesn't get very cold here, not lower than 15 or 20 degrees above, but there is a good deal of moisture in the air and it chills one. The nights so far have been a bit chilly, so that we have used all our blankets and closed up the front of our tent. We also have been issued a stove.[41] All it is, is a conical piece of sheet iron with a door in it and a little hole at the bottom to rake out the ashes.

The pipe goes up thru at the top of the tent. It is rather crude but still it warms up the tent in great shape. It is about a ft. and ½ in diameter at the bottom. We burn wood in it, of course. We filled a box with dirt and set the stove in the dirt. We are pretty comfortable now with the floor and stove in our tent. Of course, we only use our stove nights and mornings and it isn't really necessary then but very comfortable.

Yesterday A.M. we had signal work, and in the P.M. being Wednesday we washed and scrubbed our clothes—no drill Wed. and Sat. P.M.s. We drill morning and P.M., not quite 8 hours as part of our time is taken up at the picket line taking care of the horses. We have no more horses than we had at Van Cort. Park. Our drill consists of signal work mostly and some manual of arms, once in a while, a hike. Not very hard. Our food is improving and is pretty good now. At first, before we got settled it wasn't very good, awfully greasy. Last night we had creamed codfish on toast, chocolate pudding, tea, bread, boiled potatoes. Codfish was well seasoned and tasted fine. The pudding was better than ordinary, too. Our desserts or sweet things consist usually of either choc. or bread pudding, canned pears or peaches. The other night we had pancakes and sugar syrup for supper. However, whatever you send to me will certainly be most appreciated, as we get a good many plain meals. When you send, put in enough to go around the squad (eight of us) and a little extra for Uncle Dud. That is, when you send something like those cupcakes, put in say 8 or 16 and a couple extra. Get me?

Well, there are rumors galore, afloat about transferring. I know this, that 1 major (Major Sherman), 2 captains (you don't know them), 22 lieutenants, and about 1800 enlisted men are going. Lieut. Darling and Lieut. Knapp of Co H are going. Capt. and Lieut. McLean are not going. Most all of the line companies will be transferred with the exception of the 1st sergeant, mess sergeant, supply sergeant, maybe a line sergeant or two and a few enlisted men. Most of the men are going to the 7th regiment (the new 107th), a few to the 3rd Field Artillery and the 22nd Engineers.

Now to get down to our company. We don't know positively where we're going or if we are going. The band will not go, Mess Sgt. Cleveland, 1st Sergeant Tripp, Sgt. Sweet, (Supply Sgt. Thompson transfers to 22nd Engineers by his own request) will not go and a man or two on sick list will not go—I know. The rest of us, I don't know anything about for sure. Rumor says all but the few I mentioned above will go to the 7th (the 107th).

I have been writing this letter all day long, a little at a time. It is now evening—10 o'clock. I'll go on.

No definite news altho it looks just the same—as tho we are going to the 7th. It is quite probable that the transferring of our Detachment will not take place until after the transferring of all our line companies—possibly four or five days. Cap't. Davis hasn't said who is going and who isn't, in fact hasn't said a word one way or the other. All information or rumor has come thru some of our fellows who are working at Hdqtrs. or some of the sergeant-majors.

Tonight there was an impromptu serenading of the Colonel. The band and about 1000 men were up at Hdqtrs. The Colonel talked, also Lieut. Col. Cookinham and Capt. Davis and the Chaplain. I was very sleepy and after supper I lay down on my cot and went to sleep and so didn't go. The other boys said there were good speeches and that there were tears in the Colonel's eyes when he spoke of the breaking up of the regiment.

I rec'd. Father's, Ed's, and Mother's letters, also one from Aunt Nellie. Am receiving the morning paper, now.

Well, it is most time for taps. I must close and go to bed. Will write at once as soon as I find out definite news. With love to all

Bob

Am looking for the box from Ed and Father. Also am looking forward to receiving your box.

RDT

Letter postmarked Spartanburg, S.C., Oct. 14, 1917, 5 PM

Saturday Evening
Oct. 13, 1917

Dear Folks,

Will write with a pencil as my pen doesn't work very well.

Rec'd a letter from Aunt Nell a couple of days ago. I hope you take some of my letters around for her to read as I can't write everybody and I would like to have her hear the news if she cares to. Also Grandma Truesdell and Aunt Sarah. How are they?

Rec'd Ede's letter but have not yet rec'd pckg. she spoke of sending. Thank you for getting the cap. It is just what I want and I know I will enjoy wearing it. Probably will get it tomorrow P.M. Also rec'd the pckg. from the store. Many thanks to the boss and his ass't. On the box were written the signatures of several of the men in the packing-room. Please remember me to them all as well as all the other boys in the shipping room. Also everybody in the office, and the salesmen — everybody.

I heard that Mr. and Mrs. Young had gone. Very sorry. They are probably missed in church considerably.

I have never rec'd any funny pictures that Charlie Challice took. Ede says Mother sent them to me.

I had a letter a few days ago from Bill Hones and have just answered it tonight.

Well, we have just been paid off for Sept. tonight. The paymaster was certainly slow this month. To tell the truth, all I've had is about 10¢ for the last two weeks. I would have had plenty only I lent some to several of the boys. Have plenty now, in fact will send some home soon.

I have never rec'd that pckg. Ede sent me at Van Cortlandt. As I wrote you, I rec'd a post card from the NY office of the Amer. Xpress Co. telling me that they had a pckg. there and I wrote them back to forward it to me here. That was a week ago and I haven't heard a word since.

I have rec'd several issues of the Republican but not regularly and not all of them. Mail takes about 2 to 3 days to reach here from Bing.

Had a celebration in our company last night. Had a big supper — chicken pie (I think the chicken flew thru it pretty fast — I found one small piece in my helping), sweet potatoes, celery, bread and butter, coffee and apple pie — cigars. Then a speech by Capt. Davis to the men who leave to go to the 7th and also to the men who stay. He did not announce who were going or who were not. Later in the evening, however, Sgt. Major Nelson came in to see our squad and told us the pleasant news that out of our squad, two men would be transferred, Privates Mulford and Truesdell — to the 7th. Well, both of us are sorry to leave the 1ˢᵗ, and especially our squad. There have been so many rumors about who was to go and who was to stay in the Mounted Orderly Section that I haven't written anything about it to you. No one knew about Tod and I going till yesterday P.M. when Bloomer saw the orders at Hdqtrs. We hoped that we would all go or all stay and not only do Tod and I feel sorry to go but the other boys in our squad who stay also feel the same way. If we had been divided up equally, four and four, it would have been more pleasant. You know how the ads run in the papers—join the Nat. Guard and be with the home boys. Well, we are serving our country, and I suppose we will have many more unpleasant things to stand than this. It will probably be a week before we transfer, so continue to address me same as usual. There are eight men going from the Mounted Orderlies, six from the other squad and 2 from ours. Sisson goes with us from the other squad. I don't believe you know any of the other boys from the other squad who go to the 7ᵗʰ (the new 107ᵗʰ).

Tod and I are going to look up the Quartermaster Corps when we get over to the 7ᵗʰ. Possibly we can transfer to that on acct of our former experience.

Went over to Capt. Davis and took my exam for qualification card this P.M. after some studying. The Capt. asked just one question and gave me my card. I can go down to Spartanburg any night now till taps and by getting a written pass from the Capt I can stay out later than that.

Didn't have much drilling today on acct of inspection this A.M. and no drill on Sat P.M. Am on orderly duty tomorrow.

Col. Boyer had the whole regiment assemble this A.M. and had a picture taken if it.

Well, I will write soon again. I must go to bed as I'm getting sleepy. With love to all.

Affec. yours,
Bob

Sunday A.M. [Oct. 14, 1917]

Will write a bit more this morning. It is clear and cool—a beautiful Sunday. Am on orderly duty but Capt Davis excused all in the office who wished to attend church—just outside the office—so I went out. It seems a little more like Sunday today than it did last Sunday when we were digging trenches. The Chaplain gave a very good talk and we sung some old familiar hymns. It made me think of the First Presbyterian [the church of which Pvt. Truesdell was a member in Binghamton].

I will get down to Spartanburg soon and see what accommodations there are down there.

I will no doubt meet some fine fellows when I get over to the 7th but of course it seems hard to leave all the Bing. boys. I haven't the faintest idea what part of the Hdqtrs Co of the 7th I'll be put in—you know there will be a lot of new sections. Time will tell. Will write soon again.

Bob

Letter postmarked Spartanburg, S.C., Oct. 17, 1917, 1 PM

Hdqrs. Co.—1st NY Inf.
Camp Wadsworth
Spartanburg, S.C.
[Tuesday] Oct. [16], 1917

Dear Folks,

Well, I feel better about going to the 7th. There'll be nearly all the 1st Regt. over there and I'll meet some nice fellows undoubtedly. E, F and L Companies went over yesterday afternoon at 1:30 escorted by our band and the 7th band met them half way and took them over. The tents were all put up for our boys by the 7th fellows and our fellows rec'd a fine welcome, it is said. Companies A and B went over this P.M. at 1:30. The 1st Regt. begins to look like a skeleton. Each Co. as it goes takes all equipment with it, including tentage. I expect we'll go over about Friday or Saturday—although we have rec'd no orders as yet.

The Broome Co. boys had a banquet (it really was one) last night in Co. H mess-hall. Hdqrs. Co. went down. We had chicken, sweet potatoes, rolls, pickles, gravy, coffee, bread and butter, ice cream and cake—cigars. Some feed, I can tell you—all for 50¢. Afterwards Col.

Boyer, Major Sheehan, Major Sherman, Cap't McLean, Cap't Davis, Lieut McLean, and Lieut Knapp spoke. We had some fine talks and I really enjoyed it as much as anything I have attended in that line since I enlisted.

I'm going down to Spartanburg tomorrow if possible and will look around to see what accommodations there are there.

I rec'd Ede's letter and Ede's package containing apples and socks and cap last night. The socks are certainly great. I will save them till it gets a little cooler. The cap is just what I wanted, too. Where did the apples come from? They certainly had the old [New] York State flavor. They were dandy. This noon I rec'd the other pckg. containing the cup-cakes. I have tested one and they are great. We will soon finish them. All but one apple are gone, already, — we have made way with one can of peanut-butter, quite a few cigars, and three pckgs raisins, from the other pckg.

I also rec'd Father's note of Thurs. P.M. in which he tells about the new license we must have.[42] Would be glad to hear more about it.

There really isn't much use of sending me the Journals of Commerce as I don't have time to read it. We honestly don't work very hard, and still our time is taken up pretty much. The trouble I find is we don't get enough exercise and also our work isn't varied enough to make it as interesting as it might be. It consists almost entirely of signal-work except of course when we are on orderly duty about once in four days. We will no doubt get some "real" work after we change.

I am going to send a box home containing a peanut plant and some cotton in the natural state. Think possibly you'll be interested to see it. — I just ran over about 5 minutes run, and got a sprig of cotton, cut it right out of a field of it.

Well, I'll write soon again. With love from

Bob

Tuesday P.M. [Oct. 16, 1917]

Letter postmarked Spartanburg, S.C., Oct. 18, 1917

Oct. 18, 1917

Thurs. A.M.

Dear Folks,

Well, the Machine Gun Co. and C, G, K, L Co.'s went to the 7th yesterday afternoon. When we were down on the picket line this A.M., Lieut. Royce of the Supply Co. told us that the Supply Co. fellows and Hqrs. Co. fellows go tomorrow. So probably Mulford and I will pack up tomorrow morning and make our debut to the 7th tomorrow P.M. about 1:30. I had a talk with Capt. Davis as I was driving him down town yesterday A.M., during which I told him of my former experience in business again and he told me he would talk with the Adj. of the 7th and see that I had a good show. I'll get along all right, I know. There'll be some good fellows over there, no doubt. I was on orderly duty yesterday so that's how I happened to get a chance to talk with him. Address me same as ever till I let you know that I have changed.

Yesterday P.M. Bill Bloomer took my place as orderly, and as it was half-holiday (Wed.) I got permission to go down town. Did several errands for the boys as well as some for myself. Also went into a first class looking retail grocery store and visited with one of the clerks who had been there for 15 yrs. Nice fellow. They carry quite a line of Sunbeam goods, also Chase & S.[anborn] teas and coffees. They are getting 10¢ for sugar, 40¢ and 50¢ per gallon for bulk cider vinegar, $12.00 for flour. Their vinegar is made in Kentucky, he said.

Also looked up the State agent for the Security Mutual L.[ife] Ins. Co. but was unable to find him. His name is Ligon.

Had a oyster stew for supper and went to the movies. Came back about 9:30.

I went into the Bureau of Information, also, and had a very pleasant visit with a Mrs. Milan who is in charge of looking up rooms to let. She gave me her name and telephone number and said as soon as I found out just when you were coming down to let her know a few days in advance, and she thought she could get a room in a small good family and in a good respectable quiet locality for $3 or $4 a week without board. She said that would be better than staying at the Hotel Cleveland or the Hotel Finch. The former is the new high-toned hotel, which might be compared with the Arlington [a hotel in Binghamton] and the Finch is like the Bennett [another hotel in Binghamton], a little older but good. However they are both charging pretty good rates. Mrs. Milan told me that a lady told her that she was paying $5 per day at the Hotel Cleveland for a room without bath. Isn't that ridiculous? They are soaking the officers as well as civilians. As to meals, there are several good restaurants and a nice tea room or two, so Mrs. Milan said. I think this would be more satisfactory. She said of course it would be somewhat different from NY State but you would be comfortable and near a bath.

I have especially noticed several things since I have been down here. Coca-Cola, Cheri-Cola, Pepsi-Cola are advertised extensively down here and also drunk ditto. Barrels of it are drunk, it seems. It is used much more than in NY State. Also, I haven't heard hardly any birds sing or seen hardly any and I just awoke to the fact the other day that I miss them. I heard a few sparrows chattering on the city square last evening.

The leaves are turning here and it begins to look like fall although it is quite warm. The last few nights have been quite warm, too, as well as the days. Had a little shower during the night, last night.

Am going to wait till I get over to the 7th before sending any money home, as I don't know but what I might want a little over there, to chip in, in putting in a floor, or something like that.

Also went in the Y.M.C.A. down town but there are so many fellows around that it isn't much satisfaction to go in.

I heard there was a collision between an electric street car and a railroad train last night between camp and town and that there were five or six soldiers killed and 15 or 20 injured. Have heard no particulars.

I'm feeling first class. My cough is just about all gone.

I noticed by the Press [a Binghamton newspaper], which Bill Bloomer takes, that Del McLean has been ordered to duty. Well, I suppose that leaves a clearer field for you, Eddie, old scout.

We're doing "cot duty" this A.M. for some unknown reason. We never ask the reason if we have no drill. I'm reclining lazily on my cot with my head on a pile of blankets chewing gum (expectorating occasionally out the side of the tent) and taking life easy. Bud Sheak is over on his cot asleep. Tuttle and Bob Harris are on orderly duty and the other boys are around somewhere. This is my last day with the old 1st, I suppose. Four of the band fellows have formed a saxophone quartette and are now playing out on the street, along with the drums as accompaniment. Sounds good. The saxophones are now just starting to play "There's a long, long trail awinding." Sounds fine—I went out and listened to the fellows playing. Then had to go down to the picket line to water the horses. It is now noon and time for mess.

Bob Harris has been in and says that there is going to be a big parade down town this P.M. to view [to] which he is going to take some of our officers down in the Hdqrs. car.

I understand that a man from one of the line companies is going to be detailed permanently to run the Hdqrs. car. I don't know how true it is.

Well, I must close. Tuttle is going over to the P. Office and will mail this for me.

> With love from
> Bob

Letter postmarked Spartanburg, S.C., Oct. 20, 1917

> Friday 11 A.M. [Oct. 19, 1917]

Dear Folks,

Well, I have a few minutes so I'll write a little.

Tod Mulford and I have emptied our bed-sacks of straw, folded up our cots and packed up our stuff and are waiting around for the Supply Officer to send after our things to take them over to the 7th. We will

probably march over after dinner about 1:30. There are ten of us going
to the 7th, including several reservists who have attached to the Hdqrs.
Co. The two men who are going to the 22nd Eng.—Terrell and Allen of
the other squad—do not go until tomorrow.

It is quite windy out and cloudy. It rained considerably last night
and this A.M. so we won't have quite so nice a day to change as the
fellows who went the days before. Cos. D, H and M and the Hdqrs Co.
and Supply Co. fellows go today to the 7th and this cleans up the 1st NY
Inf. Our streets are bare excepting a tent or two in each street for the
1st Sergeants, Mess and Supply Sgts. The companies had fixed up their
streets so nice that now as you look across the streets with the tents
gone and a few big trees standing, and the ground cleared and planted
here and there with little pine trees, it looks like a park.

I wouldn't be surprised if, after we get over to the 7th, Tod and I
would be put in the Supply Co. and tried out for Reg't. Supply Sgts.,
although there is nothing definite about it. Capt. Davis said he would
see that we got our chance at it.

Clevey was over talking to Capt. Davis last evening and he saw
the reorganization table of the Hdqrs Co. There are to be 294 men
and 6 officers, a total of 300. There will be 2 captains, one of them the
Adjutant, 2 first lieut's., 3 second lieut's, 1st sgt, 2 color sgts., Mess
sgt., supply sgt., 17 line sgt's and numerous corporals. There is going
to be the same no. of Mounted Orderlies (on horses), two motorcycle
riders on duty at the Reg't. Hdqrs, six or seven bicycle riders, the Staff
section, consisting of the Adj. and the Reg'tal non-com. officers, signal
section, telephone section, etc. If we don't get into the Supply Co., we
certainly ought to get something good with the Hdqrs Co.

Col. Fiske is the Col. of the 7th and Capt. Despard is the Adj.

Well, the sky is clearing up and the sun is shining so I guess it will
be cleared up by the time we march over.

It is nearly mess time (noon) and I will close. I will write you soon
again—just as soon as we get over to the 7th.

Say, here's a bit of real news. Finch of our squad has just come
in from stenographer duty at Hdqrs. This A.M., he wrote an order

reducing Reg't. Supply Sgt. David Murray to a line Sgt. in Co. F. That is, he stays with the 1ˢᵗ. What do you know about that? I've been thinking that something like this might happen. You know how he is. <u>Don't say anything</u> about this for awhile as the order is not out yet. No doubt you'll hear about it from the Murray's.

They are making a great drive on Liberty Loan Bonds here. The Hdqrs Co. of the 1ˢᵗ subscribed $1200 approximately, mostly by the Mounted Orderlies—only 3 of the band bought. I did not buy any as I felt that any money I could save, ought to be used in paying up on my note. The 1ˢᵗ Reg't. has subscribed about $80,000 so far and the whole camp about $850,000.

Well, I am finishing this after dinner. It is now 1 o'clock and most time for us to fall in, to march over to the 7ᵗʰ, so I will close. I just noticed in reading over [this letter], that this is the 2ⁿᵈ time I have started to close. This is absolutely all the gossip I think of. With lots of love to you all.

Bob

P.S. I've failed to ask to be remembered to Agnes [the Truesdells' cook] for some time. I'll make up [for that] in this letter, tell her.

RDT

Letter postmarked Spartanburg, S.C., Oct. 23, 1917, 1 PM

Saturday Evening [Oct. 20, 1917]

Dear Folks,

Well, address my mail hereafter to Pvt. R.D.T., Hdqrs. Co.—107ᵗʰ U.S. Infantry, Camp W, Spartanburg, S.C.

It rained hard just as we were ready to fall in to march over here yesterday PM but stopped after having gotten the road in a nice thick mushy state of muddiness, so we didn't have to march over in the rain at least. We had to wait around quite a while before our stuff came over but finally got our tent up and cots arranged. Then it was mess

time. Everything was pretty well confused of course, it being the first
night, and more so as there are ten of us in the tent. But today we have
gotten pretty well settled. You see we had to turn in our saddle equipment before we left the 1st and this included our nice heavy horse blankets which we had been using to put over us at night, as we weren't
using them on acc't. of not having any horses (some sentence, eh?).
So we all in our tent bought us each a mattress. [Sunday P.M. — Am
finishing my letter this P.M.] I really think that it will prove money well
spent [it cost $2.50] as it will help keep me warm as well as be very
comfortable.

Our mail just came in from the 1st and I rec'd. a letter from Mother
and the Rep.[ublican] Herald and Journal of Commerce. I'll read
Mother's letter and then continue this.

Bill Sisson was just telling me about Don and Lucinda a few minutes ago.

Now to go on. After the rain yesterday P.M. it got quite a little
cooler — and cleared up. It was a beautiful evening but really cold.
Even with my mattress I was cold along this A.M. To show you how
cold it was when we got up this A.M. to fall in for reveille, I put on my
sleeveless sweater under my flannel shirt, my army sweater over my
shirt and over this, my overcoat and on my hands, a pair of woolen
gloves — issued to us over in the 1st and I was comfortable. We set up
our stove this A.M. We haven't put in a floor as we probably all will be
moved around in a week or so — except between our cots. I put in a
few boards under my cot to put my stuff on. We are pretty well fixed
now, that is, temporarily.

Tod (Ford) Mulford and I have our cots next to each other.
Between our cots, we have built a rack to hang our clothes on. In the
tent are Walt Jones, Bill Finigan, Bill Morgan (three former reservists who, when the N.Y. was called, were attached to our Hdqrs Co at
Bing.), Max Constable, Stuart Donley, Bill Sisson, Leonard Hoaks, our
horseshoer, Cook Truesdell, Tod and myself. Cook T. moved up to the
mess shack this A.M.

We all had to fill out a card yesterday giving our army pedigree and what we could do. We will probably be temporarily assigned to different sections in a few days. As it is, at present we don't do much of anything until we get straightened around.

There are now nearly the full no. of men in the Co. (294) and when we fall in for mess, it's some line. At present, while our mess shack is being enlarged (all of them were built to correspond to the old organization) we have to walk down about 20 mess shacks down the road to eat. Believe me, if you don't get up near the head of the line, you're liable to get a cold meal.

Our officers are fine, Capt. Hayes and Lieut. Brady. There are men here from Co. H, Co. M, Co. D, and other Co's of the 1st, men from the 12th Inf, and from all over, it seems.

Rec'd letters from Father and also one from Hocky. Have plenty of clothes and plenty of money. Am feeling fine. Took a bath this PM. Pretty cold but it makes you feel fine.

Well, will write soon again. Love to all—

Bob

Changed my mind—will write some more. Hope I'll get to mail this after [a] while. It's now Monday A.M. [Oct. 22] before drill.

I forgot to mention that I put on my socks that Edith sent me, yesterday as it was so cold. They're absolutely splendiferous. Can't tell you how fine they feel and how much I appreciate them. If I might suggest it, I could use another pair or two. Please excuse my "nerve" when I say that if it is convenient for Ede, I could use a pair or two more of them. If you're busy at other things, Ede, I'll buy a couple of pairs down town, as these heavy socks are much more comfortable on acc't. of the cool weather.

I slept fine last night. Warm and comfortable and feel finer'n a fiddle this AM. It was cold but is warming up. This is our 1st A.M. to fall in for drill over here in the 107th. Don't know what we will do. So long

Bob

**Letter postmarked Spartanburg, S.C., Wadsworth Branch,
Oct. 26, 1917 1 PM**

Thurs. A.M. [Oct. 25, 1917]

Dear Folks,

Rec'd Mother's letter and Ede's postal and the pckg. containing the
eats. Cakes all gone. Extra fine. The preserves are A#1.

I would like some more cigars if convenient. Mine are most gone.
Maybe you could bring some down when you come. Also candles are
scarce and high. I bought some yesterday when I was down town and
had to pay 6 for 25¢. You see there are but few of the tents that have
electric lights in as yet, and we do not have any candles issued to us for
some unknown reason.

I find it very agreeable so far here in the 107th. Of course we have
not been placed in sections as yet. All we have been doing is digging
and making our street and drilling in close order and manual of arms,
which is really interesting altho tiring. I have had more drilling here
than I ever had in the 1st.

Yesterday P.M. was our P.M. off, but our platoon had to help in
fixing up the street, while the other 3 platoons of the Co. went over to
watch an athletic meet between the 107th and 108th Inf's, so this A.M.
we have an hour and a half off, which fact accounts for the time I have
to write this letter.

Please don't come down, Father, with an idea of doing anything
on my behalf as regards a change, as that would be unmilitary. I'm
all hunky-dory right here. I hear rumors that the 1st is going to be
no more. The boys of the Mounted Orderly Section who are left over
there, say they hear they are going to be transferred to the Artillery.
What do you know about that? So I guess I'm satisfied with my change.
Rumor says that the 1st is simply going to be disbanded.

The 15th Inf. (colored) left yesterday — said to be going to Mineola.

Now, — as I said in my wire, I rec'd your wire a day late, —
ie — Tuesday A.M. I got off yesterday P.M. and went down town to

see about rooms. I got a list from the information bureau and started hunting. It certainly is some work. I have engaged nothing as yet but am going down again Sat. P.M. and will positively engage something. You did not say how long you expected to stay. I may wire and ask you as it is somewhat essential when engaging rooms. You know there are many officers rooming down town and many officers' families. I think you will have to pay about $15 per week including room & board for a good room, —$5 for room and $10 for board, possibly $3 or $4 per week extra for heat, when coal must be furnished for the fireplace. You know not many places have steam heat. If I can get steam heated rooms, not too expensive, I will get them of course. You must be prepared to get along as well as possible with such rooms as I can get you. And bring some good warm clothing as mornings & evenings are cold.

I hoped Ed would be able to come, too. I think he would be very much interested to see the camp.

If you plan to arrive Friday P.M. I thought possibly you would get rested up for Sat. I probably won't be able to see you until Sat. P.M. about 1:30 or 2 o'clock and then will see you most of Sunday I hope.

At the same time I got your telegram, I found a card from Mr. Phelps. He and Mrs. Phelps, Em Mossy & Ben [family friends from Binghamton who were passing through South Carolina on their way to Atlanta, where they apparently spent the winter] were all over to see me and I was out to drill. Isn't that rotten luck? I certainly was very sorry not to see them.

I have had letters from M.J. Kipp, Ruth Jenkins, Dewitt Bauter, Hocky, and one from Mr. German of the Y.M. who is leaving Bing to take a position in N.Y.

If those clothing markers are ready, bring them down with you.

P.M. Am waiting to take this over tonight to send by special delivery.

Just rec'd Father's wire to engage room. Will do so this coming Sat.

Bob

Private Truesdell and his father, Edwin S. Truesdell, Sr., at Camp Wadsworth

Letter postmarked Spartanburg, S.C., Nov. 6, 1917, 1 PM

Monday Eve. [Nov. 5, 1917]

Dear Mother and Ed,

Maybe by this time, tho, Father and Ede will be home.

Well, Father has been here and gone.[43] We had a good visit even tho he was here but a short time. He can tell you all about the camp and who he saw. Did you see Dave Murray, Father, just before you left Sunday night? He said he was going to try and find you.

As I told Father, the Capt. thought we of the Hqrs. Co. weren't getting acquainted with each other very well—the new men from different companies each sticking together, so today we had a general shake-up and I am in a new squad and a new tent. Never knew any of the men before and don't know them very well, now, but I guess we'll get along all right. They look like pretty good fellows. Will tell you more about them, later.

The box of eats, which Hocky and Mrs. Hotchkiss and Ed sent was rec'd tonight and partially "consumed" tonight for mess. We had some feed. You know Mrs. H. put in three jars of jelly and preserves, a pound of butter and a cake of maple sugar. I shared it with my old squad from the 1ˢᵗ and also with my new squad of today, and have lots left yet. Ed, the smokes are fine. I'm going to appreciate those cigarettes.

Here is something <u>very important</u>. Please buy something especially fine in the way of a wedding present for Pete and Alma. I have just written Pete I wouldn't be able to help him get married. Wish I could but war is h—. Tut, tut, my boy. So I want to send them a present at least. Take out whatever it costs from my pay at the store which father says he is continuing.

Took out $5000 worth of insurance from the gov't. tonight. Father will tell you of it.

Rec'd the announcement of Don Doane and Lucinda's wedding.

Father has told me about Ed's enlisting in the aviation section. Well, Ed, you know best. I suppose the gov't. needs us all and I can realize your feelings as you staid at home. I hope you'll arrange things at the store so they'll be as easy as possible for Father to look after. I don't know what he <u>will</u> do now for a bookkeeper.

We voted today. Just like I did last time in the old undertaking rooms around on Front St—for "Hi" Woodburn and Isaiah Beasley for town constable or something.

Well, it is now 10:30, I am up in the mess hall, it is pretty darn cool, I must be in my tent at 10:45 (call to quarters) and in bed at taps (11:00) so I'll call things off till next time which will be soon. Love to all.

Bob

<u>Don't forget Alma's present.</u>

Letter postmarked Spartanburg, S.C., Nov. 7, 1917, 1 PM

[Tuesday] Nov. 6, 1917

Dear Folks,

Wrote you last night—will write a short letter tonight.

Am going to send home a package with some stuff I don't need in it, soon.

Will you please send me some of my music—songs—the ones I sing the most? The Sanitary Detachment the next street over has a piano. I was in, a few minutes this A.M. talking with some of the fellows. I'm going over now and then to have a little music with them. They seem to be pleasant and agreeable.

Had a letter from Ede in NY this P.M. Also heard from Bill Hones. He is a Capt. in the Reg. Army now. That certainly is fine.

Have gotten pretty well settled in my new quarters and find the fellows are all pretty [good] scouts.

Had a busy day today digging in the streets and drilling.

Am pretty sleepy so I'll stop and write more later. With love,

Bob

[Thursday] Nov. 8, 1917

Dear Folks,

I certainly am doing some writing lately. For the last three evenings I have been writing letters—catching up with my correspondence which I have been neglecting somewhat.

Have just finished writing to Cap't. Willy Hones Jr. from whom I heard several days ago.

I have Ede's letter at hand from N.Y. and Ed's and Mother's letters written after Father's return. Am very sorry to hear of Eddie Crane's death.

Of course, I remember Mrs. Rowe. Am sorry to hear of her death.

Am interested to hear about Charlie Morris.

Some of the floors for our tents arrived today, but we haven't any in our tent yet. Probably will have it in a few days. Will also have electric lights in a few days as they are working on them now.

Am enclosing some pictures which Ed sent me some time ago. I have no place for them here, so you keep them for me. They are pictures of our camp at Van Cortlandt Park.

In our new squad—after the rearrangement the first of the week, I find eight men—Schrader (squad leader) (home in Long Island—former 12th man), Lancomb, also former 12th man, Mack, Kelso, Jessup, Henwood, Rockefeller and myself. The last five men are former 1st men—transferred from line companies there to the Hdqrs. Co. here. They are mostly from up state. They are all pretty good fellows—I get along with them very well. Henwood is a former actor, according to his story. He says this is his third enlistment and that he is 48 years old. He looks about that old, I should think. The other fellows are younger.

We are still having plenty of drill—we haven't been separated into our sections as yet. After between seven or eight hours, one is pretty tired and sleepy. We had our street finished now. Father can tell you about it. It looks fine.

I hear that the boys who went over to the 105th F.A. [Field Artillery] from the Hdqs Co of the 1st don't like it. Tuttle is going to transfer to the Base Hospital as photographer and Bud and Bill are trying to get into the Camp Q.M. Corps. Dr. Korn got Tuttle into the Base Hospital, I guess. Tod and I are figuring all the time to see if possibly we can get into the Q.M. Corps.[44] Absolutely nothing definite but just looking around.

Took out $5000. life insurance with the U.S. as Father advised.

Finished up the eats tonight from the box Ed and Hocky sent me—still have the cigars & cigts and am enjoying them immensely.

Send me plenty of letters. I like to get them. I'm speaking to Ed and Ede, too. Don't be bashful. Give me all the bits of town gossip.

Another letter soon. Good night. Love to all.

Bob

Letter postmarked Spartanburg, S.C., Nov. 15, 1917, 1 PM

Wed. A.M. [Nov. 14, 1917]

Dear Folks,

Will start this letter now as I have a few minutes.

Suppose you have rec'd my letter regarding transfer to Q.M. Corps. Application has not yet returned from Cap't as yet so I have no definite news as yet.

There is one thing I want to ask about. In Ed's letter postmarked Nov. 7, he says he just rec'd a notice from the Navy saying they were enlisting no more men at present, so he is back where he was before he tried to enlist. Then I rec'd a letter from Father postmarked Nov. 10 saying he had hired a young fellow to take Ed's place. Has Ed enlisted or not? That's what I'd like to know.

Also what did Father just mean about Reed Kellam—he said Ray but of course he meant Reed—not telling Helen? That he was home or that he was starting for France or what?

I rec'd my music OK tonight. Thank you. I've been over tonight and sung some at the Sanitary Detachment Mess Hall. Not having sung much, I am in poor trim.

Have you got a present for Pete and Alma? Hope you have.

Saw Dave Murray yesterday. Said he found Father at the Cleveland [Hotel] after I left him and had a good chat.

Write me all the bits of news about the people of Bing. I know, such as about Reed K. etc. I like to hear about them. I haven't rec'd a Rep. Herald in so long, I don't know how they look. I wrote them a card about it yesterday. Come across with a letter now and then, Ed & Ede. Father and Mother are fine about writing.

Bud Sheak, [Bill] Bloomer & [Russ] Tuttle have gone to the range to practice with the guns—with the rest of the Artillery. Don't know when they're coming back or whether they will come back at all. The range is about 25 miles distant in what direction I don't know or near what place. They took all their tentage and equipment with them.

A number of the lieutenants who were left in the 1st have been transferred to other regiments in the camp. I saw Moss McLean today over in the 106th Inf.

Went downtown this P.M. and did a few errands.

Tod [Mulford] is playing in the band now for the time being. We are both waiting to hear from our applications for transfer.

Love to all –
Bob

Letter postmarked Spartanburg, S.C., Nov. 16, 1917, 5 PM

Thurs Eve [Nov. 15, 1917]

Dear Folks,

Will write a short letter tonight. I rec'd pckg containing candles and cigars also Ede's pckg of candy and socks.[45] The candles certainly arrived just in the nick of time as I was burning my last one. The cigars also were welcome. I am certainly well stocked with smokes, cigts, small and large cigars. They're great. And now for Ede's pckg—the fudge is fine—all the squad say the same and I thank you very much for the socks. They're first class.

Rec'd. Father's and Ede's letters this P.M. Sorry to hear about Mr. Davidge. Ede, you certainly are busy. I'll accept no apologies for not writing to me, Ede, even if you send me two boxes a day. Got to hear from you, Ede, old scout—must have the town gossip. Write short letters at odd times and plenty of them. Same advice to Ed. Slip along the letters, old kid.

Well, we finally got a floor put in our tent today. It's slicker than a palace. Poles have been put up during the past day or two so we'll probably have electric lights shortly.

Was on special detail this A.M.—made duplicates of those census cards. Didn't have to drill.

Tod says the artillery boys haven't gone to the range, after all.

Haven't heard from my application yet.

Hope I'll get a Rep Herald after [a] while.

> Will write again soon.
>
> Bob

Letter postmarked Spartanburg, S.C., Nov. 19, 1917, 1 PM

Sunday P.M. [Nov. 18,1917]

Dear Folks,

Was planning to go down to Spartanburg today to church and dinner with Tod but our squad was duty squad today so we had to stay in the street. Each squad takes a turn at duty squad for one day. Its duties are to police the street and do any other jobs that come along. Not very hard, but would rather have had it come on a drill day as the duty squad is exempt from drill.

I certainly rec'd some mail last night—six letters—two from Father, one from Ed, one from Mother, one from Grandma Truesdell, and two from Mary McMahan. Thank you, Mother, for tending to a present for Pete & Alma. I sent them a telegram yesterday P.M. Wish I could have been on hand for the wedding.

If convenient, please call up Mrs. Corbett and give my love. I've had many good times up at Conklin.

Go ahead and sell my fur coat and get what you can out of it. I suppose some of my suits and other overcoats (outside garments) might be sold, too. They probably will be out of style before I get ready to wear them again. Let Ed go over them and he might as well wear what fits him. Save one suit for me and sell the rest. He might as well be wearing some of my underclothing, etc, too.

Glad to hear of Ed's raise at the store. Give my regards to all the members of the Blind Relief Committee.

Don't know whether Father told you or not that Harriette Waters and I agreed to disagree. I still hear from her once in a while—that is, she owes me a letter—I can tell you later whether she writes me or not.

Am going to send home a box containing a few unneccessaries in the way of clothing, etc. Also some holly some fellows found, when out walking.

Guess I told you we now have our floors & side walls in. We're quite comfortable.

Rec'd Father's letter with enclosures. Will submit them with my application for transfer. Capt Hayes is still sick in Spartanburg so we haven't anything regarding our transfer.

I'd appreciate it if you could mail me a copy or two of the Rep Herald. I had only a very few since I came to the 107th—a month's time.

More next time. Love to all—

                                                    Bob

Letter postmarked Spartanburg, S.C., Nov. 20, 1917, 5 PM

Monday Eve [Nov. 19, 1917]

Dear Folks,

Just a short one tonight, as I have already written Grandma Truesdell. Tod Corbett and Mr. Williams to get Marsh' address.

I rec'd a Rep Herald today (Nov. 16th issue) the first one with the new corrected address. Hope I'll continue to receive them. You see I haven't had hardly a one since I came over here—now a month's time.

Submitted the two letters which Father sent me to the top sgt. today and he will attach them to the application for my transfer. Capt Hayes returned today from the hospital at Spartanburg, so I ought to hear something in a few days.

Rec'd Mother's and Ede's letters tonight. Thank you very much for tending to the present for Alma and Pete. Take it out of my pay that is accumilating at the store. Nice of you to send them a present too. Hope I get the paper with acct of the wedding in it. Please write me all about it.

Glad to hear that Hal Murray is doing well.

No hard feelings about you, Ede, as letter writer but I really enjoy hearing from you. Write me as often as it is possible. You are certainly busy, I'll say. You're doing well.

Love to all.

Bob

Ede, the socks are fine. I'd like about one more pair if it isn't asking too much.

Letter postmarked Spartanburg, S.C., Nov. 24, 1917, 5 PM

Thurs. P.M. [Nov. 22, 1917]

Dear Folks,

Rec'd Father's letter yesterday and Mother's this noon. Wish I could see Uncle Arthur. Give my love to him. I certainly would enjoy being present at our church centennial.

Remember me to Helen Kellam. She's having a rather rough time.

Talk about mental telepathy. Night before last, I wrote Mr. Williams asking Marsh' address and today I receive Mother's letter with the address. Am very glad to get it. Will write him at once.

Also heard from Henry Hopkins at store. Have rec'd the paper regularly for the past three or four days.

Was downtown yesterday.

Friday A.M. [Nov. 23, 1917]

Was downtown Wed. P.M. with Dave Murray and met a couple of girls he had met. Had a fair time. In the evening, I went down and had a great time. You can't imagine what I did. I had a tub bath with plenty of hot water. It's the first tub bath I've had since I left home—the 18th of Aug.—three months without a tub bath. You know I enjoyed it. I had it in a barber shop where I went for a shave. Good clean place. Cost me 25¢.

Friday night [Nov. 23, 1917]

We had a very interesting lecture the other day on gas masks by Lieut. Wilson. He had borrowed one for a short time. It is carried in a case on the left side by a strap over the right shoulder. For the position of ready, it is brought around so that it hangs in front. The flap is opened. It is made of rubber and covers the entire face—two big glasses to see thru, a clip to pinch the nose closed, and the tube to place in the mouth for breathing. The tube leads down to the box in the case, which contains the purifying chemicals, which will last about 10 to 18 hours under actual use. It's very interesting.

Today about 150 men who came over here to the 107th at the same time I did were transferred back to the 1st. They are mostly fellows who are physically unfit or undesirable as to discipline. I have just been over to the 1st for a few minutes to see the fellows. They don't know what is going on, or what is going to be done with the reg't.

Last night the 1st & 2nd platoons (I'm in the 5th squad of the 1st) had two hours of night drill on advance guard work, etc. from 7 to 9. On account of that fact, we had no drill during the day. We also made out our allotment blanks and had some clothing issued to us by the supply sg't. Out of my pay, comes $5. per month for a $50. Liberty Loan Bond and $3.30 per month for my $5000. insurance which leaves $6.70 of the $15 (half my pay) which the gov't. says we must dispose of, so as not to receive more than $15. in actual cash each pay day. So I allotted $6.70 home to Father. If I need it back again I'll write Father. The allotment is compulsory if a man has dependent relatives but is voluntary otherwise. At present, Sec'y [of War Newton D.] Baker has not yet put in effect the ruling that men will receive only half their pay in active cash, but the law has been passed and I believe if we go across the water, I expect this ruling will be put in effect. I thought I might as well make out the allotment and then if I need the money I can write you for it.

Men are working on our shower baths putting in heaters and boilers for hot showers — also closing up the showers and covering them with tar paper so to make them more comfortable. It's about time they did, for the showers are almighty cold. I go downtown to the Y.M. for a hot shower usually. I guess ours is the first reg't. to have these new water heating apparatuses put in. They are evidently trying them out.

We are having some bayonet drill now, learning the different parries and thrusts and sticking our bayonets thru some dummies that are manmade.

I bought one of those little Sterno heaters a couple of days ago for 50¢. They certainly are handy to heat water for shaving etc. Also when you're sending me another box, if you include a little G. Wash. Coffee and a small can of milk, we can have hot coffee. Of course this is not a hint. Absolutely no.

Everybody in the company put in $3.00 and we bought some special agate dishes and some knives and forks which are better than our regular US issue. Little nicer to eat with. We also eat in squads—small tables along each side of the mess shack.

We are certainly getting some cold weather here tonight. The wind is blowing and the air is cold and raw. But with our floors and by closing the tent all up and having a fire in the stove we keep very comfortable. Wore my sweater and overcoat over to the 1st tonight.

Had a letter this noon from Ed and one from Ruth Jenkins telling me considerable about the wedding. Also heard from Ed Stone at the store.

As for Ed's coming down to see me over Thanksgiving, I'll say come ahead. I heard a rumor that we would go into the trenches for 48 hours beginning next Wed A.M., so that would mean we would be in the trenches on Thanksgiving Day. Men from different units are occupying them now all the time for 48 hours each. We undoubtedly will do our trick but this is only a rumor about Thanksgiving altho it might be true. Ed could come a day or two later, say the Friday or Sat following Thanksgiving if I find we are to be busy on Thanksgiving. The fare is about $60.00 both ways. I believe I can get the same room I had for Father, I think—$5 per week for room and $10 per week for board or less for less time. It costs considerable I know and for that time I won't feel hurt if you don't come altho I'd be tickled to death to see you, Ed. If you feel you can afford it, come by all means as I will enjoy it and I know you will.

Were Father or Mother or Ede invited to Pete's wedding? Somewhat surprised that Ed wasn't unless it was a small affair.

Please send me Mr. Z. Ben. Phelps address. If he is still in Greenville I am going to try to see him.

Well, the fire is getting low and the tent cold, so I'm going to quit and go to bed. Inspection of quarters and equipment tomorrow morning as usual.

Am planning to go down to church with Tod Sunday. Oh, say, before we left Bing. Mr. Waters wrote a man whom he knew down here that I and Bob Harris would be down here in camp. This gentleman is a Mr. McGee, mgr. of the August Smith Co., a department store. He has invited Bob and me to come down for Sunday dinner. Bob doesn't think he can get away but I expect to go as Tod and I are planning to go to church together Sunday A.M. at the Pres[byterian] church and as Mr. McGee is a member of same church, maybe he'll invite Tod to come. Hope so.

Haven't heard from my application for transfer. Afraid it isn't going thru as Capt Hayes has been back for several days but don't know for sure. I'm going to ask the 1ˢᵗ Sgt about it in a day or two if I don't hear anything about it. Well if I can't get it, then I'll just do my darnest here in the 107ᵗʰ and be as satisfied as I can. It isn't a bad reg't, at all. Well, I'm really going to quit now. Goodnight, love to all.

Bob

Letter postmarked Spartanburg, S.C., Nov. 28, 1917, 1 PM

Tuesday Evening [Nov. 27, 1917]

Dear Folks,

I have just a few minutes.

I waited until last Saturday to hear about my transfer but heard nothing so I asked the 1ˢᵗ Sgt. and he said that the Cap't said for me to go over to the Q.M. Corps here at camp and see if they could use me and if that was the case, he would OK my transfer here. You see the federalized Nat Guard has no QM Corps so to transfer from the 107ᵗʰ to the QM Corps is to transfer from the U.S. N.G. to either the N.[ational]A. or the Reg.[ular] Army — both the latter have QM Corps. I went over to see Cap't Evans at the QM Corps and he took my name after telling me that at present there was no opening but if there was, he would let me know and send me a blank to fill out for transfer.

Tod saw a notice in a NY paper that the Recruiting Officer at 357 Broadway NY City announced a need of men in the QM Corps of the Nat. Army so I have written him according to the advice of our 1ˢᵗ Sgt and told him my experience and asked him for information. I'll see what this brings.

Mr. McGee to whom Mr. Waters wrote some time before I came down, in regard to my coming down in camp, wrote me last week and invited me to Sunday dinner with him. Mr. Waters also wrote to him of Bob Harris and he was asked to dinner also but was unable to get away. Tod and I went down to church at the First Presbyt. Church in the A.M. and then I found Mr. and Mrs. McGee whom are members of the church, after services. They took me home in their car and we had a fine turkey dinner. There were two other fellows besides myself at dinner. Mr. McGee has three or four fellows to dinner every Sunday. They are very nice people. He is mgr. of a department store here—the Aug. Smith Co. We sat around after dinner & visited and then, they brought me back up to camp.

Am going into the trenches for 24 hours tonight at 8:00—most time now—all organizations are taking turns going in. Will write you more after I come out. Will be out tomorrow night at 9:00.

Has been very cold here for the past two days.

We have electric lights in our tent now.

Got Ede's letter and one from Mr. Williams tonight. Hope Ed comes down. Love—

Bob

Letter without an envelope

Thursday Eve [Nov. 29,1917]

Dear Folks,

Well, I have rested around and dozed and eaten a big dinner and read and now I am going to sit down and write a letter.

I wrote you a short letter Tuesday night just before I went into the trenches for 24 hours. The 107th Reg't. is going in by battalions (4 companies). The first batt. went in Monday night at 9 o'clock. With them went 25 men from the Hdqrs. Co. to act as runners,—four men (1 corp. and 3 men) for each company hdqrs. Tod went in, Monday night. All the company hdqrs. were in the trenches and the battalion (garrison) hdqrs. were just outside the entrance to the trenches. At 7 o'clock each man was issued 1 can PO Beans, a lot of hardtack (N.B.C.), 1 can BBerry jam, 3 hard boiled eggs and 1 apple for the 3 meals. At 7:55 the detail fell in. We all wore heavy clothes. I wore heavy woolen underwear, my heavy socks, woolen breeches and blouse, flannel shirt, regulation sweater, and overcoat. Also we took our blanket roll with 1 blanket, shelter half and poncho and wore our harness, with bayonet and scabbard and canteen and haversack with toilet articles, mess tins and rations and carried rifles. We had quite a load. We fell in with the battalion at the head of our street, without any noise and marched over to the trench entrances which are over toward the store houses. The detail I was in, was attached to Co H Hdqrs and consisted of Corp. Mix, Pvts. O'Dwyer, Louck and Truesdell. Tod happened to be detailed to show us the way in and after we had gone in and found our quarters in Shelter 20, taken off our roll and haversack, I came out again with Tod (who came out and went back to our street again as his 24 hours was up) who showed me how to find the way around. Then I came back again to Co H Hdqrs. The trenches are about 7 or 8 feet deep but no where near wide enough. Some places it is almost impossible for men to get thru without turning sideway. Our Hdqrs was in a shelter not a dug out as we were in the rear line trenches. A shelter is a hole dug in the ground with a roof made of timber and covered with earth. A dug-out is a hole dug right down into the ground and is quite a lot deeper than a shelter. The earth is carried out and timber supports [are] placed to hold up the earthen roof. Each company hdqrs is connected with garrison hdqrs by telephone and buzzer. We slept fitfully thru the night. I didn't even unroll my pack as there wasn't enough room. Our shelter was about 10x25 and there were about 20 or 25 men in it and rolls and haversacks & guns all over so I just sat down on my roll with my back against the side of the shelter and caught a little sleep. I woke up every little while, cold & stiff and got up and warmed myself up. However, I didn't catch cold, so I can't complain. I have had a little cough for a week or so, but nothing serious at all. I had to run out to garrison hdqrs a couple of times during the 24 hrs. but otherwise

there wasn't much doing. There were several theoretical advances
and bomb charges by the enemy also gas attacks—during the last,
everybody had to work the bolt in his gun so the gas would not injure
it. But being back in the reserve trenches, there wasn't as much to do
as in the frontline trenches. I took my Sterno canned heat outfit along
& O'Dwyer had a couple of cans of Campbell's boullion and we had hot
soup for breakfast and dinner. Also the kitchen detail brought in hot
coffee for each meal. Everything was done in the shelter. We weren't
supposed to be outside except on duty or to get a little fresh air just
outside the entrance. We started out at 9 o'clock Wed. night and got
back to our company street about 10 o'clock. Silence was preserved
thruout the whole affair and everybody talked in whispers. It was carried out just as tho we were in actual fighting. Officers from different
reg'ts. acted as umpires.

    I took a sponge bath when I got back and cleaned up and tumbled
into bed (cot). It was quite an experience. One day was quite sufficient.
The dugouts which were occupied by the other company hdqrs were
larger and fixed up better—had wooden seats and bunks.

N.B. I am finishing this on Friday PM. Got too sleepy last night.

    Nobody was in the trenches on Thanksgiving Day. The 3rd and last
battalion of the 107th goes in tonight accompanied by 25 Hdqrs. Co.
men. So you see, only 75 out of our 300 men go in.

    Yesterday (Thanksgiving) was a holiday and as on Sunday, we
didn't have to get up till 6:45. I was very tired so I played a little trick
(my first offence). I just slipped on my shoes and leggings and my
slicker (it was raining) over my pajamas and fell in for reveille. Then
I went back to my tent and went back to bed for a couple of hours.
Then after I got up I read all the Bing. papers I had and thought what
I'd be doing if I were home and what you all were probably doing. At
3 o'clock, we had our Thanksgiving dinner—boiled potatoes, peas,
pickles, beets, turkey (one for each squad) and dressing, celery—I
forgot, we had tomato soup first, cranberry sauce, bread & <u>butter</u>,
coffee, apples, bananas, oranges, Malaga grapes, mince pie and vanilla

ice cream. Some dinner—but some of it not cooked very well and there weren't enough dishes for everything—you know, potatoes & peas, pickled beets & cranberry sauce. There was so much sage in the dressing that it was not fit to eat, but on the whole, it was some dinner, a lot better meal than the ordinary. Afterwards I enjoyed a Tom Moore cigar—also treated the squad to one. Rested around the remainder of the day. Tod and I decided we wouldn't go downtown to dinner as there probably would be a big crowd and poor service and also the condition of our pocketbooks was such that we didn't think it wise to spend 1.50 or 2.00 for a meal when we could get a pretty good one here at camp for nothing.

Mrs. McGee told me Sunday P.M. that the First Presbyt. Church has a social

(over)

(guess I'll be a little more economical and use both
sides of the sheet as I am writing a regular book)

for the soldiers every Wed. evening after prayer meeting. Tod and I intended to go down last Wed. but I was in the trenches so we are planning to go down next week. Mr. McGee offered us a drink before we had dinner. One of the fellows accepted with great celerity. It's pretty scarce stuff down here and it's a great time for men who are in the habit of drinking, I suppose.

Ed, I saw Driver again the other day in town. He had his mother with him—I think it was his mother.

This morning, it was cloudy, misty and cool—very disagreeable. We went out for drill till 9:30 and then had a lecture till recall (11:30) on bombs and grenades and one on the trenches, both by Lieut. Wilson. Very interesting—to find out the most efficient methods of killing the Germans—just how to use the hand grenades. As yet, we have not been subdivided up into the different sections. We seem to be doing preliminary work, so far. This P.M. we fell in at the head of the street, expecting an inspection of the camp by Senator Wadsworth but he didn't show up. We have been waiting around all the P.M. for him until now. We have fallen out to get ready for regular Sat. A.M. inspection.

Tod got a box from home containing a chicken, mince pie, sandwiches, etc. and gave me some great [food]—it had the home flavor.
You know—ahem, I just dote on getting boxes, too. The fudge Ede
sent me some time ago was fine. It was made with brown sugar, I think.
Please make the next batch you send me, Ede, the old fashioned way
with white sugar—and don't send the kind you knead. Thank you.
While speaking in this vein, I might say that the cig'ts Ed sent me and
which have been gone for a matter of several days, were <u>much</u> enjoyed.
I can also easily say and without the slightest provocation, that the
same statement applies to the cigars I have been smoking.

What has become of those clothing markers, Mother? Aren't they
finished yet? Also, Ede, I would much appreciate one more pair of
those good socks. I am wearing them all the time now and they are
exceedingly comfortable.

In regard to sending me Sat. Posts, Ede—I am able to buy the daily
NY papers, the Post and other periodicals at the canteen and I get them
occasionally when I have time to read them. What about the Literary
Digest and Army & Navy Journal to which Father was going to sub-
scribe, for me? Do you want to do this and do you think it worth while?

Sorry that Father has been feeling ill with a cold. Hope he feels
OK by now.

Rec'd Ed's (of Wed. P.M.) and Ede's (of Sun. PM) letters and
Father's several letters. Don't know as I mentioned this before. Fine
that you have a position in church, Ede. I'm proud of you. Also congratulations on the success of your benefit for the Blind Soldier Relief. Ede,
Mother sent me no clipping about Bill's father. My last letter from her
is dated Nov. 20. Extend my best wishes to Aunt Sarah on the reaching of her ___th birthday. I have Father's letter containing sheets on
Coffee and War times. How does the trade feel about our drawing up
on credits? Are you absolutely shutting down to 30 days? I'd like to see
the statement for November when it is completed.

How are all the Newells. Give my love to them all, especially Aunt
Nell and Marion when you or Aunt Nell are writing to her.

How did Uncle Arthur find the folks in F[ranklin] Forks. Hope they are well. Must write them.

Remember me to Bob Brooks. Glad to hear about Bill Kennedy and funny about Frank Taft. He must have bucked up considerably. I notice that Ted Skinner didn't get a commission.

Let me know a couple of weeks ahead anytime, Ed, and I will arrange things and you come down. We'll have a good visit. I can arrange to have more time with you if you plan to arrive Wed night or Thursday. Of course we would have only 3 or 4 days so I don't know whether it would be worth $75 to you or not. I think I will apply for a furlough along the latter part of January if we're here till then. I'd just like to get a 15 da. furlough.

D. Parsons must have got married in a hurry, eh?

Had a Thanksgiving card from Myron Kipp and one from Herbert Phelps in Franklin. Also letters from Henry Hopkins, Ed Stone, Mr. Williams giving me Marsh's address—he said Mother asked for his address—and a letter from "Sam" Jenkins giving me a good account of "the" wedding and a letter today from Alma, who says Pete and she are settled in N.Y. and he has started to work again. Mr. Williams wrote that none of them were invited to the wedding and from what I gather, none of you were either. Somewhat peculiar, it seems. Alma seems to appreciate my present and also the telegram I sent.

Well, I have just finished supper consisting of beef, boiled potatoes, corn, cocoa, and bread. It's beef, beef, beef, never pork or lamb. Once in a while we get some so-called sausage for breakfast but it's mostly cereal.

Haven't anything new to write about my application for transfer.

The British made a great drive last week didn't they?

Remember me to Agnes. Regards to all the neighbors. This is some book, I'll say. I've been nearly 24 hours writing it, off and on. Love to all.

Bob

Letter postmarked Spartanburg, S.C., Wadsworth Br.,
Dec. 4, 1917, 5 PM

Mon. Eve [Dec. 3,1917]

Dear Folks,

A short one tonight as I am sleepy.

The box came Sat evening and it surely was a dandy. You certainly remembered me in great shape. I divided it around my squad and gave some to Tod and had plenty for myself. Our squad was duty squad yesterday so we had to stay in the street ready to do any odd jobs.

I have Father's letter of Friday and Mother's & Ede's letters of Friday P.M. and Thurs evening respectively.

As far as leaving here very soon, it appears to me that the men here need considerable equipment and quite a lot of more training before that happens. There are rumors that run wild all over the camp. You'd be surprised to see how quick they spread. One is that all the 1st men in the 107th are going back to the 1st and another that we are coming north to do guard duty but none that we leave for France. However these are but merest unfounded stories. I believe nothing till I hear the sure thing.

In transferring to QM Corps, I would only be obliged to stay in for the duration of the war.

I have read of Bill K. and others receiving commissions. Fine.

I don't know who you mean by Mrs. Sawtelle (Mr. Martin's mother) — it has just come to me that you mean Mr. Martin Sawtelle's mother — I'm a bonehead. Remember me very kindly to her and also to Mrs. Webster.

You are certainly a busy girl, Ede. I'll keep your picture and thank you.

Nothing new on my transfer.

Camp Dix men are certainly fortunate in getting furloughs. They are very scarce here. You have to have very urgent reasons. If there was a directors meeting of N.&T. after the first of the year at which I had important business to transact, and which could not be transacted by mail, I might be able to get a 15 day furlough. Of course I don't want to deceive the gov't. but maybe Father would want me to be present and so it would be OK. The colonel's chauffeur got 15 days (thru Thanksgiving) so I guess it's just pull that gets the furlough. Of course, some have legitimate reasons.

Wrote Marsh yesterday. Love to all.

Bob

PS I was in such a hurry to get a hot bath Sat when I wrote Father about cashing that check that I forgot to say to take that five dollars out of the allotment I will send home this next pay-day. The allotment is $6.70 per month.

RDT

(over)

I've just been reading about the death of Miss Fanny Morey. The name certainly brings back memories. I can just see her—in my mind—up in the window on the corner of the 3rd floor of Oak St School at dismissal time, watching us boys go home. If anyone started to throw snowballs, there was that rat-a-tat-tat—clear as a bell—on the window with her pencil and the finger beckoning for someone to come back and stay after school. Ed probably remembers. We lived at 92 Oak St. It must be 10 or 12 yrs ago. She certainly was a great character.

Bob

Letter postmarked Spartanburg, S.C., Wadsworth Br.,
Dec. 9, 1917, 12 M

Dec. 8, 1917, Sat A.M.

Dear Folks,

We have had Sat A.M. inspection and as it has been raining we had our cot inspection inside our tents. Much easier. No drill afterwards on account of rain and mud. It rained considerable during the latter part of the night. It has stopped now but is cool and windy. I am sitting in front of the stove keeping warm—on a camp chair with a back which I bought downtown for 75¢. It's certainly fine to have a chair to sit on.

We have a new schedule now. We do not get [up] till 6:30 instead of 6 on account of its being so dark. Breakfast at 7:00, drill from 7:50 till 11:30, dinner at 12, drill from 1 till 4:30, retreat at 5:15 instead of 5:55 and mess at 5:30 instead of six. Taps at 11 same as before.

If you would like to, you may send me some more peanut butter and jam. I'll eat it. I enclose a clipping from the Tribune[46] which I believe hits the nail on the head. We are furnished good food but our cooks are poor.

I sent a pair of those good heavy socks that Ede knit me, to the laundry last week as usual and they have lost them. What do [you] think of that? The ones Mrs. Webster sent me and which I received yesterday came in very handy. I had a fine letter from her, too. I wrote her this morning.

Ede, go in to Ray Douglas' and ask for Miss Tuttle, who is the sister of Tut, who was with us in the 1st, and ask her for a copy of each of the pictures Tut sent home to be developed. She will know. She has made some for the other fellows. Also ask her for an enlargement of the picture of our squad. She has made a couple of those for the other fellows,

Kitchens in Camps Called Unsanitary

Food Excellent, but Preparation Poor, Says Report of U. S. Surgeon General

WASHINGTON, Dec. 3.—Food provided for the National Army and National Guard units training in this country is "excellent in quality," says a report of the food division of the surgeon general's office, made public to-day, but conditions surrounding its preparation in the National Guard camps leave much to be desired.

"In the National Army cantonments," the report said, "the cooks have the advantage of permanent kitchens, provided with a plentiful supply of hot water, good storeroom, large refrigerators, etc. The National Guard organizations, housed in tents, have temporary kitchens, often with dirt floors, poorly constructed storerooms, smoky stoves and refrigerators too near the fire.

"The surgeon general, upon the reports of the officers of the food division, has recommended the inauguration of systematic instruction of cooks, mess sergeants and mess officers in the National Guard camps. The quartermaster general has acted upon these suggestions, and such instructions will soon begin."

too. You folks will all like to see them as there are some fine pictures
and I want to keep them (you keep them for me) especially the enlargement of the picture of our squad. Please don't forget to do this.

We had our first frost night before last—a heavy white one and
the night was pretty cool. We have been issued O[live] D[rab] cotton
quilts so we sleep good and warm. The quilts are slick.

There's nothing doing on a transfer this end. The 1st Sgt told me
yesterday that the Capt didn't want to let any men out of the company
on account of their being organized together and drilled and that it
would break things up. So he will not OK any applications. The only
way now is to have the application come from the other end and I don't
know just [how] to go at it. Maybe if I wrote some of my friends who
hold reserve commissions in the Q.M. Corps and who are on active
duty in different N.A. [National Army] camps, they might know of an
opening. Charlie Challice is one, isn't he? Where is he located? Who
else do you think of, Ed?

In regard to a furlough—I think the best way for you to do is
this. When you decide on the date for your directors and stockholders
meeting which is usually the first part of January, isn't it, send me a
night letter, formal in character, from the company with you as Gen
Mgr & Sec. Treas. informing me of same and that my presence is
necessary particularly on account of the fact that it may [be] my last
opportunity to attend for some time. Important matters to take up, etc.
Make it strong. I think this is all true. Then I'll take it up with the 1st
Sgt. Write me what you think of this. Furloughs are very hard to get
and one must have a sufficient reason.

The cake you sent me in that box, Ede, was alright as far as I know.
We ate it and it tasted OK.

What about Bill Hones' father? What did he print in his paper?

I have Father's several letters, including the one enclosing the Nov.
statement. Thank you.

I think I will take out $5000 more insurance as you suggest. It's
good stuff. Well, more next time.

Bob

Dec. 10, 1917, Monday A.M.

Dear Folks,

Talk about the sunny South—the temperature night before last was
about zero and last night 7 degrees below zero. Ede, please send
me a knitted helmet—O.D. in color—at once. You know what they
are, surely. Lots of the fellows have had them sent to them. Our
squad—what is left of them—is on mess squad detail. We have to
wash all the squad big pans and pitchers. All the water pipes are frozen
up and the men are, too. I have on my heavy underwear (issued), a
sleeveless sweater, my flannel shirt, regulation sweater and am hug-
ging the fire. The company did not go out to drill this A.M., it was so
cold. Some of Hdqrs Co are on guard, including four of our squad.
There are also 25 men with the 2nd Battalion in the trenches, but they
all came out this A.M. as it was so cold.

Guard duty for Hdqrs.Co. is somewhat new. Hdqrs.Co. has never
done guard duty before until last week and this. I haven't been on as
yet. It only takes part of the company.

I have Father's letter containing Nov. statement. Dewitt put it over
Larrie, eh? I notice that Walt beat out Will a little, too. Good total sales.

Not much to write about today. Love to you all. Hope I can get a
furlough. Let me know what you think about the plan I wrote you of.

Bob

Ed Stone wrote me that old John Harris of Morris has sold out. What
other changes have taken place, since I left? I am thinking of sending
my old customers each a Xmas card. F.S. Gardiner of W. Oneonta has
sold out, hasn't he?

RDT

PS Here's an envelope I started to use in writing about a transfer. You
might as well use it.

RDT

Dec. 13, 1917, Thursday A.M.

Dear Folks,

I received Father's letter dated Dec. 10 last night and was very glad to get it. I noticed that I hadn't heard from home in several days. I do like those letters. What's the matter with Mother's and Ede's writing? Of course I know that it takes paper, but write on wrapping paper if you have to, if it's only a few lines. Why don't you write on a schedule, say Mother on Sunday and Ede on Wednesday—and Father as often as he gets a chance—or more frequently for everybody if there is news and you have the opportunity.

So Ed has gone to Wash. Well, I await with interest to hear what he does. I hope he gets into something good. I expect Hocky will throw a little bluff and come home again to work in the bakery. However it makes a little more pleasant trip for Ed to have him along as he is good company.

We had our first snow storm Tuesday night and when we fell in for reveille Wed. (yesterday) there was about five or six inches of snow on the ground. It had snowed nearly all night. Of course we couldn't very well drill in the snow. The company went out for a short hike in the P.M. However, our squad didn't, as we were mess squad detail again. We had it last Monday, extra and yesterday was our regular day.

No drill today either as the weather remains cold and the snow is too deep for drilling. We went for a short hike this A.M. and warmed ourselves up good.

By the way, the laundry found my socks, Ede, so I now have your two pair and the pair Mrs. Webster sent me.

We had a regimental review Tuesday P.M. for Maj. Gen. O'Ryan [the commanding officer of the 27th Division] who has recently returned from France.

I haven't received the package of cigars and cig'ts that Father wrote he had sent, as yet. His letter telling of their being sent, was dated Dec. 4th and here it is Dec. 13th. However other fellows are complaining of poor service, sometimes two weeks, so maybe it will show up after a while. I have had first class service until now. I hope they arrive pretty soon as I can use them to good advantage.

Our Cap't. Hayes left Tuesday night for France with orders to report to Gen. Pershing at once. He said in a talk to the company Monday night that he didn't know anything about it except that he was to report there and that as far as he knew, he would still be attached to the regiment—away temporarily. This started lots of rumors—some that we would soon be going across and others the opposite. Personally, I believe it will be a long time before we cross as we lack equipment and clothing and training as we haven't even been divided up into our different platoons for special work, as yet. Tod was over to the 1st last night and he had a talk with Lem Larrabee and Art Nelson and some of the other boys and they told him that Maj. Gen. O'Ryan and a part of his staff had been over there at Reg't Hdqrs a good share of the day yesterday looking over old records and having a pow-wow—that on account of the lack of morale in the 107th and the lack of communication between the 1st & the 7th men (all of which I believe is true, as I know it is in the Hdqrs Co, and hear it is in the line company). The 107th was to be broken up and all the 1st men were to go back again—how soon is not known—and the 1st is to be built up I suppose with draft men. I hope this is true. Maybe it's only rumor but it hardly seems as tho Art Nelson & Lem L. would tell Tod of it if it were not true.

Bob Harris has a furlough for 15 days which extends over Xmas and New Year's and he starts home sometime next week. He's certainly lucky. There's considerable difference between the 1st and the 107th, I can tell you. If there is any possibility of getting a furlough, you bet I'll work my head off to get it. Of course the men who have been in the service the longest, have the best records, and have very urgent special reasons are the ones who get them. Possibly pull helps a little, too. Only 5% of the company can be absent at one time. The men who get furloughs over Xmas & N. Year's only get 8 days. I talked with

Lieut. Wilson yesterday and told him I would like to get a furlough after the 1st of the year (knowing there was little chance probably of getting a Xmas furlough) and said that I wanted to go home on business etc. and he said to put in my application about the 1st of the year and he would OK it. So I think my chances are pretty good to get one about Jan 4th for eight days. I'll just have to wait and see. Do you think it is worth coming home for 8 days? Of course you offered to foot the bill.

We are all waiting for pay day. We haven't had our Nov. pay as yet. We certainly ought to get it in a day or two. I am pretty low and may have to cash another $5. check. Most of my money goes for laundry (there are no facilities for washing cloths here—particularly in cold weather), buying New York papers, and buying food at the Canteen. I won't say much about the food (it's in the cooking) but as long as I have money, I'm going to buy some decent food, as what we get often is far from appetizing, to say the least.

I have increased my insurance to $10,000 as Father suggested. Also I cancelled that $6.70 allowance I was going to send home. It may come home for now.

I received a box last night from the First Presbyt. S.[unday] School. It was fine of them to send it. It was marked "Please do not open until Christmas" but as I was craving for something sweet and my pocket book was pretty low, I opened it. Maybe you'd better not tell anyone in S School about it. It contained an O.D. hdf., a pencil, Colgate's Shaving Stick, pckg. B Nut gum, two pckg. sweet chocolate, some fruit cake, salted peanuts and candy. It was a nice box and I enjoyed it.

Had a letter from Bill Hones the other day. Seems to be getting along well.

I am finishing this letter in the P.M. It is still cold, with snow in the air. The company has been over and carried back some fire wood for the kitchen. There seems to be plenty over at the switch but the reg't hasn't enough mules and wagons evidently.

Well, I've been out standing retreat and it is now time for mess. Hope to hear from you soon again. With love to you all,

Bob

**Letter postmarked Spartanburg, S.C., Wadsworth Br.,
Dec. 15, 1917, 1 PM**

Friday Eve [Dec. 14, 1917]

Dear Folks,

Here it is Dec. 14 and no pay yet. Tod and I have been over to the 1st and have seen Bob Harris. As I was out of money, I asked him to cash a check. On account of having a furlough, he had plenty of cash, but he had nothing smaller than a ten, so I gave him a check for $10.00. Otherwise I would have only taken $5.00. I hope you won't think I'm extravagant, but I have had to pay for laundry and other odds and ends like haircut, canned heat, stamps and writing paper, eats, etc. The food has been better the last day or two as Lieut. Talbot has been looking after it.

Bob has a 15 day furlough. He starts home a week from last night and has until Jan. 4th. You will undoubtedly see him.

It seems to me that we gave up that storage of Mr. Mead's at Walton before I left. Still as it is five months ago, I won't say for sure. I know we had nothing in the storehouse before I left and as I recollect, we gave it up—that is, I didn't see Mr. Mead myself, but I think you wrote him from the store.

I haven't heard from Ed as yet. I am anxious to hear. Also about Hocky. Can it be possible that Hocky has really enlisted and how can he get into the Ordnance. He doesn't know anything about ordnance, does he?

In regard to furlough, Mother, there is a lot of difference between our reg't and the Ambulance Co's, the 1st Reg't and others. Also, sergeants have a better chance than buck privates. I think I will be able to get a furlough from Jan. 4 to Jan. 11. Father, send me a telegram about Jan. 1 as you say in your letter.

Don't know as I will go to Atlanta with Dave. He suggested it to me some time ago. Tod and I are thinking of going to Spartanburg for dinner on Christmas.

Mother, I really don't know of a thing I want for Christmas. There isn't much that we would be able to use. If I can cash a little check once in a while when necessary, (I'll try and not cash too many or too often) and if you will keep writing me your good letters, I'll be satisfied. Of course I'll appreciate a box of eats now and then.

Everything was OK in my Thanksgiving box, Ede, cake, pie, and everything. Go ahead and send me another as you say you are going to in your letter. It will tickle me to death.

Love to all of you and to the Newells.

Say, I could use a good pair of gloves—I'd rather pick them out myself if you don't object.

Good night.

Bob

Letter postmarked Spartanburg, S.C., Wadsworth Br.,
Dec. 18, 1917, 12 M

Monday Eve [Dec. 17,1917]

Dear Folks,

I received Father's telegram. I had already spoken to Lieut. Wilson about a furlough around the first of the year and he said he would OK a furlough for that time. Then afterwards the announcement was made that there would be two periods for furloughs—Dec 20 to 28 (for Christmas) and Dec 28 to Jan 3 (for New Year's) and that men who wished to make application for furloughs should hand in their names to the first sgt. Since I had already had a talk with Lieut. Wilson and told him that I wanted a furlough for business reasons (I didn't know there would be the Christmas and New Year's furloughs) I thought I might better wait and not try for a Christmas or New Year's furlough. Even if I had put in an application, I believe my chances would have been pretty small as there are men who have been away from home longer than I, men who have been in the service longer and only 15 men can go in each period, anyway. I think my chances are pretty good tor about Jan 3 or 4—eight days, maybe ten. I'll try for 10 days anyway. Tod made application for a Christmas furlough (Dec 20-28) but doesn't hold much hope for it.

I bought some gloves downtown so I really don't need any as I said I did—for Christmas.

I received Ede's letter of Thursday. Any box you send, Ede, will absolutely meet with my approval. Go ahead and send, Ede. I will appreciate the helmet very much. It is a coincidence that you were just knitting one.

Yes, Bill wrote me about his engagement. He seems to be getting along well in the army.

Also received Father's letter of the 13th. Am anxious to hear from Ed. Haven't a word from him as yet.

Have never received the box of smokes Father sent me on Dec. 4. Did you send it by Parcel Post? I suppose you did. If you send any more, you'd better register the package. I've been watching every mail and hoping to see it as I need some smokes.

No pay day yet and here it is the 17th. Well, I'm in the army now.

Was over to the 1st last night with Tod and had a visit with Bob Harris and the other boys. Bob is counting the days till his furlough. Not much news over there.

Will you thank the Sunday School for the box they sent and I will also write them.

The weather is still cold. We didn't do much drilling the latter part of last week but today it was somewhat warmer and we went out and did "Squads right and left." We had a lecture Friday by Lieut. Wilson on the different sections of our company but as yet we are doing the same old drilling.

Saw Dave Murray over at the 1st last night. He has had a hard cold for several days but is getting better.

Well, this is all the news for tonight. Love to you all.

Bob

**Letter postmarked Spartanburg, S.C., Wadsworth Br.,
Dec. 20, 1917, 12 M**

Wed. Evening [Dec. 19, 1917]

Dear Folks,

I've had "some" mail yesterday and today. Letters from Bob Brooks, Ed, Father (2), Mother, Aunt Nell, Joe Valentine and Christmas cards from Mary McMahon and Mildred Harris at the store. Also a little book of Binghamton views from Henry Hopkins, Jr.

Ed wrote quite a letter telling how he and Hocky enlisted and their different experiences. Evidently, so far, they aren't rushed with work. He has seen P.F.Tichener, Eddie Jackman, Sher Smith & Charlie Challice.

I have Father's letters as of Saturday and Monday. No doubt, Mr. Sisson has Bill's telegram by this time. I guess Bill just neglected writing as he is well. He waited so long that he finally wired his father, so he told me. The "X" in your Monday letter, Father, is certainly appreciated. We finally had Pay "Night" (instead of Pay Day) last night. Started paying the company off at nine o'clock and finished about 10:30. I don't just understand why they didn't wait until this morning to pay us off, except that they didn't want us to miss this morning's drill. It would be terrible if we missed a half day of drill just to get paid off. We had several days of pretty cold weather during which it was a trifle hard to keep warm in our tents but it isn't so cold now altho it's not warm by any means. During the middle of the last two days, the snow has melted off some (making it sloppy in the afternoon and icy in the morning — great for drilling) but there is still some left. Nothing doing on the pckg. of cigars yet. You "know" I notice your frequent letters, Father, and I surely appreciate them. I will try hard for a 15 day furlough but may only get an 8 day, and will be mighty fortunate if I get that. I have been over to the 1ˢᵗ tonight. Saw Bob Harris. He starts tomorrow and will be in to see you. He has a couple pictures of the camp and a two star service pin which I am sending the family as

Christmas presents. They are my limit. Was going to send a service flag but Mother wrote she already had one. Hope they please you. The 1ˢᵗ Band was planning to come home for Christmas, as you probably noticed by the papers. Had it all fixed up at the Bing. end but Division Hdqrs. vetoed it.

You will probably receive an allotment check from my November pay check for $6.70. Keep it. I have cashed two checks lately. As I wrote you, I have increased my insurance to $10,000 and cut out my allotment. I stand as follows:

$5.00 per month for $50. Liberty Bond
<u>6.60</u> per month for $10,000 insurance
$11.60

So I will have $18.40 coming each month from my $30. pay.

Thank you for writing me the news about the business. I like to hear about it. A good statement of facts you sent out in regard to shortening of credits. The trade must begin to realize the conditions by this time, I should think.

No more news about going back to the 1ˢᵗ. A rumor, I guess, altho the conditions I wrote of, are certainly true.

I saw Dave the other night and wrote you. Didn't see him tonight when I was over.

I haven't been in the YMCA building very much, in fact the first time was just a couple of days ago. They are doing good work. They furnish a good warm comfortable place for the men to read, write and visit. They had entertainment & moving pictures and are a good influence. They furnish reading and writing material, sell post cards and stamps. The Knights of Columbus building does the same. The YMCA has had a big tent where they had good vaudeville and pictures until the other day when we had the snow storm. It fell down during the storm from the weight of the snow.

Had a nice letter from Aunt Nell and enjoyed it very much. Also enjoyed Mother's letter. I have just read it over again now.

Had a first class letter from Joe [Valentine], in which he gave me lots of good dope on the business.

Tod didn't get his furlough for Christmas. He's going to try for one after Jan 1ˢᵗ, same as I. Was downtown with him this P.M. and had a good meal. Must stop and make up my bed as it is most 11 o'clock. With love to you all.

Bob

Letter postmarked Spartanburg, S.C., Wadsworth Br., Dec. 30, 1917, 6 AM

Dec. 27, 1917, Thurs. Evening

Dear Folks,

I have so many letters to answer that I hate to start. Had another letter from Ed today written on Christmas. He had a quiet day same as I did. Also had a nice letter from Ethel Summers and a little note which Vivian wrote to me. Also have had letters within the last few days from Grandma Truesdell, Aunt Nell, Joe Valentine, Bob Douglas, Mrs. W.O. Birdsall, Miss Hoag of Yonkers, Marion Newell, Xmas cards from several of my old customers, Orrie & Frances Summers, Dorothy & Sally Ballard, Uncle Arthur, several from Ed, several from all of you and your Xmas telegram.

I received Ede's box the day before Xmas and Mother's came last night. The helmet is fine, Ede, and I thank you and your picture is fine, too. It is a very good picture of you—the photographer must have caught you unaware—I am going to enjoy looking at it. The candy is all gone long ago. Tod wants me to thank you for his candy cane. Mine was fine, too.

Have you been into Ray Douglas' to get those pictures from Miss Tuttle, yet? You haven't mentioned it in your letter. I hope you have as there are several good ones, particularly the enlarged photo of our old squad in the 1ˢᵗ.

I finally received Father's package of smokes and they are very welcome.

Mother's package was fine. The cake disappeared in about 10 minutes. The boys [wished they had] more. I will write and thank Mrs. Sawtelle and Mrs. Leighton very soon. The socks & wristlets were very nicely made. I will study up on French with my book. Nice little pencil Father sent me. In my Red Cross box there was a box of Hershey's gum and in Mother's a box of Beechnut, so I'll have plenty for a while. I'm keeping the salted peanuts for myself. I appreciated your Xmas telegram very much.

Dave Murray has been under the weather with a cold, but was over a couple of nights ago with a pair of mittens his mother sent him for Christmas. He was in bed for a few days but is much better now and has not been seriously ill at any time, I believe. Many fellows have colds and coughs here, in fact a great many. They took cold during the cold spell we had a couple of weeks ago. I have a little cold and a slight cough—nothing serious in the least and am getting over it.

It is great that Roy is going to get a major's commission. Hope he will be able to be home some to help Father. I was sorry to hear of Mr. Comstock's and Mr. Rally's death. I can just see them both in my mind, walking into your (our?) office, Father—Cummy with the dope on the flour market, and Mr. Rally, with the spat, spat, spat as his feet hit the floor and his patient attempts to sell you tea. Poor Cummy, he certainly had a hard time, didn't he?

I received Father's letter containing blank proxy. I am going to speak to Lieut. Wilson after the first of the year. If it is just as probable that I caught a furlough so to be home for the annual meeting on Jan. 21, I think I will wait until then. If he would rather I would come home about Jan. 4th, I will come then. If I can't get one at all, I will send back the proxy to you.

Sunday and Monday our squad was on mess shack detail. Sunday was our regular day and Monday was extra—for disciplinary reasons—we didn't have our floor swept quite clean enough to suit the corporal in charge of quarters on the Friday before. We were lucky not to get it on Christmas. The duties are to wash up all the squad table dishes in which the food is served to the different squads.

Christmas Day, we had our turkey dinner, with all the fixin's. Good but it didn't have the home flavor. Tod and I went downtown — after we got stalled with no gas for an hour in a Ford — the driver had to walk about 3 miles for more gas — in the evening, saw some good Keith vaudeville which has just started in S., had a soda and came back to camp. I hoped we wouldn't have any reveille Xmas A.M. (that is — we wouldn't have to get up till we pleased) but reveille was the same as on Sundays — 7:15.

Xmas eve the company had an entertainment in the mess shack. The band played a number of selections, there was music by our company Hawaiian trio on instruments, free-hand drawing by one of the men, and another fellow and myself sang. I haven't been doing much singing but got away with it pretty well. I sang "Oh, promise me" and "Mother Machree." The men of the company chipped in some time ago and rented a piano but there aren't any men in the company who play very well.

I have been writing the last couple of paragraphs later. This is Friday evening. I got so sleepy last night I had to go to bed.

I have just received Father's letter concerning questionnaire and the questionnaire itself. I took it up to the 1st Sgt. He says that all that must be done is for him to send a certificate to the local board stating that I am in this command at the present time and this he will do at once. You see I enlisted after I registered.

Aunt Nell sent me a post office money order for $5 as a Xmas present which I appreciated very much of course. Money is one of a few things which a fellow can use here. Father's X [$10] came in very handy, too. Mr. Alonzo Roberson made a very nice Christmas present to the Bing. boys here in camp — $2. to each man.[47] So I received $17. in all.

The company has finally been divided up into the different platoons. I am assigned to the Signal Platoon and my work is similar to that I had over in the Hdqs Co of the 1st — wig wag and semaphore signaling etc. We still do plenty of "squads right and left," "right front into line" and "on right into line" however.

The weather has modified considerably. The snow has all melted off. Xmas day was a nice bright, fairly warm sunshiny day — quite different from other Xmas days I have experienced.

I think I forgot to say we had a Xmas tree in our shack and lots of holly which is easily gotten by going out in the woods nearby.

We have a fellow in our tent named Sancombe who works in the regimental post office. He says there were 10 carloads of mail [that] came in for the camp during the few days preceding Xmas, so you can see there is a tremendous amount of mail coming in here. There is certainly a bunch of it coming into this reg't.

Well, inspection comes again tomorrow A.M. I expect I'll go to town maybe and get a bath and do a few errands in the P.M. With love to all.

Bob

Notes

1   Jacobson, *History of the 107th Infantry U.S.A.*, 13.

2   Seward, *Binghamton and Broome County, New York, A History, Vol. I*, 576.

3   Harris, *Duty, Honor, Privilege: New York's Silk Stocking Regiment and the Breaking of the Hindenburg Line*, 1.

4   Jacobson, *History of the 107th Infantry U.S.A.*, 13.

5   Ibid.

6   Seward, *Binghamton and Broome County, New York, A History, Vol. I.*, 576.

7   Yockelson, *Borrowed Soldiers: Americans under British Command, 1918*, 24–25.

8   Harris, *Duty, Honor, Privilege: New York's Silk Stocking Regiment and the Breaking of the Hindenburg Line*, 62.

9   Ibid., 83–84.

10   Ibid., 89.

11   Yockelson, *Borrowed Soldiers: Americans under British Command, 1918*, 25.

12   Ibid., 27.

13   Yorke, *The Trench: Life and Death on the Western Front 1914–1918*, 39–40.

14   *History of Company "E", 107th Infantry, 54th Brigade, 27th Division U.S.A.*, 50.

15   Jacobson, *History of the 107th Infantry U.S.A.*, 15.

16   Ibid., 11.

17   *History of Company "E", 107th Infantry, 54th Brigade, 27th Division U.S.A.*, 51–52.

18   Morgan, *The Concise History of World War I*, 74.

19   Ibid., 77.

20   Fussell, *The Great War and Modern Memory*, 41–42.

21   Morgan, *The Concise History of World War I*, 78.

22   Ibid., 81–82.

23   Ibid., 82–83.

24 Ibid., 85.

25 Jacobson, *History of the 107th Infantry U.S.A.*, 17.

26 Harris, *Duty, Honor, Privilege: New York's Silk Stocking Regiment and the Breaking of the Hindenburg Line*, 88.

27 Van Ells, *America and World War I: A Traveler's Guide*, 232–233.

28 Matloff, *World War I: A Concise Military History of "The War to End All Wars" and The Road to the War*, 70.

29 Stone, *World War One*, 151.

30 Morgan, *The Concise History of World War I*, 56–57.

31 Stone, *World War One*, 142–143.

32 Yorke, *The Trench: Life and Death on the Western Front 1914–1918*, 72.

33 Keene, *World War I: The American Soldier Experience*, xiii.

34 Simkins, Jukes, and Hickey, *The First World War: The War to End All Wars*, 147–148.

35 Ibid., 24.

36 Liddell Hart, *World War I*, 176.

37 Yockelson, *Borrowed Soldiers: Americans under British Command, 1918*, 31–32.

38 Yorke, *The Trench: Life and Death on the Western Front 1914–1918*, 53.

39 Pvt. Truesdell refers two times in this letter to African-Americans he encountered in South Carolina in ways now unacceptable, although not at all unusual at that time. These references are surprising, even shocking, because in his later life, he was never known to discriminate.

40 Pvt. Truesdell often refers to "Ed," his older brother, who was still living in Binghamton and had not yet enlisted in the military.

41 The stove was known as a Sibley stove, which, together with wooden floors and sides applied to the tents, helped to provide warmth.

42 Pvt. Truesdell refers to a new license that his father must have. It becomes clear in subsequent letters that his father has purchased a new Ford. Owning and driving an automobile was still a relatively new experience at a period of time when Americans were making the change from the use of horse-drawn conveyances to automobiles.

43 Pvt.Truesdell's father visited him for a few days, apparently at
    some point during the week of October 28, leaving on Sunday night
    November 4.

44 Pvt.Truesdell notes that he would like to transfer to the
    Quartermaster Corps, the part of the armed services whose
    responsibility was to provide food, clothing, and supplies to the army.
    It doesn't escape the reader that an infantryman would face terrible
    dangers in trench warfare and probably many doughboys would
    have preferred the Quartermaster Corps, whose work was done well
    behind the front lines, but in Pvt. Truesdell's case, his interest in
    such a transfer was very sensible since he already had several years
    of employment in the wholesale food business.

45 Pvt. Truesdell again acknowledges receiving packages from home.
    Families at home typically—and apparently frequently—sent
    food of various kinds, cigars and cigarettes, and items of clothing,
    especially socks. Smoking was very common, and many soldiers, if
    not most, smoked cigars, cigarettes, and/or pipes.

46 The article "Kitchens in Camps Called Unsanitary" appeared on
    Tuesday, December 4, 1917, in the *New York Tribune*.

47 Pvt. Truesdell mentions Mr. Alonzo Roberson. Alonzo Roberson, Jr.,
    a prominent citizen of Binghamton, was successful in business and
    banking; his beautiful mansion on Front Street is now the home of
    the Roberson Museum and Science Center.

FURTHER TRAINING
AT CAMP WADSWORTH
AND IN FRANCE

While training progressed in the many training camps stateside, the American Expeditionary Forces (A.E.F.) were becoming more organized in France. Probably unbeknown to Pvt. Truesdell and most of the other members of the 27th Division, Gen. Pershing formed the American II Army Corps on February 20, 1918. The new II Corps was composed of six American divisions scheduled to arrive during the coming spring months in the British sector.[1] The 27th was one of those divisions.

As noted above, gas warfare was introduced early in the war by the Germans and continued to be used by both sides. Inevitably, American soldiers would encounter gas attacks, and indeed, on February 26, 1918, American troops came under a German gas attack for the first time.[2] In *Doughboy War,* James Hallas explains that gas casualties were admitted to a hospital where they stripped and showered if they were able to do so on their own. If not, they were bathed while they lay on their stretchers. Bicarbonate of soda was sprayed in eyes, nose, and throat. If soldiers had ingested food or water contaminated by gas, they "were given olive or castor oil to coat the irritated stomach linings. Fortunately, while a significant producer of casualties, gas was not a great killer. About 27.3 percent of all A.E.F. casualties were caused by gas, but most were not fatal."[3]

During February 1918, the Germans, again seeking techniques to break the stalemate on the Western Front, were training their troops in new offensive techniques. "There was a special school in

Belgium to train infantry that would move forward, fast, dodging and weaving, giving each other cover fire. Such were the *Stosstrupps*. They were not to try to deal with enemy posts but to move forward and destroy communications."[4] Further, Gen. Ludendorff was planning the concentration of heavy artillery, light machine guns, and grenades fired from a rifle.[5] The concentration of weaponry, stealthfully done, took place near St. Quentin, where the French and British armies joined. This was a vulnerable spot since each army would likely look after itself and perhaps retreat in different directions—the French toward Paris and the British toward the Channel ports where they could evacuate to England.[6] Unbeknown to Pvt. Truesdell, of course, the area around St. Quentin would become the ground over which he and the rest of the 27th Division would be fighting later in the year.

On March 3, 1918, the Treaty of Brest-Litovsk officially ended the war between Russia and Germany. By signing the peace treaty, Russia lost Ukraine, Poland, the Baltic provinces, and other large Russian territories.[7] The many divisions that Hindenburg and Ludendorff had moved from the Eastern Front to the Western Front gave Germany a superiority in manpower on the Western Front for the time being—until the Americans arrived.[8]

The shifting of the divisions from the Eastern Front to the Western Front, the special training of *Stosstrupps*, and the concentration of weaponry near St. Quentin had been done for the purpose of beginning a series of German offensives on the Western Front before American soldiers arrived in great numbers. On March 21, more than 6,000 German guns opened a five-hour artillery bombardment on a 60-mile front against the British near St. Quentin.[9] The massive barrage was the beginning of an offensive code named "Michael." The offensive eventually penetrated 40 miles.[10] Regaining the lost ground during the coming months would be a severe challenge for the British and their allies, including the 27th Division.

After the British fell back to Amiens during the German "Michael" offensive, Gen. Ludendorff continued the offensive, which finally lost steam just short of Amiens. The British brought up reserves, some in red, double-decker London buses. At the same time, the German troops fell upon "masses of British stores" and gorged "themselves in a way unthinkable behind their own lines."[11] The offensive was finally called off around the beginning of April, but by that time, the British had suffered 178,000 casualties, the French about 77,000, and the Germans around 250,000.[12]

On April 9, the Germans began another offensive known as Operation Georgette. This offensive was south of Ypres near the Lys River. Just as they had done in Operation Michael, the Germans began the attack with great intensity and by the next day had seized Armentières. The British were forced to abandon Messines Ridge (its continuation, Mount Kemmel, briefly held by the French, was also lost) and Wytschaete, which the British had struggled to occupy the previous year. On April 11, Field Marshal Haig issued an order in which he told his men that they had their "backs to the wall" and that "every position must be held to the last man; there must be no retirement." Although the British were gradually able to strengthen their position,[13] the outlook was dire. The Allies finally agreed that their efforts must be coordinated, and Gen. Ferdinand Foch was named the Allied commander in chief on the Western Front.[14] When the Germans continued Operation Georgette in the latter part of April, they were met by a strong British and Australian defense. By the end of the month, they had run out of momentum, and the offensive wound down.[15]

Meanwhile, German U-boats were carrying out constant attacks on Allied shipping in the Atlantic and the North Sea. The attacks had become so devastating that the British devised a plan to try to halt the losses. The British Royal Navy staged a raid on Zeebrugge, a major U-boat base on the Belgian coast, on April 23, 1918. "Two...block-ships were sunk across the narrow channel as planned, the viaduct was cut and Zeebrugge was neutralized as a U-boat base, but for just three days. By the end of that time the Germans had cut a new channel that by-passed the two sunk cruisers."[16] The British plan had appeared to be promising, but in fact, passage of U-boats was barely inconvenienced.

Back in the United States, on January 8, 1918, President Wilson gave his famous "Fourteen Points" speech,[17] in which he recommended the basis for a peace plan that included the self-determination of nations, but meanwhile, men at Camp Wadsworth were trying to keep warm in the unusually cold winter. After the weather finally improved, the doughboys were sent in March to the rifle range at Glassy Rock, 12 miles from Campobello, South Carolina, in the foothills of the Blue Ridge Mountains.[18] As a city boy, Pvt. Truesdell had to get used to using a rifle. At the end of the first day of rifle work at the range, Pvt. Truesdell writes, "First we shot ten shots at 100 yards prone (lying down) with bayonets fixed. Then back to 200 yd. line where we shot 10 shots from a trench, standing. Then to the 300 line where we fired from trench, standing, 15 shots....They say we keep it up every day we're here, Sunday included."

Later in March, Pvt.Truesdell writes that he will soon be going into the trenches for 72 hours. The 107th was originally scheduled for the 72-hour stint in mid-February, but the weather had been so bad that Gen. O'Ryan had postponed the assignment. Even though the weather had improved, heavy rains causing the trench walls to be dripping wet and the trench floors to be flooded were a huge challenge for the men.[19]

During the spring months at Camp Wadsworth, training was clearly becoming more intense. The next destination was the artillery range. On April 10, the 107th regiment hiked to the artillery range about 24 miles from the camp, where the men had their first experience moving forward under a rolling barrage.[20] The return hike from the artillery range to the camp was particularly memorable. The men had to cover a distance in one day that would ordinarily take two days. Jacobson confirms that on the return hike from the artillery range, "purposely the men were put to a severe test, and they met the test admirably."[21]

The men at Camp Wadsworth received official word of an imminent departure on April 15. Aside from having to send home all unserviceable items, their preparation included receiving "the new American Enfield rifles in place of the Springfield rifles which had been used in training."[22] Although the men were told that they would be leaving Camp Wadsworth, they were not told where they would be going. That information was undisclosed.

As directed, Pvt. Truesdell, having been duly vaccinated against smallpox, packed up and prepared to depart from Camp Wadsworth. After the last days of intense preparation, he and the other men of the Headquarters Company of the 107th Infantry Regiment boarded a train—perhaps with a mix of excitement and apprehension—on Sunday, April 28, 1918, for an overnight trip to an unknown destination. That destination turned out to be Newport News, Virginia, the second largest embarkation port during World War I. Hoboken, New Jersey, was larger, but nonetheless, 288,000 soldiers left the United States for Europe from Newport News.[23]

At Newport News, the men were housed for 10 days at Camp Stuart, where they slept in spring beds in comfortable barracks rather than the canvas cots in canvas tents at Camp Wadsworth. The barracks were also furnished with excellent bathing facilities.[24] Held in quarantine, the men could not leave Camp Stuart, but friends and relatives could visit them at the camp.[25] Pvt. Truesdell's parents were among the visitors. It was probably during the weekend Friday—Sunday, May 3—5 that his parents traveled from Binghamton to Camp Stuart to visit their son shortly before his regiment left for France.

On May 9, Pvt.Truesdell boarded the U.S.S. *Susquehanna* along with other men of the 107th Infantry Regiment "with the exception of the 2nd Battalion and Machine Gun Company and one platoon of Company D, which was quarantined.... Soon after she received her quota of troops the *Susquehanna* left her pier and went out into the bay, where she lay until the following morning" when both the *Susquehanna* and the U.S.S. *Antigone*, on which other units of the 107th were sailing, "quietly and unostentatiously moved out to sea."[26]

Both the *Susquehanna* and the *Antigone* were former German liners, which had spacious dining rooms and staterooms for officers on the main and upper decks; below decks were the mess halls and bunks for the men.[27] In fact, the men on the *Susquehanna*, previously known as the *Rhein*, referred to their quarters as " 'the black hole of Calcutta' because they were located so far below deck." It took about two weeks to reach France, a period of time during which seasickness was prevalent.[28]

The two ships traveled in a convoy with 14 other ships initially accompanied by the U.S. Cruiser *Frederick*. On the sixth day at sea, the convoy was surrounded by a dozen destroyers, which were to provide protection against German submarines, and the *Frederick* turned back.[29] Fortunately, no submarines were sighted during the trip, during which the weather, except for two days, was pleasant.[30] It was during the Atlantic crossing that soldiers' letters began to be censored. Pvt. Truesdell's first censored letter was read by Lt. R.H. McIntyre, who also read some of Pvt. Truesdell's other letters.

Brest, France, located at the western tip of Brittany, was the destination of the 27th Division. The main American Navy base in France, Brest was located in a sheltered rocky inlet and had been an important French naval base in the past, but, because France concentrated on its land forces during the war, the Brest port had been allowed to languish. Consequently, there was plenty of room for American ships to moor, and, after the U.S. built up the port facilities, it was here that transport ships brought nearly a million doughboys.[31] After the transports arrived at the Brest harbor, flat-bottomed barges called lighters carried the soldiers to the docks.[32]

After the *Susquehanna* arrived at Brest on May 23, the men were ferried to an old stone quay and formed into battalions. They then marched to the outskirts of Brest and bivouacked. The hike to camp took the men through the city, up a hill, and out past the old walled-in Pontanezen Barracks, more familiarly known as the Napoleon barracks. With little emotion, French women quietly watched the soldiers marching through the town, but many children followed the battalions, noisily begging for treats and cigarettes. Just beyond the barracks, the men put up shelter tents in the hedged-in fields and settled in for the night.[33] The following night, the 107th received orders that it would leave Brest the next morning for a trip by rail.[34] After riding two days in French box cars (8-chevaux—40-hommes boxcars, each of which could carry 8 horses or 40 men), the men arrived in Noyelles sur Somme on the Somme river basin.[35] The next day, the regiment was ordered to move again. Rue, another town near the Somme, became the regimental headquarters with

the men billeted in various little nearby towns. The billets were anything
that could provide shelter—barns, woodsheds, spare rooms in houses.[36]

It soon became evident that the 107th regiment, along with the rest
of the 27th Division as well as the 30th Division, would train with the
British. American rifles and other equipment were replaced by British
Enfield rifles, bayonets, gas masks, and steel helmets.[37] Training with
the British was probably expected. Once the United States had declared
war, the British were eager to have American soldiers sent to the British
Expeditionary Force (BEF).[38] However, President Wilson, Secretary of
War Newton D. Baker, and Gen. Pershing, the commander of the A.E.F.,
staunchly resisted amalgamation.[39] It was important to Wilson that
the U.S. Army must fight as a separate force; if the U.S. didn't have its
own expeditionary force, Wilson feared that he might have diminished
influence at peace negotiations.[40] In any case, training under the
tutelage of the British in France was essential for the newly arrived
American infantry. Gen. Pershing had somewhat softened his position
and became open to the idea of British "assisting in the training of
American troops as long as it was 'strictly supplementary to our own
regular program' of fielding an American army."[41] In January 1918,
Gen. Pershing had made clear that his divisions were being loaned
to the British and that he might need to recall them at a time of his
choosing.[42] As it turned out, however, two American divisions, the 27th
and 30th, spent their entire service on the Western Front with the
British Army."[43]

Meanwhile, elsewhere on the Western Front, the Germans began
a third offensive on May 27th northeast of Paris on the Aisne River at
the Chemin des Dames. The Germans experienced great success and
"reached the river Marne, from where a heavy gun, 'Big Bertha' (named
after the wife of the arms manufacturer, Krupp), sent shells to Paris, 40
miles away."[44] By this time, Gen. Pershing believed that the 1st Division
was now ready to take up offensive action, and indeed the "Big Red One"
launched into battle at Cantigny, May 28-31.[45] The Americans proved
their fighting stamina and held their ground despite seven German
counterattacks.[46] Then, with Paris in danger during the Germans' third

offensive, the American 2nd and 3rd Divisions were sent to the Marne where they fought with the French at Château Thierry to halt the German onslaught.[47] If Pvt. Truesdell and others in the 27th Division were aware of these American successes, perhaps they gained confidence that they too, with further training, would be successful in battle.

The 107th Infantry Regiment of the 27th Division was indeed undergoing intense training with the British in the vicinity of Rue. It was at this point while they were training that they were sent to Noyelles in company detachments to retrieve any personal belongings that they wanted to have with them because their barracks bags were to be sent into storage in Calais.[48] Of course these personal belongings would have to be carried, so only the fewest and/or lightest articles could be kept.

A decent meal soon became a prime concern of the men after they started training with the British. Pvt. Truesdell tells his parents about a good meal that he had in a local restaurant, and he also writes about some special arrangements that he and several other men have made regarding meals probably because army food became monotonous. Staples were stew, rice, canned tomatoes, bacon, potatoes, canned corned beef or salmon, and hard crackers.[49] To simplify the distribution of food, the British took on the responsibility of delivering rations to the Americans training with them. Although Pvt. Truesdell is not complaining about the British food, many of the doughboys "found the food disagreeable,"[50] so it is not surprising that, during this time in and around Rue, the men sought out local restaurants whenever they were free from duty.[51]

While the 27th Division was training with the British in the area of the Somme, other American forces continued to try to push the Germans back after the latter's third offensive and became engaged, beginning on June 6, in heavy fighting in the Battle of Belleau Wood. The Second Division's Marine Corps brigade suffered terrible casualties, but the U.S. forces had decisively captured the wood by June 26.[52] Meanwhile, the Germans launched another offensive on June 9, but the French held the advance to nine miles. Within five days the offensive came to a close.[53]

Because the 27th Division was training with the British, Field Marshall Sir Douglas Haig reviewed the division on June 12.[54] Unfortunately, just at this time, the commanding officer of the 107th Regiment of the 27th Division, Colonel Willard Fisk, became very ill and received orders to return home. His longtime leadership of the regiment was much respected, and his men were reportedly very sorry to learn of his departure back to the U.S.[55]

Regimental headquarters was soon established in Vaudricourt, also in the Somme basin, and the battalions were again billeted in surrounding villages. British officers and NCOs reviewed the use of gas masks to make sure that the Americans were prepared for German cloud gas attacks. Following a lecture on the different kinds of gas warfare by a British officer, gas was released from cylinders, and every man had to be able to don his gas mask instantly.[56] After further training in offensive and defensive tactics, "the regiment packed up and started east on a long hike that extended over several days."[57] Indeed, Pvt. Truesdell writes that the regiment was subjected to some very difficult hiking in mid-June. He reports that "it has been hike, hike, hike....Man, I have done some of the meanest hiking for the past week I have ever done." The men marched in hobnailed shoes over hard and flinty roads and had to carry heavy loads: rifles, blankets, overcoats, and other clothing as well as personal belongings. To make matters worse, the weather was very hot.[58]

After about a week of hiking, regimental command was established in Haute Visée with the battalions in nearby villages, all of which were near the city of Doullens. Here the 27th Division was to be in reserve against an anticipated attack by the Germans.[59] The 27th Division was now attached to the British Third Army, commanded by Gen. Sir Julian Byng.[60]

In one of his letters, Pvt. Truesdell mentions that there are "lots of aeroplanes flying around." At the beginning of the war, it had been only 11 years since the Wright brothers succeeded in their test flight in 1903, but despite an initial lack of confidence in the military use of aircraft, military commanders learned that planes were essential in various ways as the war continued: reconnaissance, bombing, and fighting enemy planes.[61] Even before the United States entered the war, American pilots had formed the American Squadron, known as the *Escadrille Lafayette*, which first proved its usefulness at Verdun and thereafter gave invaluable support to France.[62]

**Letter postmarked Spartanburg, S.C., Wadsworth Br.,
Jan. 3, 1918, 11:30 AM**

Wed A.M., Jan 2, 1917[8]

Dear Folks,

I went downtown yesterday afternoon (we had New Year's Day off) with Tod, had a hot shower at the Y.M., saw the Keith vaudeville and had something to eat. When I got back about 10:30, I found your wire. Thank you for your good wishes. I have written about 10 or 12 letters the past week and have about 7 or 8 more to write. I am pretty sure I wrote you the day after Christmas, but I have written so many letters I may be mistaken.

I have written Ed four letters lately. I did fail to write him after I received his first letter, for a few days but since then I have written, as I say, four times. I presume the mails are slow. He has probably received my letters by this time. I received a box from the store, I think it was last Friday night. It contains 6# sweet chocolate, 200 Fatima cig'ts and 2 pckgs N&T raisins. I don't know just who sent this to me as I have heard nothing about it. If Father sent, I thank him. If somebody else sent it, please let me know. It was very acceptable.

The weather since Xmas has been snowy, cold, sloppy, windy etc. The Negroes blame us soldiers for bringing this weather as they say they never have had so much snow and cold as there has been this winter. Superstitious, eh?

Monday night (New Year's Eve) I went over to Co C mess shack to a beefsteak supper. There is a fellow named Zimmer in our company who was transferred from Co C a short time ago. He is a member of the Collegiate Quartette of NY City and has a very nice baritone voice. He also plays the piano well. Same fellow who accompanied me at our Xmas eve entertainment. Well, he wanted me to go over to Co C and sing for them. So I sang the same songs I sang for our entertainment—"Oh, promise me" and "Mother Machree" and then later I sang "Love's Old Sweet Song" which is the favorite song of Major Engle (in command of the 1st Battalion) who was present as were also the officers of Co C. I was in pretty good voice and got along very well. I enjoyed myself very much and met some nice fellows. The feed was OK. We had all the beefsteak we could eat (I had a piece as big as a dinner plate), vegetable soup, baked potatoes, creamed carrots, olives, coffee, bread & butter, delicious fruit salad, bananas & oranges, two bottles of pop, cigarettes & cigars—the best feed I've ever had in an army camp—it was well cooked and seasoned. Then the entertainment was first class afterwards,—some colored fellows from town, lots of "home" talent, which was really fine—instrumental.

I think I told you I had a nice letter from Uncle Arthur. He wrote that he was sending me a Khaki Testament but as yet I have not received it. Hope it gets here. However if it is not addressed any better than the letter was, it may never arrive. My letter was addressed as follows:

Mr. Robert Truesdell
Spartansburg, S.C.
Soldier's Camp

"Some" address, eh, but I suppose he didn't have any more of it. It was a wonder that I ever received the letter.

Had a letter from Ed the other day, written on last Thursday evening. Said he talked with P.F. Titchener on the phone.

Also have Mother's letter written last Thursday night, Ede's, written Friday P.M., and Father's of the 26th and 27th.

I'm glad if the pictures and service pin pleased you. I wrote on the box which contained the service pin that it was for both Mother and Edith, Ede, from what you wrote in your letter, you seemed to think it

was for Mother alone, I thought maybe. Mother writes you very gener-
ously offered to let her wear it. It is very nice of you. However I want
both of you to [take] a turn wearing it, if you care to, that is.

So Tod Corbett called up. I wrote him some time ago and haven't
heard a word. He's not much of a correspondent.

I'm glad you saw Mrs. Humiston. She's a great woman. I used to
enjoy calling on her.

Great sales for the year, Father. I'm anxious to see the statement
for the year.

You ask me about my squad, Father. Well, I don't like to be uncom-
plimentary, but if I tell the truth, I'll have to be. The squad leader or
temporary corporal (Schreider, by name) is a combination of Jew and
German, I should say. He hails from Southampton, Long Island (came
from the 12th) and is a rather coarse and ignorant fellow and also somewhat disagreeable in his manner. Can't hand him much. The next man's
name is Sancombe. His home is in Malone, N.Y. and was transferred
to the company from Co K of the 1st Inf. While he isn't what you would
call a really high-class fellow in civil life, he is at least agreeable and
"get-along-able." He works at the regimental post office. The next man's
name is H.P. Mack. He comes from up around Loon Lake, N.Y. He is a
farmer and a pretty good fellow. He came from Co K of the 1st. The next
fellow is "Mouth Almighty." His real name is Glenn Kelso and he comes
originally from Perry, N.Y. which is near Buffalo although he enlisted
in Southampton in the 12th and came here from there. He had very
little education, evidently, for he is an ignorant, no-nothing fellow, full of
noise, noise, noise and always telling what a first-class lineman he is (he
worked for the New York Telephone Co) and how much he knows about
signaling. Honestly I get so sick of hearing him talk about what a fine
fellow he is, and he don't seem to know any better. He has just come in
and he's talking now. He has come down from non-com. school where
he received a warrant as corporal in the Signal Platoon. Believe me, if I
had to talk about myself as much as Kelso has, to get a corporal's warrant, I'd rather be a private forever. I believe I know as much as he does
and I know Sisson does (we are all in the Signal Platoon) but the loud

talking won here. I doubt if he gets along very well with his men. The next fellow is Neacrato, an Italian, pretty good clean quiet sort of chap who came here recently from the 10th Inf. The next man is LaFave who came from Co K of the 1st—another Malone fellow. He was bugler in Co K. He is pretty lazy and a fellow who thinks if he can put a thing over on anybody, it is all right. He is forever trying to get two fellows arguing. Next is Jessup. He hails from Southampton, came here from the 12th. Nice pleasant little fellow, gentlemanly and easy to get along. The last is Rockafellow. He is an older fellow about 35 yrs old, I'd say. The rest are 20 to 25 yrs old. His home is in Middleton. He came from Co I of the 1st. Pretty good fellow. We call him "John D" for short. Schreider is assigned to the Sappers & Bombers Platoon, Mack, Jessup and Rockafellow to the Pioneer Platoon, Neacrato, Kelso, and myself to the Signal Platoon and La Fave to the 1 Pound French Mortar Platoon. The Pioneers have to repair dug-outs, shelters, trenches, etc. sort of general work. I can't really say I enjoy the squad, at least I don't enjoy it some of the time on account of some of the fellows in it. The squad leader doesn't take much interest in the squad, but we seem to get along. I get along all right, don't have such a bad time, things might be worse.

Tod is attached to the band so he doesn't have anything to do with the rest of the company.

You should see the tents up and down the street. Every little while, a live spark will drop down and start a hole burning. Usually they are discovered before burning very long, so that the tents have anywhere from one to a dozen holes in them, ranging in size from a half dollar to a dish pan. They are the same all over the camp. Sometimes the fires aren't discovered until too late and then up goes the tent and contents in flames. [There] have only been a couple in our regiment burn[ed] up so far. We have four holes in our tent, all burned recently. We were lucky until lately, our stove didn't seem to spark any. One of the holes is right over my cot, just where I lay my head each evening upon retiring (ahem). I have stuffed the hole with paper and I guess I'm all right, now.

It's getting pretty near my turn to go on K.P. (kitchen police). Each private in the company takes his turn in alphabetical order for five days and the Ss and some of the Ts are on at the present. The K.P.s do the dirty work around the kitchen—wash out the big pots and pans, pare the "taters," tote water, etc, etc, a dirty job but it doesn't come very often.

You're having good snappy weather, eh? It's chilly here but no where as cold as it is in B. I'm sitting in front of the stove now, toasting my shins, very comfortable. Everything is fine and dandy as long as we are issued wood enough. This P.M. we had no wood, so we sat around in our overcoats.

It's fine that Roy is going to be home for a while. It will help you out.

Our col.—Col Fiske and also Col Boyer of the old 1st have gone to the field and staff officers school at San Antonio, Texas, which starts Jan 2. Don't know how long it lasts.

Well, I have told you all the news. Will write again soon. With love to all

Bob

Letter postmarked Spartanburg, S.C., Wadsworth Br., Jan. 8, 1918, 11:30 AM

Sunday Evening [Jan. 6, 1918]

Dear Folks,

I'm on kitchen police. Get off tomorrow night after five days at it. Each private in the company gets it in alphabetical order. I've handled garbage, quarters of beef, scrubbed pots and pans etc. and am dirty.

Haven't time to write much and am too sleepy anyway. Will write you a regular book in a few days.

Am waiting to see Lieut Wilson about furlough. He returns in a few days. Am going to try to get home for the annual N&T meeting. Don't get your hopes too high for I may not get it, but I will do my best as I certainly would like to be home for a few days.

Love to all.

Bob

**Letter postmarked Spartanburg, S.C., Wadsworth Br.,
Jan. 10, 1918, 11:30 AM**

Wed. Night [Jan. 9, 1918]

Dear Folks,

Well, I'm off K.P. as I wrote Father this P.M. It was some dirty job but I won't get it again for a long time.

Our hot shower-baths are going now and I was down about 5:30 after I got [back] from town and had a good bath.

As I wrote to Father, I cashed a check this P.M. for $10.00. I bought a pair of boots which cost me $7.50. I have them on now and they are certainly fine and also they come in very handy. Price pretty steep but everything is down here. Tod went downtown with me.

You have certainly had some cold weather. Of course it hasn't been anywhere near as cold here and still cold enough if one lives in tents.

Very sorry to hear about the death [of] Milton Steele's father. It must have been a great shock and especially so, occurring at the dance as it did.

I have received Father's several letters, Mother's and Edith's also—written recently. I liked the stuffed prunes very much, Ede, and more would be quite acceptable. I assure you Tod says he would like a pair (or two) of socks very much. I will follow your instructions when mine begin to wear thru.

I received the insurance check Father sent me. Thank you.

Hope you all have had plenty [of] coal and wood to keep you warm.

I received a fine meerschaum pipe from the salesmen for Xmas. It was fine of them.

Well, I had the best visit over to the 1st last night. Bob Harris told me all he could think of about his visit at home. Lem Larrabee is going to the officers' school which started today here. Art Nelson has rec'd a second lieutenant's commission and is still over to the 1st helping them in the adjutant's office as Capt Davis has been transferred to the Military Police. He (Art) hopes to be assigned to the 1st permanently.

You know the different skeleton regiments here are going to be made into Pioneer Reg'ts. The 1st is now the 1st U.S. Pioneer Inf. An officer told me this P.M. that there were 25,000 men coming here soon to fill up these skeleton reg'ts. The job of these reg'ts. is to rebuild and reconstruct what has been torn down and blown up over in France. They are weeding out and giving all officers and enlisted men S.C.D.s (Surgeons Certificate Discharges) who are not fit for good hard service. You undoubtedly know that Major Seymour is out, also Major Sheehan is coming home. Geo Lenz of the band may get one as several others of the band may. I had a visit with Dave Murray. He went to Atlanta over New Year's & saw Charlie Morris. They staid with the Phelps part of the time while there. He says the Phelps are all well. [He] and Sid are now living there with them as Sid has been transferred to Atlanta. Fine, eh? Dave says he is coming home on a 30 days furlough for a short operation, nothing serious. This is on the Q.T.

I saw Lieut. Wilson this P.M. and I hope to be able to get home for the annual meeting. However don't get your hopes too high. I will let you know at once when I get anything definite on it.

Had a letter from Marian Ford Hackensack. She's a fine girl. Hope the young man is a good chap.

Had a letter from Mr. Williams.

There are a number of men from this reg't who leave for Camp Greene, No. Carolina tomorrow, and who are going over soon to act as interpreters, etc. I guess with the Vermont troops. Sancombe from our tent goes. They don't know just what they're going to do. I think 85 go from this reg't.

I must close now. Will write again soon. Love

Bob

Am in an awful hurry.

Letter postmarked Spartanburg, S.C., Jan. 17, 1918, 5:30 PM

Tuesday Eve, Jan. 15, 1918

Dear Folks,

Well, <u>many glad</u> tidings have I for you. I haven't written for several days as I have been busy studying and doing other things. I honestly don't know what they are, but it doesn't seem as tho I'd had a minute to sit down and write.

It is now after taps (11 o'clock) and I really shouldn't be doing this but here I am lying in cot (can't say bed) writing you by the light of a candle. (Electric light makes too much light, somebody might see the light in the tent.) Well, I won't keep the good news away from you any longer. My furlough is assured. But that isn't all. Here's my story.

About the middle of last week a division order came thru and was read to the company that an exam would be held on Jan 21 for enlisted men to try for commissions as second lieutenants in the QM Corps. My wire to you [explained the] necessity of having recommendations in quick order and I thank you very much for your kindness in getting them for me. They were certainly excellent recommendations from excellent men. I don't believe I am as fine as they make me out. I filed my application and had plenty of time. Tod Mulford did also. We decided we would try it although the time to prepare for it is very limited. We have sent for books to study and are attending a school which the captain of the supply company is conducting for the men who expect to try the exam. There are about 35 or 40 trying in this regiment. Well, several days before this order came thru, I had spoken to the lieut. about a furlough for 10 days starting the 18th, as I wrote you — so here's what I thought I'd do. If my furlough didn't come thru, I would try the exam — meanwhile studying and preparing anyway, but if I got my furlough, I'd let the exam go as the Cap't of the Supply Co. told us there would be another exam later in the year. I felt all the time that there was hardly time to adequately prepare myself to try this exam, but figured I would study along and attend this school and take the exam the next time maybe, giving myself plenty of time to plug. When I came in from school tonight (7 to 9) I found that the corporal in charge of quarters had been down looking for me. So I went up. There was my furlough all OK for 10 days and starting tomorrow the 16th. Well, I went up to the Lieut. to see if I could get a pass permitting me to leave camp tonight in order to catch the midnight train to Washington. I told him I had put in my application to try for the exam for the QMC commission and all about how I had it figured out. He was fine and said "Don't give up this chance to try for a commission by any means. I will have your furlough postponed until the 22nd or 23rd and you go ahead and try the exam." He also said he would arrange to have me excused from duty in the company in order to give me more time to prepare for the exam. So I am to go up to see him in the QM and make things definite. I will finish this in the A.M. after seeing him.

Wed. A.M. [Jan. 16, 1918]

I have been up to see Lieut. Wilson and everything is OK.

Thurs. A.M. [Jan. 17, 1918]

Well, I am absolutely going to finish this letter now and get it off. My hands are pretty cold so please excuse the writing.

I haven't seen the Lieut since yesterday A.M. but he told me he thought there would be no trouble in getting my furlough postponed. I will get it around the latter part of the month, I can't tell you just exactly the day. I'll let you know just as soon as I find out.

I was down to do some errands yesterday P.M. and while there [I] wired you a night letter which you have undoubtedly received by this time. I haven't written you for several days and having such good news, I thought I'd send a wire.

I'm sorry I won't be able to attend the annual meeting, but I thought it over and decided that as I might be in the service for some time to come, trying for the commission was more important than being present at the meeting for you are "master of the situation" and whatever you say, goes, as far as I am concerned for my reliance on your judgment is "colossal." Anyway we'll have a good visit when I do come home—which won't be long at that.

I have received Mother's letter of last week Thursday, Ede's of Friday last, telling of the box she had sent and which I received yesterday P.M. and Father's of the 11th and also of the 14th which contained the original recommendations from Mr. Phelps and Judge Lyon. Did you forget to enclose the original of Mr. Moon's or was there none? I have read over this last letter several times. It certainly is a "pippin," pop. I am afraid you're going to the dogs, Father, and losing all your Christian spirit, now that I can't be there at home to guide you. It certainly has been a fine year for us if things are as you write. Those profits are tremendous. When I get home I suppose I'll greet you as president of the N&T Co.

Now as to Ede's box, I'll say it was a success. I now have six pairs of good heavy socks (I suppose they are for me—I know you asked if Tod wouldn't like some—but you said nothing about there being any for him—so I took them) which is about right. I also thank Mother for the clothing-markers. They are first class. About the bags of candy Ede put in, I'll say that 1 and a half bags are gone already.

Had a good letter from Ed in which he says they are in their new building and that he is very busy.

Please don't expect to hear much from me for the next week as I must do a lot of studying and will [be] very busy. I am feeling great. In a week or 10 days time if all goes well, I ought to be on my way home on a 10 da. furlough. If anything particularly interesting happens I'll wire you a nite letter. Love to all.

Bob

**Letter postmarked Spartanburg, S.C., Wadsworth Br.,
Jan. 21, 1918, 6 AM**

Sat Eve [Jan. 19, 1918]

Dear Folks,

More developments. I am attending the school which the C.O. of the
Supply Co is conducting evenings. I spoke to Lieut. Wilson again about
my furlough which he told me to put in my pocket for a couple of days
and he said to keep it and after the exam he would just change the date
on it.—So I will surely see you.

In regard to the exam—I have heard today that it will be conducted as follows—of the men whose applications are accepted (no
men will be allowed to try the exam unless their applications have been
accepted) part have been notified today to appear on Monday next
for physical exam, part will be notified tomorrow (Sunday) to appear
Tuesday for physical exam, and the remainder will be notified Monday
to appear on Wednesday for physical exam. Then on Thursday the
mental exam will take place. The reason for the 3 nights for physical
exam is probably on account of the large number applying to try the
exam. A few men have been notified but so far Tod and I have not been.
Of course we have plenty of time to hear as yet—Sunday and Monday.
I am not "building too many air-castles" about getting a commission in
the QMC as the time is very short and the subject tremendously large
and yet I believe I have as good a chance as any of the fellows for none
of them have had any more time to study than I. The examiners can't
expect the applicants to know a lot about the QMC as it takes years to
learn half about it. Of course, if they are after men for Remount Stations
(part of the exam is to be about hypology[63]) men who have previous
experience in that line will have the advantage over the others, but if
they want men for the QMC in general I believe I have had as valuable
experience as any. Lieut. Wilson is giving me some time off from drill
to study up for the exam. He certainly is fine to me and I don't know
why particularly as he has paid no special attention to me before.

Mr. Ben Phelps dropped in yesterday P.M. for a few minutes and it was certainly fine to see him. He says he is working hard and that all of them are well. Will tell you all about it when I come home.

As I have said, I hear that the mental exam will not be until next Thurs. the 24th and if my application is accepted and I try the exam, I will probably start about the 26th or 27th—a little later than I wrote in my last letter. Don't get nervous—I'll get home pretty quick. The particulars about the exam seem to come thru from the Division Q Master rather slowly. If my application is not accepted I may get started before. Will let you know as soon as I find out for sure. Meanwhile I am continuing to study.

Had a letter from Ed tonight. Have written him about the furlough and expect to stop off and see him of course.

With love to all.

Bob

**Letter postmarked Spartanburg, S.C., Wadsworth Br.,
Jan. 24, 1918, 11:30 AM**

Wed. P.M. [Jan. 23, 1918]

Dear Folks,

Just a short note. Have Ede's letter of the 15th and Mother's of the 18th at hand.

That was quite an article in the Press about what you've done for the P.B.R.W.F.S.S. Ede, I think you and I went around with the Ford and picked up those boxes, when you first took over that work, didn't we?

I notice in the paper and from what Mother says, that Dave M. is getting along well.

What I am really writing this letter for is to mention the fact that the cost of transportation for one from Spartanburg to Binghamton is between $25. and $30. and if agreeable to the writer's "old man," it might be well if the former has the aforementioned sum in hand at as early a time as possible. (P.S. Send it any way you think advisable.) I have been studying since last Monday or Tuesday a week ago. The C.O. has been fine about excusing me from drill. I take my physical exam tomorrow A.M. at 8:30 and the mental test comes tomorrow night at 8:00. Some of the fellows seem to think that there will be several mental tests taking up several evenings, and starting tomorrow night so possibly I won't be thru till the middle of next week. I don't know definitely about this but will be quite apt to find out about it tomorrow night. If possible I want to arrange for my furlough to start about the 31st or the 1st so I will be home over a Saturday and Sunday and I think this can be arranged all right. Tod had to report yesterday A.M. for physical exam and came thru OK. I expect to do the same.

Haven't heard from Father about his trip to N.Y. Probably will, soon. Love to all.

Bob

**Letter postmarked Spartanburg, S.C., Wadsworth Br.,
Feb. 10, 1918, 1:30 PM**

Sat A.M. [Feb. 9, 1918]

Dear Folks,

Just a short letter. Will write again tomorrow.

I enclose check Father sent me for expense in coming home. Found it when I got back.

Also found a letter from Marsh. A short one, in which he said he was well and busy.

Also found that Bud Sheak and Bill Bloomer are back from the range and are looking fine. Tuttle comes in a day or two.

Bud Sheak wants Father—would like to know if Father would write a letter of recommendation for him. He asked me to write about it as he has no writing material. Only a small part of his company are back and none of the baggage. His address is:

Pvt. Robert Sheak
Hdqrs Co
105th Field Artillery
Camp Wadsworth

When I got back here, I found the company had all been rearranged in their tents, so now I have to settle again and get acquainted with more new fellows. Am at home now. It doesn't take long for me to settle.

The weather is warm here. Yesterday was beautiful and clear as was Thursday. Today is warm & cloudy. The mud is dried up considerably. Quite a change in weather from Binghamton.

I got that express package, I told you about, last night — the one Ede & Ed sent to me at Van Cortlandt last Aug. The cupcakes were like bullets, but there were 100 cigts & 50 cigars which came in very handy.

Will write you more fully tomorrow. Feel fine. Tod is fine. Was glad to see him. He has heard nothing about exam as yet. Will write more about it tomorrow.

My trip home was certainly short, wasn't it? Better than none, however. With love,

Bob

**Letter postmarked Spartanburg, S.C., Wadsworth Br.,
Feb. 11, 1918, 1:30 PM**

Sunday Afternoon [Feb. 10, 1918]

Dear Folks,

Well, I'll try and tell you of my return trip. I called up Mr. Maltby while I was waiting in Elmira as Father suggested and had a pleasant chat. My train was on time but as we went along we lost time. I had an upper berth. Below were two ladies — I think they slept together — evidently schoolteachers from the New England States. The train was quite crowded so it was a good thing I had the Erie wire ahead for a berth for me. In the morning when I got up, I found that the train was about five hours late and as the day went on, we lost more time so when we arrived in Washington, it was about three o'clock—six hours late. I went up to the Ordnance Bldg. and found Ed. We went up to the room and visited until about six when we went down and met Hocky and Bob Brooks and went to supper. Afterwards Bob left us and we returned to the room where we visited until it was time for me to go to the train. Ed went with me to the station. Thursday morning when I awoke, it was much warmer and the sky was clear and beautiful—no snow on the ground. It was quite a contrast to Binghamton. I arrived in Spartanburg about two o'clock—an hour late. Did a couple errands and went to camp on the electric road. The roads are drying up rapidly but no cars (jitneys) are running as yet between camp and town. It is a beautiful day here today warm and clear and was yesterday. Our tent is wide open and I am sitting here with no coat or sweater on. I had a good visit with Ed and Hocky and—

5:30 I had to stand retreat and will now continue my story. —told them all the home news. I told Ed about seeing the many interesting things in W. while he has the chance, etc.

When I got back to my company street Thursday afternoon about 4 o'clock,[64] I found everybody had been changed around in the tents to conform to the new platoons.[65] I am now in a tent with Proudy an old 7th man from NY as corporal—a good fellow; Wright, an agreeable chap—old 1st man from Walton; Wade, another old 1st man—good fellow; Julian and Olseski, former 12th men and latter from 10th, pretty fair fellows; Loushay, from the old 1st, pretty fair; and Gross, who used to be in Tod's tent—a good chap—a New Yorker, old 7th man. Gross and Proudy are fairly well educated fellows and agreeable. Wright and Wade are more ordinary but agreeable; Julian, Olseski and Loushay are agreeable but rather ordinary fellows. All young fellows, around twenty to twenty-five. My stuff was all here and O.K. except that there was some mud on it. We moved around last Sunday in the mud and rain. I have built myself a new shelf and put up some coat hooks and am now quite at home in the new tent.

Tod is now in one of the band tents and on the next pay-roll will be classed as 3rd class musician, a regular member of the band.

While I was home, Bill Sisson left (Father remembers his father told us in Dean's Drug Store) and is now at Fort Hancock. Tod had a letter from him in which he says he is leading a life of ease, while the regiment is being formed.

I told you yesterday that Bill and Bud are back from the range and are looking fine.

Ede, don't forget that enlargement of the picture of our old squad at Ray Douglas'.

Tod tells me of a rumor that the 27th Division is still due for 18 weeks more training before leaving here. Don't know how much truth there is to it but I guess we need that much more training all right.

I have been over to the 1st this P.M. Tod and I went over for dinner. Saw Bob Harris, Clevey, Lem Larrabee. They have all the tents up and ready for the men who are expected to arrive soon to fill up the regiment. It looks like a real regiment now with all the tents. All the new officers are there so evidently the men will come soon.

I sent Mr. Bunys [?] the panorama view of camp that he asked me to—the one he spoiled as he was framing, so he will probably send it over in a few days.

Also I sent Ede a couple of Gas Attacks as she asked me.[66]

Tod finished the exam for QMC. Says it was fairly hard. He says that men who fail in the exam will have the privilege to try again this month—a special order. Men who are recommended for commission will be notified next week. I expect to see the C.O. next Monday (tomorrow) and see about getting some time off to study. No notice has come about when the exam will be held except that it will be the latter part of Feby. The nights I missed on the exams, they had tests on Field Transportation, Courts-Martial, Rules of Land Warfare, Hypology on Monday, Tuesday, Wednesday & Thursday nights respectively. No test on Friday night and a test on Sat. P.M. on bridling a horse etc. So the whole exam lasted from Thursday to a week from the following Sat

Panorama view of Camp Wadsworth.

Pvt. Truesdell has drawn an arrow pointing to his tent.

P.M.—over a week. I'm going over to the camp's Q Master tomorrow and get all the dope I can on the coming exam.

It has been a beautiful day today. I had a dandy hot bath this A.M. and have felt fine as a fiddle all day.

It is now 6:30 and beginning to get twilight so I can't see to write without a light. I guess you have all the news so I'll close.

Tuesday is Lincoln's birthday and I think we have the day off. The massed bands of the 27th Division give a concert in Spartanburg in the evening and I think I'll go down with Tod, who plays, of course.

Will close—with love from

Bob

Letter postmarked Spartanburg, S.C., Wadsworth Br., Feb. 14, 1918, 10:30 AM

Wed. P.M. [Feb. 13, 1918]

Dear Folks,

You make me a good correspondent even if I don't want to be—you write me so many good letters and of course I have to answer. I have two letters from Mother and two from Father and one from Ede.

Was interested to know about Bee Powell. I remember Bob Nichol. He and Bee were quite thick altho I didn't know it continued afterwards.

Sorry I didn't see Mrs. Matthews. Please tell her so next time you see her.

Ed says that he wrote you a letter and asked that you send it on to me, so I'll be expecting it.

Don't know whether I thanked Father or not for sending me the allotment check of $6.70. I thank you again if I have. It came in very handy.

Am very sorry to hear about Mrs. Sawtelle. Remember me very kindly to Mr. S.

I was called into active service on July 15th, so my pay started then and I got $30 per month for the remaining 5½ months which totaled

$165. This dope is for Father to make out my income return.

Ede, I have subscribed to the Gas Attack for 3 months to be sent to you, so please let me know whether it comes to you regularly. It is published weekly.

I have just heard that the next exam for Q.M.C. has been put off till April. I don't care if it is put off till then providing we stay here so I can take it, for it will give me so much more time to study. However I hope it isn't put off too long. It looks to me as tho we would be here for considerable time yet.

We had a regimental review yesterday P.M. Don't know what it was for except for the exercise. They are thrown in for good measure occasionally.

I had a very nice letter from Margaret Harrington day before yesterday. I have just written her. Grandma Truesdell told me she had sent her my address, when I was home.

Altho yesterday was Lincoln's Birthday we had no holiday except that in the evening we were allowed to go down town with late passes. The occasion for it was a concert given by the Massed Bands of the Division at Converse College. It was fine. C. College has a good big auditorium which holds a couple of thousand people, I should estimate and it was practically filled. I enclose a program so you see what the bands played. I certainly enjoyed it immensely. Tod played in the 107th Band, of course. I expected to meet him after the concert but he had to come back up with the band.

Well, this is all for now. With love from

Bob

Hdqrs. Co. — 107th Inf.

Dear Folks,

I certainly have some dad all right. Before me I have five letters from him dated Feb. 11, 12, 13, 14 and 15 — a letter a day — it's great, but it's almost too good to be true. I certainly appreciate them.

Thank you for letter of recommendation from Mr. Moon. Also Mr. Moon is due my thanks.

Also received letter containing 50¢ check of Equi. Life Ins. Co. It came in handy, altho it was small. Tell Henry I'm obliged for the calendar, please. Hope Joe will get to Washington to see Ed. I know he would enjoy himself and if he cared to get down here to see me, it would be great. It would give him a good idea of what the camps are like.

You'll be director of everything in town, Father. Do [you] have to spend much time on the Cold Storage Co?

I have Father's letter on hand containing recommendation for Bud Sheak and thank you. I will get it to him soon. Am glad that some of my old customers up the N.B. Branch still send in for some tea and coffee. It is gratifying to me. I thought that Ed Stone had let it all go to pot. On what grounds was Ed Parsons stricken from the draft? Am interested to know.

Please tell Mary McMahon I received her letter and enjoyed it very much. — I guess I'll enclose it just for the fun of it. She certainly is a great one. She says such funny things. Notice what she says about Father in his deacon suit and brown hat.

I also acknowledge Ede's letter of last Monday and contribute thanks.

I also rec'd Mother's letter containing Ed's letter. It's quite a book from Ed, eh? When I was in W. I told him to visit and look around and write long letters home. He evidently is taking my advice.

Hdqrs. Co. had to do interior guard duty again last Friday and Saturday, but it only took part of the company and I was not called upon.

Also while the different battalions of the 107th are in the trenches, details of the Signal Platoon of the Hdqrs. Co. have to go in with them but again I was not chosen and I am mighty glad for the trenches are in awful condition on account of the very heavy rain we have had lately. However they are improving rapidly, so that if I do have to go in tomorrow or the next day, they will be most dried out. You should have seen some of the men who were in when it was so muddy, just plastered from head to foot with that slimy red clay and all their equipment covered, too. The clay was ground right into their clothes. Some of the trenches caved in and some equipment was lost. There was four or five feet of water in some places. About as bad as over across, I should think, and all the men who are going in now, do a 72 hours trick—three days of it.

I wouldn't be surprised if we would go to the rifle range in a week or two. The 2nd battalion (Co's. E, F, G & H) is there now, or at least part of it is.

I'm not getting any Republicans lately. I wonder what's the matter?

Also will you send me a can or two more of G. Wash. Coffee? My supply has run out. How about some big cigars, too, while you are sending?

Went to regimental church this morning, Mother dear, and enjoyed it. A Dr. Strayer[67] (don't know whether that's the correct way to spell it or not) of Rochester spoke. He returns tomorrow to his church after having spent some time here in Wadsworth. A good talk. Afterwards, I went over to see Lieuts. Darling and Knapp at Co. H. Lieut. Darling is at the range. Had quite a chat with Knapp. Then I went over to the 1st. Saw Clevey, Dave Murray, Lem Larrabee. Also saw Cap't. Floyd McLean for a few minutes. Roy wanted me to see the above officers when I returned.

This is all for tonight. With love

Bob

**Letter postmarked Spartanburg, S.C., Wadsworth Br.,
Feb. 26, 1918, 10:30 AM**

Monday Eve [Feb. 25, 1918]

Dear Folks,

Just got off K.P. tonight—three days of it. Didn't have a opportunity to write yesterday and am tired tonight. Will write you a complete book tomorrow. Feel finer than a frog's hair. Have received your many good letters from all during the past few days and they read "fine." Good night till tomorrow. With love

Bob

**Letter postmarked Spartanburg, S.C., Wadsworth Br.,
Feb. 27, 1918, 10:30 AM**

Tuesday Eve. [Feb. 26, 1918]

Dear Folks,

I borrowed a typewriter from one of the fellows and thought I would try writing a letter to you on it. I may find it slow going and change to pen and ink before I finish, but I'll finish the letter somehow, anyway.

I have quite a lot to say for I haven't written in several days. Here I go right down the list.

When you send me another box please include some peanut butter. I have already mentioned G. Washington Coffee and cigars.

A week ago Sunday I went over to the 1st and had a good visit with Clevey and Dave Murray. Also saw Lem Larrabee. Bob Harris was out. By the way, I hear that Art Nelson was married today down here in Spartanburg. Clevey told me that Art expected to be married soon. I guess that he was just waiting for his commission.

Was on mess shack squad one day last week but that was a soft job. Just wash a few dishes and sweep out the mess shack etc etc.

Also attended a lecture in one of the Y.M. buildings an evening last week which was very interesting.

Miss Hoag also sent me the newspaper containing the article about Mr. or rather Rev. Wendell Prime Keeler and it was interesting although I do not remember him very distinctly.

Ed sent me a first-class picture of himself last week which I prize very much. It is really about the best picture I have ever seen of him. Undoubtedly he sent you one, too.

Went to town last Wed. P.M. with Tod Mulford and raised the d—l as usual. That's me all over, Mabel.

Had a good meal at the Quality Shop, went to the vaudeville and came back "home."

Quite a little is being said here about the "Smileage" Books. The officers behind the movement are anxious to have all the people back home furnish the soldiers with them. Don't happen to have an extra one about, do you?

Last Friday was Washington's birthday as you probably recall. In the morning we had a concert by the massed bands over on the drill field. Also several pictures were taken. The Hdqrs. Co. happened to be down in a little gully so all we could hear was the bass drum. The concert was beautiful—maybe. After standing around all the morning, we marched back to the street about noon and were given the rest of the day off. A certain number of men were also given 48 hour passes extending over Sat. and Sunday. This was quite a surprise for we have never been given this privilege before. If I had only known sooner I would have been tempted to come up to Washington [to see] Ed. I thought, too, of Father's being there to see Ed and how fine it would be if we could all be together for a few hours (I would have had about 24 hours in W.) but after figuring it out, I knew Father would be back home by that time, and I decided to give it up. I also thought of taking a trip to Asheville or Atlanta for I considered it a chance to see something of the country down here as we very rarely get two days time off. But Tod wasn't feeling very good and there wasn't anyone else to go with, so I gave it up. I expected to stay in camp and do some studying, but there must have been bad luck around me for Sat. A.M. the corp.

in charge of quarters put me on for 3 days kitchen police. So instead of having 24 hours off, I went on K.P. I came off last night and took a good bath.

There was no retreat on Sat. or Sun. and no reveille on Sun. Great stuff.

By the way, Father, if there are any jersey gloves left at the store, will you please send me a couple of pairs?

I was a little surprised not to be invited to Art Nelson's wedding for I have known him pretty well for a long time but of course I don't know his girl although she is a Binghamton girl. She has worked in Ray Douglas' picture store for some time. I don't know her name.

Tuttle is back from the range and he has been over here a couple of times but I haven't happened to see him. Haven't seen Bud [Sheak] and Bill [Bloomer] lately.

I have Mother's letter dated Feb. 17, Edith's of the 20th, containing Ed's letter, Father's of the 21st, Mother's of the 21st, Father's of the 22nd and 23rd and tonight I received Mother's letter of last Sunday. I am glad Father had such a good visit with Ed and am glad Ed is getting along well. I would like to be remembered to Marg. Stoker West. Hope Ede has a good time in Syracuse.

I don't know just when we will go to the range but I will be able to write to you the same as ever when we do go. I don't know anything about Bill Sisson. Haven't heard a word from him or about him. Haven't heard anything more about the Q.M.C. exam. Am studying.

The weather is somewhat springlike altho we have cool spells now and then. The wind blew an awful gale last night—that really is no exaggeration—it nearly blew our tent down. I heard a robin this morning.

Well, no more for tonight. Love to all,

Bob

Letter postmarked Spartanburg, S.C., Wadsworth Br.,
Feb. 28, 1918, 10:30 AM

Wed. Noon [Feb. 27, 1918]

Dear Folks,

Just a note to enclose an article which Ed wrote and sent to me to read on "The Ordnance Dep't." Pretty good little article, I tho't. Maybe he sent you one, too.

What he wrote about Father's and Mother's pictures, I second. I would like your pictures very much.

Nothing new since last night except that we signed the pay-roll.

Am going down town this P.M. Received an invitation in last night's mail from the First Presbyterian Church of Spartanburg to a reception tonight. Think I'll go maybe. It's for all the men (the Presb'n. men) of the 107th Reg't.

Love to all

Bob

P.S. Am sending home my N.Y. discharge which I just got via Parcel Post—under separate cover. I rolled it in an old issue of "Life." Watch out for it.

RDT

Letter postmarked Spartanburg, S.C., Wadsworth Br.,
Mar. 4, 1918, 10:30 AM

Sunday PM [Mar. 3, 1918]

Dear Folks,

Haven't seen anything of Republican Heralds as yet. I miss them— I haven't seen hardly anything of Binghamton news lately.

Art Nelson was married last week down here. He had his girl come down here but I don't believe any of his girl's or his folks, either, came to attend the wedding. Col. Boyer gave the bride away (rather different, to say the least), Capt. Davis was best man, and most of the guests were officers. Clevey gave me the dope — he and Tuttle were the only enlisted men present. Tut knew Art's girl before she was Mrs. Nelson. She used to work in Ray Douglas' store. I was a bit surprised not to be invited, but Clevey said it was a rather peculiar affair, anyway.

Had a very nice letter from Marg. Harrington and also one from "Neudge."[68] Also heard from Orra and Frances Summers and Bob Brooks. Bob says he has his commission and is in Paterson, NJ.

Friday night I was over to the 1st. Ed Terrell and "Grandpa" Allen, formerly Mounted Orderlies of the 1st and now of the 102nd Engineers came over too. Bud Sheak, Bill Bloomer and Tuttle came over from the artillery, too, so we all had a regular reunion. Tod was with me. The second battalion of the 102nd Engineers to which Terrell and Allen belong leave tomorrow for schooling in a camp in Virginia near Washington. Saw Dave Murray, too.

The weather is fine today. It is warm and clear. The front of our tent is open and some of the fellows are playing quoits and others, baseball in the street. I have a touch of spring fever. I heard a robin singing a day or two ago.

Bud, Tut, Dave M. and I went down to the second concert by the massed bands last night and had a very pleasant evening. Mr. House who was a soloist sang very nicely. Has a very pleasing voice. I met him when we were in Van Cortlandt Park (he was then in the 71st Inf., also at Van Cortlandt Park at the same time we were) up at the YWCA canteen in Yonkers. We were standing around the piano singing and we got talking. We came back together in the car. A pleasant chap. He sang "Because" — I think I have the song at home — and "Carry Me Back to Ole Virginy."

Had a letter from Alma Jenkins a couple of days ago. She says Pete is sick from being inoculated for typhoid. He'll come out of it all right in a little while.

Had a postal from Ede in Syracuse last night.

Don't believe we'll go to the range for a week or ten days yet. We are getting quite a course in bayonet work and also special platoon work in telephone and telegraph, at present, with plenty of "squads east and west."

I have three letters in front of me from Father postmarked Feb. 25, 26, 27 for which I extend my thanks.

I wrote you once what I received from Uncle Sam last year, Father. Probably you mislaid the letter, or at least I'm pretty sure I wrote you.

I was in active service from July 15th to Dec 31 — 5 1/2 months at $30. per month — total $165.00.

Haven't received cigars and G.W. Coffee as yet but expect they will arrive soon. Thank you for sending them.

By the way, I gave Bud your recommendation yesterday and he appreciated it very much.

I can't write Ede in Syracuse for I don't know her address. She will have to wait till she comes home till she hears from me.

Love to you from "Mama's pet and Father's joy."

Bob

**Letter postmarked Spartanburg, S.C., Wadsworth Br.,
Mar. 8, 1918, 10:30 AM**

Wed. Evening [Mar. 6, 1918]

Dear Folks,

Am receiving the Rep. Heralds now and am certainly glad to see them again. Thank you, Father. Well, I did my first trick at guard duty yesterday. A new experience and I learned quite a little. We went on at 4 o'clock Monday afternoon. As usual when the Hdqrs. Co. goes on guard (it seems that way, anyway), it rained but it soon stopped although it didn't clear up. However, we had informal guard mount on account of the inclement weather. I was on the 2nd relief, No. 9 Post, which is down back of the shower-baths from Co. D to the Supply Co. My relief went on at 6 P.M. — off at 8 o'clock. The tricks are 2 hours on

and four off. So I went on again at 12 o'clock midnight, coming off at
2 in the morning. Then from six till eight Tuesday morning and from
12 till 2 in the afternoon. I didn't mind it very much in fact I rather
enjoyed it except that I missed some sleep. Major Mazet, acting Col.
gave us "some" long and stiff inspection about an hour long. Well, I'm
through anyhow and none the worse for wear.

Was made a first-class private a couple of days ago. My pay is
increased from $30. to $33. per month — that's about the only difference from what I was as private.

The company was on reg'tal detail today. My job was to do a little
remodeling on some bayonet dummies. This afternoon I scrubbed my
cot — also myself and feel much better.

We have a new top-sergeant. Our old one was reduced on account
of conduct unbecoming a non-commissioned officer. The new one was
formerly a corporal who worked in the top-sergeant's office.

I found Father's box containing canned figs and peanut-butter
and candy and gloves when I came over to the street a few minutes
yesterday. I am very much obliged and will watch out for the other box
which Mother says is coming from the store. The candy is all gone
also two cans of the figs and I have made pretty good headway in one
can of the peanut butter.

I heard today that the next exam for the Q.M.C. will be in April.
There's no very definite information about the exam and I think I'll go
over to the Div. Q.M.C. office and see if they will give me any real dope
on the matter. Enlisted men aren't supposed to know anything about
it, I guess (that's the way it seems to appear, anyway) but I'm going to
study up.

It's fine that Ed has received his warrant as corporal, isn't it? Both
your darling boys have been promoted, eh?

Thursday, March 7, 1918

Got too sleepy last night to finish, so I'll finish this morning. As you
will probably notice, the date above reminds one that it is Mother's
birthday. I hereby offer my most hearty congratulations to you,

Mother, and greetings on this day. May you have many happy returns of the day. I have also wired the same sentiments to you in order that they may reach you today. I also hope you will enjoy the little gift I have ordered to be sent to you. Hope I'll be home on your next birthday to extend my best wishes to you personally.

I am enclosing a clipping from the "New York Times" about Nomina Twining, Ibbie Phelps friend from Troy. I just happened to notice it as I was looking over last Sunday's edition.

Is Ede getting "The Gas Attack" [the divisional weekly] each week regularly? I hope she is. If not, let me know. They are putting out some pretty good numbers, now. How did you like the last one?

Have been up to dinner and meanwhile the mail has come in. Mine consisted of a postal from Uncle Wirt in St. Petersburg, saying that he might drop in to see me on his way home. Hope I'm not at the range when he comes. It is reported that we go to the range next Wednesday the 13th for ten days. I wouldn't be surprised if this is right. Uncle Wirt didn't give me his address so I couldn't write to him to tell him about my going to the range. Do you know what it is?

Today we are having an exam in the Signal Platoon on flag and buzzer work by an officer of the 102nd Field Signal Battalion. I am making a fair show, I guess. I don't know what the exam signifies except that it is to find out what our officers have been giving us and how much we have learned in signal work, — in other words to see how much we have progressed and to see how efficient our officers are.

I have Father's letters of Feb. 28, Mar 1, 2nd, 4th and Mother's of Mar. 4th. Also a postal from Mary McMahon. Father says Mother keeps all my correspondence — if she does, she must have a roomful of it by this time. I saw Pvt. Payne the other day and he told me he had seen Father when he was home. I was very much surprised to hear of Stuart Bieber's death and very sorry. He was sick but a very short time, wasn't he? How did Ed Hotchkiss happen to come home? Much obliged for the article about the N.Y. Guard. Was very much interested in reading it. Art Nelson's wife's name was Laura Wright and her people now live in Binghamton but they formerly lived in Deposit.

Tod knows them. Had a first-class letter from Rollin Harrington. He seems to be getting along well at his camp. Will you please tell Mary McMahon, Father, that I appreciated her post-card.

It is a fine day, warm and clear. I have been plugging away at this all day during my spare time. It is now after mess time—ten minutes of six—mess is at 5:30 but I don't feel very hungry so I guess I won't go up tonight. Don't worry, I haven't been doing any physical exercise today, that's the reason. I'm feeling finer than a frog's hair.

Mail just came in. I went up to see if there was any for me but there wasn't. The package containing G.W. coffee and cigars which you have written is on the way has not shown up as yet. It should be here as the other arrived last Tuesday. Will keep my eyes open for it.

You have all the news for this time. With love to all of you and regards to Agnes and my friends up and down the street and also everybody at the store.

Affectionately

Bob

**Letter postmarked Spartanburg, S.C., Wadsworth Br.,
Mar. 13, 1918, 3 PM**

Sunday A.M., March 10, 1918

Dear Folks,

I have Father's three letters, one of which contains statement of New & True for Feb. Fine sales but just fair percentage of profits, eh? I also received Mother's papers containing articles about the new 4th N.Y. Guards and picture of the officers. I wonder sometimes about Ed Parsons. After I looked at the article and pictures last night, I did some "wondering"—whether he displayed good judgment, after being accepted for the draft, in making a claim for exemption on the grounds he did, for he is in as good physical shape as most any other fellows are.

Sunday Evening [Mar. 10, 1918]

Tod came in this morning (by the way, before I started this letter this morning, I went to church at 9 o'clock—special attention, Mother, please—at which service a Dr. McKay, I believe, of Brooklyn gave a very good talk) and interrupted me. Wanted me to go over to the YW Hostess House for dinner. Have never been there and decided to try it. They have a fine building and very nicely furnished inside. One side is given over to the cafeteria, where one can buy good wholesome food at moderate cost from 12 till 2 and 4 till 7:30 daily and on the other side is a large lounging room. Both rooms have fine big fireplaces in them. I don't believe it's any exaggeration to say that one can put 8 to 10 ft logs in them. They are really tremendous. There is a piano and a Victrola and plenty of reading material. There is also a small writing room. We had a first class meal finely cooked and seasoned. I had a bowl of tomato soup, roast beef and gravy, string beans, bread and butter, coffee, ice cream and delicious chocolate cake—total cost 70 cents. It would have cost me $1. or $1.25 downtown probably. After dinner, Zimmer, whom you probably remember played my accompaniments when I sang New Years, and I made a little music which seemed to be appreciated. He happened to be over there for dinner, too. Afterwards, Tod and I went over to the 105th F.[ield]A.[rtillery] to see Bud and Bill and Tut. Had a good chat with them after supper, Bill and Tut stopped by for me and we went over to the 1st from where I have just returned. Tod had to play for church tonight, so he couldn't go over with us. Visited with Bob Harris and some of the other fellows. Didn't see Clevey or Dave Murray, this time but will see them next time.

I am having some work done on my teeth up at the regimental hospital. The dentist (a lieut.) is a young chap but seems to be conscientious in his work. I was up Friday and he filled one tooth and I am going up tomorrow A.M. and have a couple of other small cavities filled. That will put my teeth in good shape again. This is done without cost to me, you know.

Friday, most of the Hdqrs Co were on regimental detail—for some unknown reason—my work was to pile up some bags of oats down on the picket line. Managed to get thru with it OK.

Father, have you received or has a letter come addressed to me containing my gov't ins. policy? If it hasn't, please let me [know] and I will jog Washington up on it.

Let me tell you what happened Friday night. We have been getting pretty punk food for the past month and over. The men have complained about it. It seems that the mess sgt. (by name Walds) is trying to see how much money he can save from what the gov't allows so that we will have some extra money for food when we get across (if we ever do). This is a good idea if not carried too far. Therefore some of our meals have been pretty scarce and most of them have been poorly cooked and seasoned due, according to my way of thinking, to the fact that the mess sgt. isn't on his job enough. Friday when the men went up to mess, it wasn't ready to serve out, right on time and so as the fellows stood around waiting in the mess shack, they began to shout and holler and occasionally hiss (for the mess sgt.). Lieut. Mulaney (a recently commissioned 7th man, formerly a sergeant-major and now assigned to our company) told the 1st Sgt. to order the men out of the mess shack. So they, being peeved and having been dissatisfied for some time with the mess, came down the street to their tents and decided not to eat any supper at all. Then Lieut. Mulaney ordered them all to fall in for mess by twos with their mess-tins. Of course, as this was an order, they had to do it. So the company marched up, into the shack and out again without a stop and down to their tents. — "You can lead a horse to water, but you cannot make him drink." The above illustration fits the occasion. I was down in my tent when the trouble just started, cleaning my gun and getting ready for inspection and hadn't started up for mess. So when I heard the fellows coming out of the mess shack and found what was going on, I decided that "Uncle Dud" would better keep out of it, although I agreed with the men. Shortly after, the C.O. had the men fall in and gave us a big call down and also took away the privilege of getting passes from camp last Sat. and Sunday and the Sat. and Sunday & Wed. following our return from the range. (We go Wed. A.M.)

Tuesday A.M. [Mar. 12, 1918]

Taps came Sunday night before I could finish and we were on regimental detail all day yesterday so I didn't have a second to finish this until last night. Then Bud Sheak and Finch came over from the artillery and wanted Tod and I to go over to the show at the big tent. So we went and your letter waited.

Tuesday Night [Mar. 12, 1918]

(More delay—didn't have time to finish this A.M.)

Well, I will write you in a day or two from the range and will make it a more intelligent letter. This one is cut all to pieces. We are all ready to leave tomorrow AM at 4:45. We have been getting ready this PM.

Since I started this letter, I have received a letter from Mother and one from Father. I received a postal from Aunt Nell in Atlantic City tonight. Am glad you are enjoying the flowers I sent you, Mother.

We will be at the range about 10 days. Address me same as usual and mail will be brought up to us. Will write in a day or two. Had a letter from Ed, too. Says P.F. Titchener's mother is down visiting them. Must get to bed. With love

Bob

Letter postmarked ?, S.C., Mar. 16, 1918, AM

Thursday Eve [Mar. 14, 1918]

Dear Folks,

Well, I have a few spare moments tonight and will "take my pen in hand to let you know that I am well and happy."

I think I wrote that I received Father's second box. The contents were very welcome and I thank you very much.

I forgot to tell you of the opening of our new regimental building. We really have a building that is superior to any of the YMCA buildings—Father knows how large they are as he saw them when he was down here. It is a building nearly as big as our 1st Presbyt. Church auditorium with a good sized platform at one end and benches and tables around the outside for writing. Also we have a moving picture machine. Well, Maj. Gen. O'Ryan, Brig. Gen. Lester, Senator Calder, and several British and French officers were there and gave addresses. Then we had some movies. It was quite a success.

Some of the fellows say they have seen a schedule up in the Adjutant's office which has it arranged for the different companies to come up here to the range till Sept. So it may be that we will [be] here for five months or so yet. I honestly believe we'll be here for two months yet.

Well, now I will tell you about our trip to the range. As I wrote you Tuesday night, we arose Wed. A.M. at 4:45, had breakfast and started away at 6:00 after loading the wagons. We walked over to the siding on the Southern where we detrained when we first arrived down here, where we took a train to Campobello. Off we got and walked about 12 miles, mostly uphill. Arrived at 5 P.M. It is beautiful here, and it is such a nice change to get into the mountains here. The air is fine—among the pines. The hike was pretty hard as we hiked with full pack. I was good and tired and after I had washed and eaten, I went to bed—on the hard ground—and slept fine. Just laid my poncho (rubber blanket, used as rain coat) on the ground and wrapped up in my blankets and went to sleep. Somewhat hard but it didn't keep me awake, I'll tell you that.

This A.M. we arose at 6:30, mess at 7 and fall in at 7:45. Were served out bandoleers of ammunition and went to the range—just a step away—in sight of our camp. Part of the company went into the pits to work the targets. I was in the bunch that shot. First we shot ten shots at 100 yards prone (lying down) with bayonets fixed. Then back to 200 yd. line where we shot 10 shots from a trench, standing. Then to the 300 line where we fired from trench, standing, 15 shots. There are about 100 targets on our range (there is another just like this one and also a 1000 yd target) and when you get men firing at all of them and some firing at rapid-fire, it sounds quite like real musketry-fire. I made a fair showing, my score was 114 out of a possible 175. A man qualifies if he makes 105. This P.M. I was in the detail which went into the pits. I won't go into detail how we work the targets, except to say that after each shot, we pull down the target, see where the hit is, pull it up again and point out the hit to the man shooting. Interesting work in a way but a little hot and dusty, when the wind blows. We didn't quit this noon until 12:15, started in again at 1 o'clock and finished tonight at 6 o'clock. A long day. They say we keep it up every day we're here, Sunday included. No time to ourselves, much. I'm going out tomorrow night and get some leaves and pine needles to sleep on. Tonight I went down to the brook and took a bath, cleaned my gun, shaved and wrote a letter—this is it. It is now 9:15 and taps are at 10 up here. More shooting tomorrow, no doubt. Mail service is not very good up here. No mail yesterday or today. Will get some tomorrow, probably. Will get this out as soon as I can, probably tomorrow. With love to all

Bob

Mail address same as ever—mail will be forwarded to us up here.

**Letter postmarked Spartanburg, S.C., Wadsworth Br.,
Mar. 20, 1918, 10:30 AM**

At the range, Monday Eve
[Mar. 18, 1918]

Dear Folks,

It's pretty hard to write letters up here but I'll do the best I can. The accommodations for writing are not the best.

I received a grand total of six letters and two Rep Heralds tonight, one from Mother of last Thursday, two from Ed and three of Father's "daily letters" of last Monday, Tuesday, and Wednesday respectively. The mail comes in by bunches—just as the wagons happen to bring it, so that accounts for my receiving such a bunch tonight. Didn't receive any yesterday.

Well, I qualified on Table #3 this A.M. (was on Kitchen Police)

which is as follows: 10 shots on the 100 yd., 10 shots on the 200 yd line
and 10 shots on the 300 yd line at rapid fire which means that each ten
shots must be fired in 1 minute. If a man can shoot more than 10 shots
in the minute at the 100 yd line, he can take up to 20 shots, but on the
200 and 300 yd lines, the maximum number of shots is 10 to a minute.
I made 7 hits out of 10 shots at the 100 and 200 yd lines and 4 hits
of 10 at the 300 yd which just qualified me (18 out of 30 qualifies for
Table #3). Table #4 is same as Table #3 except that in order to qualify
a man must make 25 hits out of his 30 shots. That is where Pvt RDT
[rates], I guess, for today was the first time I ever did any rapid-firing.
There are lots of details up here. Of course there is a pit detail for the
butts, that is, for the targets everyday, and duty squad detail, kitchen
police and guard duty. I have been in the butts a couple of half days
and had the day at K.P. so far. I may get a detail tomorrow, don't know
yet. We will probably go back to Camp Wadsworth next Thursday as
our ten days will be up then. We shot yesterday (Sunday) the same
as any day and it didn't seem much like Sunday to me, in fact, I have
about lost track of the days.

It is certainly beautiful up here. There are quite a lot of trees
around here in bloom — pink blossoms — some say they are peach
trees, — I don't know. They are very pretty, anyway. The trees are
budding and the birds singing. This P.M., most of the company had to
police the camp and after finishing at 2:30 we had the rest of the P.M.
off. So I and two other fellows went walking and went half-way up Glassy
Mount which is on one side of the camp. The P.M. was absolutely beautiful and the view was wonderful. I took several pictures and also have
taken some others of the camp here so I hope to have some good views
for you later. Then we came back to camp, washed up and went over
to a farmer's house for supper. It was the most ramble-shackle looking
place you ever looked at and the family certainly lives pretty primi-
tively, no glass in the windows, no paint on the house, holes in the roof,
etc. but, they gave us a good meal altho plain. There were six fellows
who sat down at the table — and there were three dozen eggs fried for
us — none left when we got up. We also had fried potatoes, ham, coffee,

hot biscuits and corn syrup. Plenty of everything and well cooked. Cost us each 75 cents and well worth it. These farmers, or mountainers, whatever you call them, are certainly a great bunch. It is a regular vacation for me up here—such a nice change from Camp Wadsworth.

Very, very sad about Mrs. Sawtelle. It is certainly too bad. Well, I will close as this is about all the news. You may not hear from me till after I get back to Camp W.—if we go back next Thursday.

With love to you all

Bob

Received Mother's letter with Uncle Wirt's address. Thank you. RDT

PS Got hold of a "home-made" cot yesterday from a fellow in one of the companies who was going back to camp. It is set up on four crotched sticks and made of saplings. Very comfortable—more so than my canvas cot in camp—so now I am as comfortable as can be. Pine needles are great to sleep on—they smell so good.

RDT

Letter postmarked Spartanburg, S.C., Wadsworth Br., Mar. 23, 1918, 10 AM

Friday Eve [Mar. 22, 1918]

Dear Folks,

Pardon the pencil but I can write a bit faster.

Well, here I am back in Camp Wadsworth again and feeling finer than silk.

I qualified on all tables (four) at the range. Three and four are rapid fire silhouettes, on three one must make 18 hits out [of] the thirty and on Table 4 one must make 25 hits out of 30 shots—ten shots on the 100 yd, 10 on the 200 yd and 10 on the 300 yd—each 10 shots in one minute. Then I shot on Table 5—on the 500 and 600 yd range but didn't do very well as I couldn't find out how my gun shot at the distance as I didn't shoot enough. One doesn't have to qualify on

Tables 5 and 6—he simply shoots to see what he can do. Table 6 is on 1000 yd range. I didn't have a chance at that.

I guess I wrote you how I went out to a farmer's with a couple of the fellows and had supper. For seventy-five cents we had fried eggs, ham, potatoes, hot biscuits and coffee. There were six of us who sat down to the table and we finished thirty-five eggs between us. Fine hot biscuits, too. We also took a dandy walk up on a mountain and got some pictures which I will send you if they turn out well. It was a fine vacation and I really enjoyed it except that we didn't have as many conveniences as we have here. The scenery was beautiful and the weather fine, most of the time. We left the range at 11 o'clock Thursday A.M., stopped on the way for dinner and got into Campobello at 3:30 P.M. At 5:30 we left on the train and got into camp at about 8 o'clock. Got settled and had a good hot bath which was certainly OK. The hike wasn't as bad as going up as it was more downhill coming home. Today we got cleaned up and settled, that is, we did this A.M. This P.M. we had a couple of hours of drill. I was also notified that I am on the detail of 25 men from the Signal Platoon to go into the trenches with the Second Battalion of the regiment for 72 hours. I will be in K O—Battalion Hdqrs.—in a dugout 40 feet down in the ground. Will come out Tuesday A.M. Go in tomorrow A.M. at 7:30. So I won't be writing to you again till Tuesday or Wednesday. I expect we'll be going up to the range again in a short time.

I have Ede's letter containing Ed's letter and enjoyed it. I wish I could have attended the St. John Ave School play. I'll bet it was fine. The cake and socks haven't arrived as yet but I will be on the lookout for them. Go to it on your Red Cross and singing, Ede. I also have Father's letters of last Friday, Monday, Tuesday and Wed. By the way, Father, are you going to have the stationery changed to show your new office? Also have Mother's good letter of Wed. Glad you enjoyed Alma Gluck.

I wouldn't mind if you sent me some Fatima cigts and a few pckgs of 10 cent kits of Harmony tob[acco]. I find these go pretty well. Must close as taps have sounded. With love from

                                    Bob

Letter postmarked Spartanburg, S.C., Wadsworth Br.,
April 2, 1918, 10:30 AM

Easter Sunday Evening
[Mar. 31, 1918]

Dear Folks,

I have been a bit neglectful in writing this last week. I haven't written since I was in the trenches last Monday. However I'll try and make up on this one.

I have six letters from Father in front of me. Two before he left for NY and W., one from NY, two from Washington, and one from home after his return. I also have Mother's letter of Friday the 22nd and Ede's of a week ago today. I thank you all. I'm glad you liked the flowers, Father. They, themselves, don't amount to much but they are something tangible before you to remind you that I think a good deal of you and that I remembered how young you were on a week ago tomorrow. I didn't know that Bob McClane was going over. He's in the Ordnance Dep't, isn't he? I had a letter from Ed written Thursday night in which he wrote that the orders to go to Edgewood, Md were all off and that he was hanging around the personnel office waiting for something to happen. I imagine he's written you regarding this. Wonder where Hocky will go. Hope Ede's better from her cold now. You are all to the mustard, Ede, with your Red Cross work. Do you get the Gas Attack each week OK? Let me know if you don't. Also I sent you a copy of the Seventh Regt. Gazette and a program of our Division play "You Know Me, Al" of which I will tell you in a minute. Let me know, please, whether you received them. I also sent home a couple of days ago a small box containing my old 1st Inf. collar ornaments. Please save them for me.

I was somewhat surprised to hear about "Sam" [Jenkins] as I didn't know just how "W." would feel. Pete and Alma told me Sam and Mr. Stowell were pretty thick. Wish I had seen him when I was in N.Y. I wonder why he isn't in the army. He ought to make as good cannon-fodder as the rest of us. Well, there's another of my old-timers getting ready to be hooked up. Was glad to hear about Pete and Alma as I didn't know just what was going on. I had a good letter from Bill Hones several days ago. Also one from Frank and Ethel Summers.

Am sorry to say that I haven't received that box you sent me, Ede. The mails are somewhat slow. I'm on the lookout for it. I have plenty of socks, Ede, and I have everything in the way of clothes.

Well, I haven't enjoyed myself so much in a long time as I did last Wed. P.M. I went down town and saw our Division play "You Know Me, Al." It is a musical farce in three acts and it is a corker. The orchestra is fine—it is made up of members of the various bands around the camps who played the proper instruments. The members of the cast are professional and amateur actors and they do <u>very</u> well in fact I believe the show is as good as many Broadway hits. The fellows who take the women's parts are certainly funny and they do remarkably well. There are several very catchy songs written by the men in the show. They played all last week at the Harris Theatre in town including a Wed. and Sat. matinee and had good houses every performance. The proceeds go to erect a portable theatre in the camp for the 27th Division. They are going to New York the latter part of the coming week to play for a couple of weeks. Several members of the 107th Band are in the orchestra. Tod is a good friend of the fellow who takes the part of the leading lady "Arline" and he does wonderfully well. His name is Walter Roberts and he lives in Windsor, N.Y. He is a member of the 108th Ambulance Co., the old Binghamton company. His father is an inspector for the State. Roberts went to Syracuse University where he took part in theatricals and was a member of "Tambourine and Bones." He appears to be a fine young fellow. The chorus is OK too. You'd notice by the program where the costumes came from. Now if Mother or Ede or any of you can get to NY to see it you'll enjoy it immensely and be helping the 27th Division at the same time. I don't know at what theatre they will play as yet but will let you know later. I enjoyed the play so much that I went twice. Tod couldn't get down to go with me Wed. P.M. so we went Sat. P.M.

On Good Friday, we had no drill. We went to church services at the Reg'tal. building in the morning. The day was beautiful—clear and warm. In the P.M. Tod and I went over to the Base Hospital to see Tuttle who has had a minor operation on his throat. He is coming along in good shape. The base hospital is really a wonderful place—there are about 40 wards (building units) each one with a capacity for probably 40 or 50 men. That doesn't seem right, for it must have room for more men than that. Anyway it is a great big place and they are getting it pretty well fixed up now.

It has been a beautiful Easter Day just as fine as Good Friday was—warm and clear, just like a day in June in Binghamton. It just happened that my turn came on Mess Shack Squad so I worked the same as any day on Easter Day. But my job really wasn't very hard—just wash a few pitchers after each meal and wash off the tables and sweep out the mess shack. It doesn't take more than a half or three-quarters of an hour after each meal but you have to stick around all day. Fortunately, I hadn't planned to do anything, that is, leave camp, so I didn't mind it. I went over to see "Tut" again this P.M. with Tod.

Bud and Bill have gone to the artillery range again. The 1st Inf. have received about 500 Kentucky draft men to help fill them up. Some of them can't even write or read their own names. I haven't been over as yet but they are under quarantine on account of measles. Our second battalion goes to the range again in a week or so, so I suppose the Hdqrs Co. will go again before very long.

Tod expects to get a 10 day furlough in a few days. He will undoubtedly be in to see you.

We all set our watches an hour ahead last night. Suppose you did the same.

We signed the payroll for March yesterday A.M.

If I could have gotten a 48 hour pass over yesterday and today, I think I would have gone and seen Ed for a day—but I couldn't get the pass.

The massed bands went to Asheville last weekend to give a concert. If I hadn't gone into the trenches, I would have tried to go with Tod on the trip. He said it was a beautiful trip. Something always seems to keep you from carrying out your plans.

From what I hear around, I wouldn't be surprised if we moved in a couple of months—it's hard to tell, really. Maybe we'll go north and do guard duty. That wouldn't be so bad.

Well, taps will be sounding soon and I must make up my bed. Love to all of you.

Bob

P.S. I enclose three snapshots of your youngest son, taken the morning I came out [of] the trenches. #1 shows front view with full equipment including gas mask at alert position. #2 shows gas mask on. #3 shows how full equipment looks. It is the new pack—haversack at top.

Yours truly,

Bob

**Postmarked Spartanburg, S.C., Wadsworth Br.,
April 8, 1918, 1PM**

Sunday Evening [April 7, 1918]

Dear Folks,

Well, I haven't written quite as frequently the past week as you have
said. Nothing the trouble—just been busy, that's all.

I have Father's letters of last week—Friday, Saturday, last Sunday,
Monday, Tuesday, Wednesday, and Thursday. The mails are slow for
some reason or other. Your letters take four or five days sometimes,
to get here. I'm sorry if I caused you any worry by not writing quite
so often. I received the allotment check, Father, and thank you. I have
asked them to cancel it but it seems to take considerable time for
them to do.

I also have Mother's two letters of Thursday a week ago and last
Wednesday, the latter enclosing Ed's two letters for which I thank you.
It's very nice about Helen Kellam. Glad they are getting along nicely. I
saw an announcement of Reed Jr's arrival in the Rep Herald, too. Tod
Mulford thought he was going to get his furlough by this time but one
can't be absolutely sure till he has his furlough in his hand. The only
way to do is to wire home when you get it and come. I'll think he'll get
his pretty soon and I certainly hope so for he's mighty anxious to see
his folks and his girl. It's just as hard for us while we're waiting to see
whether we get one as it is for the folks at home, for we can't help planning on it and we're not sure whether or when we'll get it, so we fret
and stew, and can't do anything but wait. I wasn't on K.P. after coming
out of the trenches just on Mess Shack Squad which is much easier. I
am feeling OK and have been. Recently quite a large number of men
have had an attack of "trench" fever, not a very serious ailment, this is,
it didn't last but a couple of days—high temperature and headache etc.
but I have escaped it. I guess I'm too tough—have been brought up
in a "rough home," eh? I have had a couple of letters from Ed and with
the two that Mother sent, I have a pretty [good] idea of Ed's doings.

Am glad Ede is feeling better. I saw about her singing at the M.[onday A.[fternoon] Club and am pleased that she did well.

I have Ede's letter of a week ago Thursday. Sorry to say I haven't yet received the box yet.

The past week has been taken up considerably with gas mask instruction—that is, the first part. Last Wed. A.M, having been thru the course of instruction, I went thru the gas chambers. First, having put on our gas masks, we went into the lacrymatory chamber (tear gas). The mask is an absolute protection and one has quite a feeling of respect for it after going into the chamber. I am enclosing some pictures, one of which shows me with a gas mask on. There is a clip on the inside of the mask which goes over the nose and all the breathing is done thru the mouth—somewhat disagreeable at first but one gets used to it, after [a] while. After we were in the lacrymatory chamber for a short time, the officer told us to take our masks off, just to see how the "tear" gas would affect us—and the minute or rather the second we got too much of it, to "beat it" out the door. So we took off our masks. It wasn't two seconds before my eyes began to water and the tears rolled down my cheeks—and I made a dash for the door. If a man is subjected (so said the officer) to this gas for a length of time he will go temporarily blind and partially out of his mind. Then we went into the gas chamber full of chlorine gas, much less dense, of course, than is used in actual warfare. However it was thick enough. We took a slight sniff of it and it was enough. The officer said that the gas used across the water is so strong that one whiff will kill a man instantly. That is why every man must learn to put on the mask in 6 seconds. I have it down pretty well.

We also had some regimental maneuvers last Tuesday.

Wed. P.M. Tod and I borrowed some horses from the Mounted Orderlies and took a ride.

Am going to quit for tonight as I am very sleepy. Will write more tomorrow night. With love to all

Bob

**Letter postmarked Spartanburg, S.C., Wadsworth Br.,
April 9, 1918, 10:30 AM**

The envelope contains 24 snapshots taken at Camp Wadsworth and the area of the range.

**Letter postmarked Spartanburg, S.C., Wadsworth Br.,
April 10, 1918, 10:30 AM**

April 9th, Tues. Night

Dear Folks,

The 107th Regt. goes to the range tomorrow A.M. for five days. That is, we take two days to get there, stay one day and take two days to come back. We hike 14 miles tomorrow. It's more for manouvers than shooting. I doubt if we do any shooting at all. The band goes too — in fact the whole company, — so Tod will be along. Nothing new since I wrote you last night. Weather cloudy and rainy and windy and cold. Some weather, eh?

I may not have a chance to write you while I'm out on this hike so don't worry if you don't hear from me till next Wed. or so. Am feeling <u>extra</u> <u>fine</u>. Most time for mess (six o'clock) so must close.

Tod's furlough hasn't come thru yet and it may be some time before it does. I guess I was lucky to get mine. I'm keeping him as patient as I can.

Will wait till I see if I hear from you in tonight's mail before I seal this up.

Nothing from you tonight. With love to all.

Bob

**Letter postmarked Spartanburg, S. C., Wadsworth Br.,
April 17, 1918, 10:30 AM**

Monday Eve [April 15, 1918]

Dear Folks,

Back from the range. Arrived yesterday at 6 o'clock after a nine hour hike and a holy terror, it was, march 50 minutes and rest 10 minutes of each hour. I have a blister on my right heel, the size of a quarter, and several others on each foot, and feel pretty tired. Will write you a full account in a day or so. Am going to bed now. Feel OK. Went over to Hostess House with Tod for supper. Saw Bill and Bud. Bud's mother was down to see him but I didn't see her as I was at the range. Will try and write again tomorrow night. We had today off to get rested and cleaned up. Love to all

Bob

**Letter postmarked Spartanburg, S.C., Wadsworth Br.,
April 25, 1918, 10:30 AM**

Tuesday P.M. [April 23, 1918]

Dear Folks,

I have a new job temporarily. I am in the regimental supply office doing clerical work for "a few days." I was detailed this afternoon. Haven't done enough so far to know anything about it.

Well, we have our new Enfield rifles and are getting used to them. They weigh about a pound more and are good rifles for short range stuff.

Well, I am rested up in good shape again and feel fine. Didn't do anything special last week. Went down town Wed. with Tod and did a few errands. Thursday, Tod and I went over to the old 1ˢᵗ and had a fine visit. You see we haven't been over there in a long time on account of the quarantine. The old men are now out and so we went over. Bob

Harris's birthday was last Saturday, the 20th and he had a nice box of eats which he passed around. No change in the men except that the 1st is now filled up with men (old N.G.) from all over the country—Ohio, Kentucky, New Jersey and I don't know where all. A good many are sick and some are "bums" so they tell me, but there are some good ones, of course. Bob Harris was willing to bet me that they will leave here before we do. He looks fine. The 1st Anti-Air Craft Machine Gun Battalion left a couple of days ago. Saw Floyd McLean a few minutes. Didn't see Clevey or Lem Larrabee. Lem is thru the O.T.C. and is waiting for his commission.

Last Saturday, Sunday and Monday, it came my turn to go on Kitchen Police (nice time for it) so I have been scrubbing pots and pans for the past few days. It's not as bad a job as it used to be.

Quite a lot of newly drafted men have been coming in here recently, from Yashank, I understand. Our band has had to play them into camp—three different batches, so far.

Folks, it's going to be a mighty short time before we leave here—I suppose we'll come north somewhere. I don't know where. I wouldn't be surprised if we were out of here in 10 days. We are being issued new clothing, fully equipped, new rifles, new bayonets and belts, new blankets, new packs, etc. etc. We must send home at once all property which cannot be carried in our duffle-bags. So I am going to send home a box and my old duffle-bag. Tell Edith I would like two or three pair more heavy socks. I am sending some home as they have shrunk in the laundry and are too small. Also my books unless I can sell them. Also a clip of empty shells which I picked up at the range and a bullet, to show you how they look. And then some more junk, odds & ends. Camera, meerschaum pipe, which the boys gave me for Xmas, all my knitted stuff,— (I simply can't carry it—I may send for it later) and some other stuff. I am taking my boots with me. I may make some changes in these things when I come to box it up and send it tonight or tomorrow.

Wed. Night [April 24, 1918]

Well, here I am just finishing up. I sold all my books and got cost price out of them—better than sending them home. I also decided to keep my knitted stuff. I also gave what socks were too small for me, away, to some of the fellows. Had to send the box by Xpress COD as it was the only way they would take it.

I am at my new job—keeping a book in the office, as I said. Easy work. Had to work this P.M. and almost had to work tonight, but got out of it.

The band is playing most every night for the draft men—Tod says they're a pretty punk looking bunch.

Had a letter from Ed tonight in which he gave me all the recent news.

Before me I have letters from Father dated Apr 16, 18, 19 and 22. Also Mother's of April 20 and Edith's of Apr 18. I also received your telegram and thank you. [Pvt. Truesdell had turned twenty-four on April 18.] I received the box tonight. The cake is all gone. It was delicious. Also the peanuts. Thanks for the cigars and gum, too, and the stamped envelopes. I can't tell you how much I will value the case you are sending, Mother. It is just what I want. I hope it arrives before we leave here. Father, I don't hear a thing about another QMC exam. In fact, I haven't heard of a fellow who tried the 1st exam who has received his commission. Tonight I received Father's letter containing allotment check and thank you. I don't understand why the gov't. does[n't] stop it. I wrote the gov't about my insurance policies and they will send them to me at 100 Murray St. soon, so they say in their letter which I received yesterday.

If you want to see me, you'll have to come down before May, Father, in fact I think it much more probable that you'll visit me near New York City before long or else I'll see you for a day or so, on a short leave. I wouldn't be at all surprised if we left here by next Sunday. Of course I hope we come north before going across. We are making considerable preparation for moving and at considerable speed.

I am sorry that Mother hasn't been feeling well—hope you are better by now. I am anxious to get your photograph case. It is a fine birthday present and I appreciate your sending it.

By the way, I hope that the Suskana Flower Shop never presented my two bills for yours and Father's birthday flowers to Father for payment. I gave them explicit directions to send me the bills here. Let me know about it please.

Am glad to hear about Marsh Williams.

The cake was fine, Ede, and I thank you for your part in the box. Please send me about 3 pr more socks and be sure they are good and big—size 11.

Must close. Feel finer than silk and hope I'll see you soon. I really believe I'll be closer to home very soon. Good night with love—in a hurry

Bob

Letter postmarked Spartanburg, S.C., April 26, 1918, 2 PM

April 25, Thurs Eve

Dear Folks,

Your letter of Tuesday at hand. I wrote you a long letter last night but will write again tonight. I have been exceptionally busy for a week or so. I want to write you every day—would like to but I can't do it. I haven't the time—besides, dad, you'll have to get used to hearing from me much less frequently than you have been—much as I'd like to have you receive a letter from me every morning. I know that however much you appreciate my letters, I enjoy yours twice as much. You may not [receive] my last night's letter promptly as it is rumored our mail is being held up. The same applies to this letter.

Rapid preparations are being made to move and we will be ready to move by Saturday and may move then or in a day or two, in a week or ten days at the most—is my belief.

I heard the results of the QMC exam today. About 25 men out of the 2 or 300 men who tried it go to Jacksonville Flo. for school in a day or two. No one has been commissioned as yet. The next exam is May 5 so I hear but I'm out of it, I guess.

Of course I'm hoping we'll come up north to an embarkation port and then I'll have a chance to see you probably, but I don't know. An enlisted man doesn't find out much and neither do many of the officers, I guess.

We aren't allowed to go down town on pass—since Wed noon. Can't cash a check for myself but will probably find a way all right. Our canteen closed tonight and the officers mess closes Sat night.

Must close with love to all of you.

Bob

Letter dated April 27, 1918 without an envelope

April 27, 1918, Camp Wadsworth, S.C.
[Saturday]

Dear Folks,

Just a short note to tell you that I sent home a suitcase last night addressed to Newell & Truesdell Co. containing 1 pr. red rubber boots belonging to me and 1 pr. of black ones of Tod Mulford's and a package or two of Tod's. The suitcase also belongs to Tod! I sent it by insured parcel-post. We will be issued boots and as my space is very limited I concluded that I had better send them home. Tod has written his father to call at the store for his stuff and will you please take care of mine?

Went over to the 1st last night for a few minutes to say good-bye to the boys for a while. Bob Harris has received his warrant as battalion sergeant-major. Fine, eh? They expect to leave very soon, too.

I worked here in the office till 2:30 this morning and I feel kind of dragged out now (11:40 A.M.). We are pretty well packed up now so we can move at very short notice and I think we'll be out of here by Monday night at the latest,—quite possibly sooner.

Cashed a check for $50.00 last night and with what I had, I now have $58.00. I understand that we will get paid for April today or at least before we move so that will make about $20.00 more. Total, $78.00—that's enough, isn't it?

I am positive we are going across, but whether we will come north to an embarkation port, I don't know as there are some rumors that we go to Charleston to embark. I don't know. I'll just have to wait and see where we go and let you know as soon as I can. I'll write as soon as I can and as definitely as I can but you know it is against orders to give any information about the movements of troops, in advance, even to members of families by any officers or enlisted men.

Feel finer than silk and <u>HOPE</u> that we come north so I can see you.

We (the 107th Reg't.) had quite a bunch of drafted men from Yaphank come in last night to fill us up to war-strength. Haven't had a chance to look them over very much as yet.

Must go over to dinner now. Hope this letter isn't held up for I know you are probably anxious to hear about things. With love,

Bob

P.S. Please send this along to Ed, as it will save me some time.

P.S.S. <u>Note well</u> Put the Q.T. on anything I have said in this letter.

RDT

Letter postmarked Wash. & Charlotte, R.P.O., April 29, 1918

Apr 28, Sunday

Dear Folks,

Am writing this on the train, so please excuse the scribbling.

Well, we're on the move just 7 months and a day after we arrived at Camp Wadsworth.

Hope you have rec'd my two letters written a couple days ago in regard to the situation. Got orders to pack up and move, that's all—eventually, across the water.

At present it is 10:30 P.M. (we started at 2 P.M.) and we are on the Southern, have passed Greensboro, N.C., going north. Don't know where we're bound for—altho I'll have to admit we may not come up further than Newport News, possibly. However I'm hoping we come up further, so I can see you.

We've just arrived in Dansville.

Bob Harris and Clevey also Tuttle, Bud and Bill were over to say good-bye.

We are on the first section — each section an hour apart — we, meaning HQ Co, Supply Co and Sanitary Det.

Will write again as soon as possible.

With love

Bob

Letter postmarked Newport News, VA, Stuart Branch, Apr 30, 1918, 3:30 PM

Monday Evening, Apr 29

Dear Folks,

Arrived at Camp Stuart, Newport News, Va. this A.M. at 9 o'clock. We are told we may be here from four days to a month. Feel fine.

A number of aero and hydroplanes flying about (aviation camp near). Camp has capacity for about 20,000 troops but there are not that many here now. Haven't had a chance to look around much. May get a chance to get into N.N. and see the town. We live in barracks (iron cots) (two story) — some comfortable and our mess shacks are OK.

Will write more tomorrow.

Do you suppose you'll get down to see me? Love to all.

Your son
Bob

Address
Pvt R.D.T.
H.Q. Co 107 Inf.
Camp Stuart
Newport News, Va.

Tuesday A.M. [April 30, 1918]

Beautiful A.M. Clear and warm. We marched down to the water and saw several battle ships this A.M. Slept great. Nice iron cots with springs and a bed-sack full of straw. Great.

Forget to state that I rec'd two letters (Wed & Thurs last) from Father before I left C.W.

Will probably be issued what equipment we are short in a day or two.

Must go to mess. Will write again soon. Let me hear from you here at Camp Stuart.

> With love
> Bob

Letter postmarked Newport News, VA, Stuart Branch, May 1, 1918, 3:30 PM

Apr 30, Tuesday A.M.

Dear Folks,

Am going to try & wire you my address today. We are restricted to regimental limits on account of quarantine but expect we may be able to get into town later. People are allowed to come into camp to see friends and relatives, providing they first obtain permission at the Adjutant's office in Regimental Hdqrs.

Am also going to try and wire Ed today and have written him to see if he can get a 48 hr pass or so and come down and see me.

Finally situated here. It certainly is great to live in wooden barracks and sleep on an iron cot with springs after the way we have been living. Just had a good shower and feel OK.

We only have to drill 4 hours a day. Our 3rd battalion arrived this A.M. We now have HQ Co, M. Gun Co, Supply Co, A, B, C & D, I, K, L, M here. It is reported around that our 2nd Battalion (E, F, G, H) has gone up to N.Y. But there is nothing official, at any rate they are not here.

I was on K.P. yesterday P.M.—just for the P.M.—but it was a cinch in the kitchen we have—a tremendous improvement on those at C. Wadsworth—two nice big stoves, regular ones, which burn coal, two sinks with sewage connection, big boiler of hot water, two big refrigerators—everything OK.

I wouldn't be surprised if we were here for a month—but, one never knows. We get no advance information and in an hour, must be ready at any time.

Will close and mail this.—With lots of love

Bob

**Letter postmarked Newport News, VA, Stuart Branch,
May 2, 1918, 3:30 PM**

Wed AM. [May 1, 1918]

Dear Folks,

Have just written Ed all about things and tried to get him to come down and see me—he ought to be able to get a 48 [hr] pass,—if he is O.K. on finances.

I sent you a wire last night and tried to wire him, but the W.U.[69] refused to take the telegram as they said they had no office in Edgewood Md.

The weather is great here and the air is fine—you see we are right on Chesapeake Bay. The scenery is beautiful—many boats on the water and very often, planes in the air.

I was mistaken in telling you that our 2nd Battalion wasn't coming here. The 3rd just came in, the 2nd came yesterday,—the whole regiment is here now.

Lieut. Nelson, our senior 1st Lieut and C.O. in the absence of Capt Hayes who is across the water, has just arrived. He has been out at Fort Sill at the School of Musketry for several weeks of instruction.

As I told you the camp will accommodate about 20,000 so a Y.M. fellow told me but at present there are only the 47th Regs., the 11th

Cavalry Regs., and ourselves.

There is a nice YM and a K of C building here. If we can get into N News in a few days, we will undoubtedly find it very interesting, too.

Was vaccinated for small pox just before we left C.W. and my arm is healing very nicely without any pain or inconvenience to speak of.[70]

If you come down and are not able to get accommodations at any hotel, ask the Y.M.C.A. for a list of boarding houses.

Haven't had any mail here yet but I expect our C.W. mail will be forwarded here so will be receiving it today or tomorrow.

I feel splendid and sleep like a log on these spring cots.

With love to all,

Bob

P.S. Will you please call up Mrs. W.O. Birdsall and give her my kindest regards and a little news from my letters. I sent her a Gas Attack and still owe her a letter, but I have so many people to write to, that I can't keep up. I simply can't write so many people.

RDT

Letter postmarked Newport News, VA, Stuart Branch, May 8, 1918, 8:30 AM

Monday Eve [May 6, 1918]

Dear Folks,

Nothing much new to report tonight.

Tod got a pass last night to go over to the YMCA and phone his folks to come up for a little while. When he got over by the Y.M. and gate, he saw a couple of other HQ men who were going to try and walk out if they weren't stopped by the guard. Well, somehow or other they weren't stopped and so Tod got down town. It was just a happenstance. If he had been caught, however, anytime before he got back into his company street, the consequences would have been pretty severe. Of course, the temptation was pretty big, as he wanted to see his girl. I went to bed as I was tired.

Yesterday I felt kind of punk—the swelling in my arm didn't go down very much—went over at sick call to the hospital where they looked it over again and said to take it easy.

Tuesday A.M. [May 7, 1918]

I did this morning—it is much better and I feel better—a good deal. I think by a day or two the swelling will be gone and then it won't be long before my arm heals up.

I'm going to try and go over to the Supply Office this A.M. I think I feel good enough.

We were paid off yesterday so I now have $95.

I guess you have all the news for now. With love

Bob

PS Now here is one of those little things I wish you would be sure and do. Please tell Aunt Nell how much I appreciate that box of candy she sent down by you. Also don't forget about phoning to Mrs. Birdsall.

Ede, I was sorry you couldn't come down to the family reunion but I understand the reasons you stayed home, so don't worry. You are doing splendid work with the Red Cross, nowadays, Ede, and I know your efforts are appreciated by the people in B.

Must close with love

Bob

**Letter postmarked Newport News, VA, Stuart Branch,
May 9, 1918, 3:30 PM**

Wed. May 8, 4:10 P.M.

Dear Folks,

Haven't anything to rest my arm on so this doesn't look very good.

It's warm and a bit cloudy. Not much of anything doing. My arm is progressing OK. Swelling gone down and the wound beginning to heal.

We had a regimental review last night. They seem to be in favor.

The Colonel complimented the HQ Co on their appearance.

I am taking things easy with my arm so it will get well as soon as possible—tho I'm not sick at all.

No more to write about today. With love

Bob

**Letter written in transport, postmarked New York, N.Y.,
Times Square, June 14, 1918, 10:30 AM
Letter received June 15th 1918**

Sunday Morning, May 19th, 1918

Dear Folks,

You know, it doesn't take much to please some people, and just at present, I'm sitting in a folding chair, for the first time since I got on board so I feel real pleased and comfortable. No doubt the chair belongs to some non-com, and he will come along and claim it, so every fellow who passes me, I am afraid will say, "That's my chair, you'll have to vacate" and then Uncle Dud will do so and content himself with sitting on the soft side of the deck or a hatch or something. So far, so good, anyway.

I presume you have figured it out that I am on the water as I said I would write everyday until we embarked—which I did. I am going to try and give you some dope on things without actually telling you out and out—I believe it will pass any censor as I will refer to more or less personal matters so that only you will know what I mean. You remember the day, of course, you left camp. Well, the fourth day after that we came on board and the following day, weighed anchor.

By the way, I'll tell you here that my arm is much better—the swelling went down before I left camp and there is not much of any soreness. It will take a little time for it to heal, of course, as there is a hole about a quarter of an inch deep and the size of a dime—but it really doesn't bother me a great deal at that. I go into the infirmary each morning and have it dressed.

After you left camp, things ran along about the same as I told you—nothing new.

The name of the transport we are on is the same as the body of water near which we, when we had our garden, and the Newells lived for several years. So it's a rather familiar name. I'm going to make very few comments one way or the other on these statements—you'll simply have to figure them [out] and draw your own conclusions. Now take the figure representing the date of Edith's birthday in July [14]—and that is the number of days it takes us to get across. That same figure also represents the number of transports in our convoy.

Tuesday P.M. [May 21, 1918]

(Have been busy and am going to finish this, now, I hope.)

Quite likely, some will go to one port some to others. It is rumored that we will land at Q but no one knows definitely as yet, not even the crew. Taking the figure which represents the amount of preferred stock I own in the company and dividing it by four gives approximately the number of troops on board. Then take this last number and divide it by five and there is that number in the crew in addition (approximately). As to our protection on the water I will say it seems quite sufficient, in fact, it hardly seems as if anything could happen to us.

The weather has been fine except for one or two days when we slipped around considerably, particularly at mess time. You would have laughed if you could have seen the fellows. They would get their mess pans full of food and then would come a lurch and away they'd slide and fall down with stew all over them. During that particular time I wasn't eating very heavy—I spent most of my time in my bunk except when I was giving—you know the Bible says "It is more blessed to give than to receive"—well, I didn't receive much food—(I didn't want it) but I gave freely—to the fishes. However with the exception of that time, I have felt fine and do at the present time feel O.K. There is a canteen on board where one can buy crackers and candy etc.—if one can get near enough for there is always a crowd around it. I have been able to get some peppermint candy and ginger snaps which taste pretty good as our mess is plain. Evenings, Tod and I sit around wondering what you are all doing and as we munch some ginger snaps and candy, we have a dinner fit for a king, from tomato soup thru a nice thick beefsteak and fruit salad to ice cream and mince pie such as Mother used to make. This is all a mental elusion of course—but when that is as close as one can get to such a meal, it is best for the peace of our minds to be satisfied, eh? Tod is well and in good spirits.

There are several fellows from Bing. in the crew among whom is a chap named McCarthy. Don't know where he lives or much about him. He says he expects to get a leave to come home when he gets back to U.S. on this return trip and if possible will come in to see either Tod's father at the store or Father at N&T Co. Hope he gets to B. and sees you.

In regard to my transferring as I talked with you, everything is OK with Capt. Smith and Sgt. Jacobson of the Supply Co. but my C.O. doesn't "hanker" after it, as he thinks my six months training in the Signal Platoon is too valuable. However the Supply office needs a man and he must be taken from some company and must be a man who has been trained along other lines rather than Supply Co work so I can't see why I can['t] transfer as well as some other fellow. Sgt. J. thinks the same—he seems to be quite anxious for me to transfer and is going to take it up further with Capt. Smith and I believe will put it thru eventually—after we land. I am going in to see him and Capt. Smith in half an hour.

There are certain things I have written in this letter about which I want to speak most <u>forcibly</u> to you. The rules about writing letters are going to be most strict and I want to ask you to repeat certain things I have written to <u>no one</u>. <u>Don't</u> <u>discuss</u> <u>them</u> <u>with</u> <u>anyone</u>. They are for the <u>family</u> <u>only</u>. If you get this letter which I surely hope you do and anyone asks you about me just say you heard from me while on board and give them the more trivial news. Otherwise it may bring you and me in trouble. One of our company officers is going to act as censor and we will submit all letters for him to read. If we have anything which we do not want him to read, we can send letters once a week to the base censor who doesn't know us from Adam or does not want to as he reads about a thousand letters a day. So our personal matters are nothing to him. But I won't be able to give you anything but general news with which you must be satisfied.

We begin to hear much about the poor moral condition in France—you can rest assured that I will act the same as I have at home. You needn't have any fears about me. I will come back in just as good shape as when I left—and maybe better. You know I'm young and I can't help but feel that I'm coming home again pretty soon perfect, physically, with no effects of warfare upon me, although there will be certain dangers. I am reading out of the Testament Mother gave me and find it a great help. Although things are quite peaceable. Of course there are certain dangers now but we have such good protection that it seems impossible for other than a safe trip.

I am leaving it to you to write Ed about this letter as this is all I can write at present. But don't <u>write</u> him anything of which I spoke on the back of page 3. If you see him, tell him but don't do any writing on those subjects.

I will look forward very much to a letter from you after we land. Address me as I said—Pvt RDT, HQ Co, 107 Reg't, American Expeditionary Force. A.E.F. will be enough—Via New York.

Well, I must close for now. With love to all of you—and I will write again soon.

Bob

Letter written in transport,
stamped "Passed by Censor May 22, 1918"[71]
Envelope signed "Censored RH McIntyre 1st **Lt."**[72]
Letter received June 5th **1918**

Dear Father,

Am writing this on board. Expect we'll see land before long. Have had a good trip—weather has been fine except for a day or so when we had a slight storm. I wasn't used to the rocking so I helped "feed the fishes" and held my bunk down for a short time but feel fine now. Tod is feeling well and is in good spirits. All I can say about our trip is that with such protection as we have it seems impossible that we should have other than a safe journey across the water. My arm is better. There is a hole about the size of a dime and a quarter of an inch deep but it is beginning to heal in good shape and there is hardly any soreness. The swelling has all gone down. It is a <u>remarkably</u> positive vaccination—as the doctor told me at Camp S.

My address is the same as I told you—

Pvt RDT
Hdqrs. Co.—107 US Inf
A.E.F. (American Expeditionary Force)
Via New York

I am looking forward very much to a letter from you when the first mail arrives "over here."

There is a canteen aboard where we can buy smoking material, crackers and candy which we find handy now and then—when we can get near—there is always a mob around it.

Well, write Ed as I haven't time to write him as I must turn this in to the first sergeant now. With love to all of you. Will write more just as soon as we land.

Your son
Bob

Letter #1 written abroad and sent from the continent
Letter postmarked Field Post Office, 5 ? 18, passed by Censor No. 1987
Signed "Censored RH McIntyre 1st Lt"
Received June 29th 1918

Saturday Evening, June 1st, 1918
"Somewhere in France"

Dear Folks,

I'll bet you'd like to know where the above "Somewhere in France" is, and I'd like to tell you but it can't be done. However I'll give you as newsy a letter as I can "for the money."

I am using this writing paper which I got in Camp Stuart but the Y.M. here (with quarters in a fair sized tent) has some headed "With the British Forces" so I guess it will do no harm to say that we are in a sector controlled by the British.

We have now been in France about a week. We had an uneventful trip across the water, were well protected and saw no submarines. The first night after disembarking, we slept in our "pup-tents" after a hike of four or five miles—and we slept well. The night was beautiful—full moon and clear sky. After resting a day and another night we traveled "de-luxe" in box-cars (we named ours "Hotel de Gink") to a point about five miles from where we are situated at present. Everything is very interesting to me, of course, as it is to everyone. The railroad cars are much smaller and the passenger coaches are split up into compartments. The freight cars are all marked "So many men or so many horses capacity"—I had to laugh—it must be horses are valued as highly as men. We traveled thru beautiful country—of course it is summer-time here as in the States and the trees and grass are green and many houses have beautiful little flower-gardens around them. One of the many things I noticed is that most every building is built of stone or brick with tile roof—hardly ever a wooden structure. I noticed an advertisement for "Heinz's 57 Varieties" and the European Edition of the New York Herald as we rode along in our "Pullman." We stopped

at certain stations along the way where hot coffee was served and we
filled our canteens. We had our rations on board. We arrived in the village mentioned at the top of this page about midnight. We received a
welcome not only from the French and English but from the Germans.
They were making an air-raid on a town four or five miles away. As
soon as the anti-aircraft gunners caught sight of them, away went the
guns and there was considerable banging until Fritz went back or was
brought down. I don't know which. Since I have mentioned air-raids, I
presume you will want to know that the distance from here to the nearest battle field is about 40 miles as the aeroplane flies — so I have been
told at least. We have been here about four days and during that time
there have been a couple of other air-raids but not on this village — I
have slept so well, I haven't heard a thing of them. We slept in the place
where we detrained for one night and then after getting some addi-
tional equipment from our barracks-bags — we marched here. We are
told we may not see our barrack bags for some time, possibly. I hope
we do as I have a lot of things I'd like to have with me. One pair of my
eye-glasses are in it as well as my sewing kit and most of my extra toilet
articles [such] as tooth-paste, some soap, razor blades, etc.

We are billeted (the Hdqts Co) in barns and other buildings
around the town — a place of about 4 or 5,000 population, possibly not
so large — I haven't had a chance to look around a great deal. I sleep
up in the hayloft of a barn. It is dry and clean and until tonight I have
slept on the wood floor. This afternoon after drill I bought some hay for
1 franc 3 pennies (about 20¢) from an old woman. You'd laugh to see
me trying to talk to the French people. I look up a word in the French
dictionary I bought (3 francs 50), talk with my hands a bit, and then we
"comprendre."

The fellows have found a restaurant or two where we can get
a good meal. We had an egg omelet, French fried potatoes, bread
and butter, and coffee for about 2½ francs (50¢) — not unreasonable,
eh? But candy is scarce — one can get only sweet chocolate, figs,
etc. I bought a couple of oranges for 50 centimes (½ franc) — about
10¢ a piece. Some things are higher and some lower. I went into a

barber-shop and had a shampoo and a shave which cost me the grand total of 1 franc—about 18¢—cheap enough, I'd say. I was much interested to look around a pretty good-looking grocery store. I discovered Quaker Oats, Carnation milk, some Alaska-packed salmon and a few other American articles. There were lots of sardines, bottled liquors, French packed canned goods, coffee, etc. As I mentioned liquor, I'll say a little about it. There is a café on every corner and several between on most every street and avenue. One can get light wines and beers, cognac, champagne, etc., most anything. Of course the French drink a good deal but here at least, it is mostly light wine and beers. Drinking water is not very plentiful—that is—the water must be purified before we drink it. I presume that is one reason why so much wine and beer is drunk. Our fellows, having been prohibited all kinds of liquor in the US, have taken to drinking a bit in excess—that is—a few of them have—I'll modify my statement. About a half dozen in our company have been "subjected to disciplinary action" and I guess the rest who imbibe will do so moderately as they either want all their privileges or wish to keep their stomachs in good order.

Sunday P.M. [June 2, 1918]

I'll finish this letter now.

I have tried a glass of beer and also some wine. I derived very little pleasure from it. In fact it would take some time for me to learn to like them and I am not going to try. Water and "du lait" are good enough for me. One can get a cup of milk for the equivalent of 5¢.

The bathing facilities here are not very good but I have managed to keep fairly clean taking baths in a pail and basin. Yesterday A.M. our company took a swim in a creek nearby but it was pretty muddy. I had some clothes washed very reasonably.

Today we have had no drill. Church services were held this A.M. This noon Tod and I and another fellow went out to dinner. We bought a bottle of pickles and a small can of apricots (Libby's) and with these made a very good meal with our dinner of ham omelet, bread and oleo and coffee.

My arm is getting better and should be healed pretty quickly.

It is a beautiful afternoon, warm and clear. I am sitting in a little court-yard in front of our billet (barn) and in the rear is a good-sized field. It is beautiful now but in the winter I am told it is pretty cold.

By the way, who should come to see me in our first camp after disembarking but D.C. McNamara. He is in the 58th Coast Artillery Corp. and came over in the same convoy I did. He looks fine.

I might say we did not land in any port that we talked of before I left, so did not see Reed Kellam or Col. Wright.

There are all nationalities represented by soldiers around here. I have seen English, Canadian, French, Australian, Chinese, Scottish—the Chinese are laborers—soldiers. They are all very interesting. One can get quite a bit of information from the British "Tommies." I have talked with several.

We are allowed to go around quite a lot and it is really very interesting.

I have just been out looking at a religious Catholic ceremony. It is in the form of a parade with lots of children also many older people—streets strewn with flowers and grass. Stops were made at various places where altars were erected. The priests were all in vestments and many of the young girls were in white. A very quaint and pretty ceremony.

Tod is feeling fine and I am, too.

I believe we are the first American troops to be quartered in this town. We saw quite a few of our boys as we were traveling here.

There are quite a few planes in the air around some of the time.

Haven't received any mail as yet—it is rather soon for it. I hope you'll send me the Rep. Herald and I would like it if I could get the New York Tribune. We don't get half as much news here as we did at Camp Wadsworth.

I must apologize for not writing before but everything is so new and interesting that I neglected writing for two or three days. However I'll try to write twice a week hereafter or once a week anyway.

Well, I presume the Lieutenant will call this a regular "book" to censor and I have written all the news I can think of anyway as I'll close. Will write soon again. Love to all. Please send this on to Ed as it will save me writing five pages of this stuff all over again. Regards to Agnes, everybody at the store and all my friends around home.

Bob

My family art gallery looks good to me over here, 4,000 miles away.

RDT

Letter #2 written abroad and sent from the continent
Letter in <u>ACTIVE</u> <u>SERVICE</u> envelope postmarked FIELD POST OFFICE.

Tuesday, June 4, 1918

Dear Folks,

Hereafter when I write you I will number my letters so you will know whether you are receiving all of them or not. I wrote you my first one last Saturday and Sunday, June 1 and 2 and gave it to the lieutenant to censor on Sunday evening.

Sunday afternoon our C.O. was going to issue passes for us to go over to [censored][73] but afterwards the order was rescinded and we couldn't go. [censored] Tod and I could have borrowed a bicycle and ridden out.

This morning our company went down and had a hot shower-bath at the British baths. Was OK.

Tod and I and three other fellows in the band all eat together at a ladies house near our kitchen—that is, we get our own mess and eat it at the table and have the comfort of sitting in chairs. Along with the meal, we learn to speak some French and get the right pronunciation. I have bought a French-English dictionary and a French conversational booklet and am learning a little.

Wed. Noon [June 5, 1918]

We have quite a lot of fun talking with the Madame where we eat. There are three nice well-behaved children — 2 girls and 1 boy — Lily and Odette and Bernard. I haven't learned their last name yet. They are from twelve to sixteen years old, I should say.

Last night, I met Billy Guilfoyle who is in our company and an older man than most of us — Irish and nice old chap and he took me to the Catholic church to a service. They have a very fine church for the size of the town, I'd say, and a good organ. I enjoyed the music and singing as well as the service as I had never attended a Catholic service before.

This morning I was instructed to report to Capt Smith of the Supply Co and so I am again in the Regtal Supply Office doing clerical work the same as I did in Camp Wadsworth — for a week or ten days. Things have not worked out just as I hoped — as I talked with you and I don't know as they will. I'll have to take them as they come anyway.

We had our first issue of English tobacco Sunday and understand we get it every Sunday from now on — 3 pckgs of cigarettes and a pckg of smoking tobacco — also 1 pckg matches.

I am able to get the "Daily Mail" (Continental Edition) every morning here and get a little news. I noticed that [censored]. I also read that New York City had its second hottest June 2nd in 47 years — 91 degrees Fahrenheit. I suppose it must be getting quite hot in Binghamton. The days are quite warm here but the evenings are cool.

Wed. P.M. [June 5, 1918]

We have turned in all our extra issued clothing which we carried in our barracks-bags so we are going to travel light. The personal stuff we had in our barracks-bags, we must either carry in our packs or give away. Was obliged to give away all my Red Cross knit goods except my helmet as I didn't need it and could not carry it. I kept my heavy socks of course. I also had to give away a few other things that I could not possibly carry.

Please send this on to Ed and tell him I think just as much of him even tho I don't write direct to him but it's much harder to write letters here. I haven't only these two to you, so far — none to others.

Am going to write Marsh Williams a note if I get time. How about Pete Jenkins' address?

The boat we came over on was occupied by colored troops on its previous trip and they left a few "kouties" on board for us. I haven't been troubled so far but several of the fellows have. We are having an exam for them this P.M. altho the fellows are rid of them by this [time]. However it will do no harm.

Must close for now. With love to all. Will be glad to receive my first mail. Regards to everybody at the store.

Bob

Censored and signed by RH McIntyre

Letter #3 written abroad and sent from the continent[74]
Letter postmarked Field Post Office July 26, 1918,
passed by Censor No. 6461
Signed "OK L.L. Shaw"
Received Aug 15th 1918

June 11, 1918, Tuesday Evening

Dear Folks,

Well, night before last, I received "some" mail. It was the first I had received except one letter from Ed. I got eleven letters — as follows -

Father's	of May 8	to Camp S.
Mother's	" "	"
Ede's	" "	"
Mother's	" 10	"
Father's	" 13	"
Father's	" 15	Addressed Amer. Exp. Forces
Ed's	" 13	to Camp S.
Ed's	" 13	"
Ed's	" 15	"
Ed's	" 20	A.E.F.

and one from Pete Jenkins at Mineola. Pete says he came home and bade good bye to his folks expecting to come across but now expects to stay in the States for a while. Was expecting to go to Arcadia, Florida in a few days for an unknown length of time. There was a note from Alma enclosed in his letter, too.

Of course by this time you have received my card stating I have arrived in France.[75] I figure you received it a few days after you wrote the latest letter in this batch I just received (letter of May 15).

You spoke of staying overnight at the Waldorf on your way home from Camp S. It reminds me of the time I came down to dinner with you when we were in Van Cortlandt Park.

I have just stopped a few minutes while we had a 10 minute prayer service (I am writing in YM tent). The man in charge is an English man—an elderly minister and a fine old man. He has this little time of prayer every evening at the same time—a little before eight o'clock. While I am speaking of the Y.M. I will tell you a bit more about it. They have a good-sized tent here and plenty of tables and benches. They sell cigarettes, tobacco and tea and sweet crackers. Believe me, it is crowded every evening. I forgot to say there is a piano, too. It is certainly wonderful how the YM follows one everywhere.

We certainly did a good visit at Camp S, didn't we, Mother? Altho my bounds were pretty much restricted. I am glad Father was able to go over to Jay D's and get his annual fishing in and have such good luck, too. Please remember me to all the Parsons.

I enjoyed your good letter, Ede. I am sorry you didn't feel like coming down to Camp S. but will have so much the better visit when "I come home." That sounds good anyway, tho it may be some time away. Hope not, at least. You probably have received the last Gas Attack for some time. Don't know when more will be published. Am interested to know that Sid Farnsworth has received his orders. The "devil" of it is, that even tho my friends may be in the next town, I don't and can't know it. I have written Marsh W. a note. I am also interested to know about Mainy Wilson and K. Niles. The case containing all your pictures is fine and is getting worn with handling, already. I am sorry to hear of Mrs. Drewer's death.

I am very proud of Ed—to become top sergeant from a corporal. The Colonel has not informed me of any advancement, so I presume I am still a private, first class.

My arm is improving rapidly and will soon be completely healed.

Seems to me Hocky gets a good many leaves—how many times has he been home? Two or three, hasn't he?

I can't tell you how excited we were to get our mail—believe me, everybody hung around in a crowd and when it was given out, there was complete silence as each read his letters. Dad, you do write such good letters. After I had read over my letters, I went to bed feeling like a million dollars. It was just about a month since I had received any mail. I was surprised to get Ed's letter of May 20 quite so soon.

I'd just like to see Father driving the "Henry" around. I'm glad you got it, Father, for it will [be] fine to get around with and save some steps. I expect Mother and Ede will both learn to drive it, too.

I hope you'll send me some Rep Heralds and the NY Tribune, too, if you will.

I was much interested in Ed's letter telling about having Stetson, the son of the hat manufacturer, in his company. Kind of tough to give up a $15,000 salary to become a $30 a month private, eh? All of Ed's letters were very interesting and mostly concerned with his work.

I am working in the Reg'tal Supply Office as I wrote you last week. Am detailed over there. The work is very interesting.

Don't get very much news. We get the Daily Mail (English) every A.M.—a two or four page paper. Here's a good one. In the report of the baseball game results the other day, I noticed in the International League that there was no game between Bing. and Jersey City, I think, on account of a trolley car strike in Binghamton. So you must be having another street car strike.

We have a good place to take shower baths now and we can keep ourselves in good shape. I got a shave today in a French barbershop for five cents. Cheap, eh?

There is a canteen here now where we can buy sweet chocolate, smokes, sweet crackers, toilet articles, American baked beans (Armours) and other small articles. Candy is unknown over here. It is some different from our canteen in Camp Wadsworth but very popular, for "extras" are hard to get. We have an issue of tobacco every Sunday now.

There are lots of British and French soldiers around and some Canadians and Australians. It seems as tho every French soldier has a different colored uniform on.

Have I told you about Madame DuBois in whose house Tod and I and three other band fellows take our "chow" in and eat? We have the advantage of sitting in chairs at a table, which is somewhat of a luxury. Then we occasionally buy something extra in the way of fresh vegetables, canned fruit, pickles, etc. We learn some French and teach the Madam and Odette (age about 14), Lili (age about 12) and Bernard (age about 16) some English. The Madame's husband is in the army. She has a niece whose father has been a prisoner for nearly the whole length of the war. The [family] lived in Amiens but was obliged to move out.

The people here have to buy bread, meat, sugar, etc. on ration cards I believe. I have come up to my billet since starting this. The light is getting poor and I will finish tomorrow.

Wed. A.M. [June 12, 1918]

Most of the people are in very moderate circumstances and some are quite poor, judging from appearances. Of course, this isn't a large town and there naturally wouldn't be very many people of means. The women dress very much like American women and the men do too when they get on their Sunday clothes. The country is very fertile around here and is well covered with tilled fields and gardens. There are fine looking horses and live stock. The wagons both for business and pleasure are mostly two-wheeled affairs and some of the farm-wagons have immense wheels.

The time here is set one hour ahead the same as at home. It gets light as early as 2 or 2:30 o'clock in the A.M. and is not dark until about

10 at night. We get up at 6, have reveille formation at 6:30, mess at 7, drill from 8 till 11:30, mess at 12, drill from 1 till about 4:30, retreat at 5:45 and mess at 6:00. The rules are strict for the evening on account of possible air-raids. All men have to be in their billets by 9 and to bed by 10. No lights after sunset—nor smoking.

Tod and I are both feeling fine and are in good spirits. Must stop. I have written all the news for this time. With love to all.

Bob

P.S. You might send this on to Ed. I have written him a long letter—day before yesterday.

Letter #4 written abroad and sent from the continent
Letter received July 15th 1918

Monday, June 24, 1918

Dear Folks,

I haven't written to you since June 11 and to Ed since June 14. We have been on the move since a week ago today. We left the town from which my last letter was written on Monday and have been doing some awful hiking until today. It has been hike, hike, hike and when you finished at night, you were ready to eat and go to sleep. We have been thru many towns, stopping and billeting in one each night. I'm sorry to say that a good many of the things which you bought and made for me and which I appreciated, I have been compelled to throw and give away and sell—I simply couldn't carry them all on my back. Man, I have done some of the meanest hiking for the past week I have ever done. I gave my nice Regulation army sweater which Mother got at Franklin Lunor's to a woman in one of the towns we slept in. I sold my spiral leggings. My entire personal belongings now consist of the little khaki bag Ede made for me to hold my extra toilet articles in which I have saved just a very few extra things and a needle or two and some thread (had to throw away Ede's sewing kit), my regular small toilet kit in which I keep soap, razor etc. and a few packs of Fatima cigts which I brought over from Camp Stuart. Everything else has gone and if we hike much more, more stuff will go. It's either me to fall out or have a lighter pack. I did have to fall out for a short distance a couple of days on account of my feet being blistered. They are better now—getting tougher.

Well, here we are in a small town about 16 or 18 miles from the lines, on reserve. We may be here for three days or three months, depending on whether the Germans make a drive this way.

My arm is about healed now and I feel OK.

I have a good place to sleep. Haven't had a bath in about 2 weeks but am going to try to get some kind of a one today or tomorrow.

I have been writing this while waiting for dinner. Will finish later as mess is ready.

Tuesday P.M., June 25

Well, here it is Tuesday P.M. and I am just finishing this up.

I am detailed at present to the Adjutant's Office working on the pay-rolls. Will probably be here for several days. We haven't been paid for May as yet but will be in a day or so. Have plenty of money so far. Worked last night till 9:30.

Had a letter from Marsh Williams yesterday. He has a new job—has charge of all the hospital supplies in his unit and is evidently well and busy. I figure he isn't very far from here but I can't tell for sure, of course.

There is a good sized town about 2 or 3 kilometers from here—twice as big as the one we came from. Haven't been down yet. The country is beautiful—nights cool.

Lots of aeroplanes flying around and occasionally considerable banging—when the wind is right.

We have had mail only once since we arrived here. I wrote you about it. I hope we get some more pretty soon.

Tuesday Evening [June 25, 1918]

Tod is well and sends his regards. Mail this on to Ed. Will send via a Base Censor.

Love to all and regards to my friends.

Bob

Further Training at Camp Wadsworth and in France: Notes

1   Yockelson, *Borrowed Soldiers: Americans under British Command, 1918*, 34.
2   *World War I: A Day-by-Day Chronology.*
3   Hallas, *Doughboy War: The American Expeditionary Force in WWI*, 161.
4   Stone, *World War One*, 163.
5   Ibid.
6   Ibid., 161.
7   Persico, *Eleventh Month, Eleventh Day, Eleventh Hour*, 213-214.
8   Stone, *World War One*, 159.
9   Liddell Hart, *World War I*, 224.
10 Yockelson, *Borrowed Soldiers: Americans under British Command, 1918*, 39-40.
11 Stone, *World War One*, 165-166.
12 Simkins, Jukes, and Hickey, *The First World War: The War to End All Wars*, 155-156.
13 Yockelson, *Borrowed Soldiers: Americans under British Command, 1918*, 42-43.
14 Persico, *Eleventh Month, Eleventh Day, Eleventh Hour*, 222.
15 Yockelson, *Borrowed Soldiers: Americans under British Command, 1918*, 43.
16 Stevens, *The Great War Explained,* 118-119.
17 Keene, *World War I: The American Soldier Experience*, xiii.
18 Jacobson, *History of the 107th Infantry, U.S.A.*, 16-17.
19 Harris, *Duty, Honor, Privilege: New York's Silk Stocking Regiment and the Breaking of the Hindenburg Line*, 99-100.
20 Seward, *Binghamton and Broome County, New York, A History*, 576.
21 Jacobson, *History of the 107th Infantry, U.S.A.*, 17-18.
22 Seward, *Binghamton and Broome County, New York, A History*, 576.
23 Van Ells, *America and World War I: A Traveler's Guide,* 88.
24 Jacobson, *History of the 107th Infantry U.S.A.*, 18.
25 Ibid.
26 Ibid.., 19.

27 Ibid.

28 Yockelson, *Borrowed Soldiers: Americans under British Command, 1918*, 52.

29 Jacobson, *History of the 107th Infantry U.S.A.*, 19-20.

30 Seward, *Binghamton and Broome County, New York, A History*, 576.

31 Van Ells, *American and World War I: A Traveler's Guide*, 102-103.

32 Ibid., 135.

33 Jacobson, *History of the 107th Infantry U.S.A.*, 21-22.

34 Ibid., 22.

35 Seward, *Binghamton and Broome County, New York, A History*, 577.

36 Jacobson, *History of the 107th Infantry U.S.A.*, 27.

37 Ibid.

38 Yockelson, *Borrowed Soldiers: Americans under British Command, 1918*, 9.

39 Ibid., 10.

40 Ibid., 12.

41 Ibid., 17.

42 Ibid., 19.

43 Ibid., xiv.

44 Stone, *World War One*, 168-169.

45 Van Ells, *America and World War I: A Traveler's Guide*, 163-164.

46 Morgan, *The Concise History of World War I*, 62.

47 Van Ells, *America and World War I: A Traveler's Guide*, 169-170.

48 Jacobson, *History of the 107th Infantry U.S.A.*, 29.

49 Hallas, *Doughboy War: The American Expeditionary Force in WWI*, 183.

50 Yockelson, *Borrowed Soldiers: Americans under British Command 1918*, 60-61.

51 Jacobson, *History of the 107th Infantry U.S.A.*, 30.

52 Morgan, *The Concise History of World War I*, 64-65.

53 Matloff, *World War I: A Concise Military History of "The War to End All Wars" and The Road to War*, 96.

54 Seward, *Binghamton and Broome County, New York, A History*, 577.

55 Harris, *Duty, Honor, Privilege: New York's Silk Stocking Regiment*

and the Breaking of the Hindenburg Line, 125-126.

56 Jacobson, *History of the 107th Infantry U.S.A.,* 32.

57 Ibid., 33.

58 Ibid.,32.

59 Ibid., 33-34.

60 Harris, *Duty, Honor, Privilege: New York's Silk Stocking Regiment and the Breaking of the Hindenburg Line,* 127.

61 Yorke, *The Trench: Life and Death on the Western Front 1914-1918,* 56.

62 Stevens, *The Great War Explained,* 57.

63 Pvt. Truesdell mentions the word "hypology" in two of his letters. No such word appears in *Webster's Collegiate Dictionary,* but since the word "horse" is derived from the Greek *hyppos* and since Pvt. Truesdell refers to "Remount Stations," one must conclude that there was a section dealing with horses on the Quartermaster Corps exam.

64 Pvt. Truesdell's 10-day furlough apparently started on Tuesday, January 29, 1918, as he notes later on, and lasted until Thursday, February 7, 1918, as confirmed in his letter mailed on February 11, 1918.

65 Although the men of the Headquarters Company of the 107th Infantry Regiment had been divided into specialty platoons about the end of 1917, they apparently weren't grouped together in tents according to their new platoon assignments until the first week in February 1918. Pvt. Truesdell reports that the change took place while he was away on furlough, and upon return, he had to get to know new tent mates—once again.

66 The "Gas Attack" was the weekly news publication of the 27th Division

67 Dr. Strayer was the minister at the Third Presbyterian Church in Rochester, New York.

68 "Neudge," was Marion Newell, Pvt. Truesdell's first cousin. Their mothers were sisters, and their fathers, Frank Newell and Edwin S. Truesdell, Sr., established Newell and Truesdell Co., Importers and Wholesale Grocers. Marion Newell later became Mrs. Robert Bates Guy and a leading citizen in Binghamton, New York.

69 "W.U." stands for Western Union, the company that transmitted telegrams. Telegrams were the normal form of communication when one needed to send a short message that would be delivered quickly, usually the same day.

70 Pvt. Truesdell mentions his vaccination for smallpox in several letters. The immediate swelling and soreness eventually went away, but the scar, at least the size of a dime, remained on his left arm for the rest of his life.

71 This letter, which is undated, certainly seems to have been written after the previous letter was penned, but it was received by Pvt. Truesdell's parents ten days before the previous letter was received. Both letters were written on board the *Susquehanna*.

72 In *Duty, Honor, Privilege: New York's Silk Stocking Regiment and the Breaking of the Hindenburg Line* on p. 168, Stephen Harris tells us that Lt. R.H. McIntyre was a graduate of Williams College and a lawyer at the New York law firm of Harris and Towne. According to Gerald Jacobson in *History of the 107th Infantry U.S.A.* on p. 461, Lt. McIntyre was assigned to the Headquarters Company of the 107th Infantry Regiment on October 9, 1917; during the Battle of the Hindenburg Line on September 29, 1918, he became a prisoner of war and, following the Armistice and his release, he returned to the Headquarters Company on December 20, 1918.

73 The censorship of letters began on board the *Susquehanna* on the way to France. Pvt. Truesdell was generally very careful about what he wrote in his letters, but on two or three occasions, the censor blacked out a phrase that could conceivably be helpful to the enemy. The outside of the envelope could have the sender's name and unit, but generally, Pvt. Truesdell simply wrote his name, followed by U.S. Infantry, Amer. E.F. As an alternative to writing letters, doughboys could use the Field Service Postcard, which had fixed statements such as "I am quite well," "I have been admitted into hospital," "I have received your letter dated _____," and "I have received no letter from you." Only rarely did Pvt. Truesdell use the Field Service Postcard in preference to writing a letter, but when he did use the

postcard, he simply crossed out the inapplicable statements before sending the card home.

74   Although this letter was written on June 11 and 12, the mail was apparently delayed with the result that the letter didn't leave France until late July and wasn't received until mid-August.

75   On Friday, May 31, 1918, Pvt. Truesdell's parents received the Army's official postcard indicating that their son had arrived safely in France. Pvt. Truesdell had signed and addressed the postcard before sailing; the postcard, shown below, was held stateside until confirmation that the soldier had "arrived safely overseas," then mailed to the addressee.

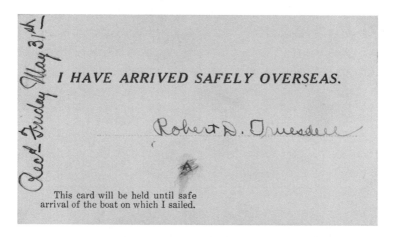

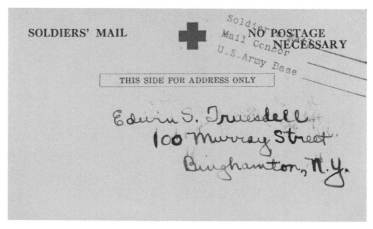

COMBAT IN BELGIUM AND FRANCE

Because there had been signs that the Germans were preparing to launch an attack in the area of Doullens, the British stockpiled vast stores of ammunition. As the 107th approached the reserve line, they could see great camouflaged ammunition dumps with shells of various sizes piled everywhere. However, perhaps because German airmen discovered all this British preparation, the anticipated assault did not take place. Instead, British intelligence began to report that German shock troops were moving in the direction of Belgium.[1]

Thus, on July 1, Pvt. Truesdell's regiment received orders to entrain the next day for a new destination, which, the men soon learned, would be Belgium. During the long trip by rail, the men got used to seeing the effects of enemy shelling: ruined towns and widespread wanton destruction. By late afternoon, the troops reached their destination. Part of the regiment, including Regimental Headquarters, detrained at Wizernes, the rest at nearby St. Omer. The British military authorities had ordered the citizens of St. Omer to leave the city because it was too close to areas that might come under attack and because the British needed their rear unimpeded should they need to move backward. The British had learned in the past that when fleeing peasants choked the roads, it was difficult to shift troops to other positions and to move forward reserve artillery, ammunition, food, and water.[2]

When the 107th Headquarters plus the 1st and 2nd Battalions were ordered to hike from Wizernes to Broxeele while the 3rd Battalion hiked from St. Omer to Buysscheure, the men had to endure a march close to 20 kilometers on a hot day over flat land that sometimes was brackish and ill-smelling. Because there were very few places to billet in Broxeele and Buysscheure, most of the men put up shelter tents in nearby fields. On July 5, the men were on the march again with Regimental Headquarters and 1st and 2nd Battalions ending up that day in Arneke and the 3rd Battalion in the neighboring village of Ledringham. Then the regiment moved on to St. Laurent and Winnezeele, small towns near Steenvoorde, a city that had been experiencing steady shelling by the Germans almost every day. Here again, much of the regiment pitched shelter tents after digging in to gain as much protection as possible against enemy shells.[3] Despite all this movement from place to place, the Y.M.C.A. was able to keep pace. Pvt. Truesdell tells his parents that "along came an American Y.M.C.A. truck, and believe me, everybody was mighty glad to see it. We were able to buy Little Bobbie cigars, Sweet Caps, Prince Albert, Lowney's sweet chocolate, etc, and it certainly seemed good to get American goods." The division was now attached to Gen. Sir Herbert Plumer's British Second Army. The reason for the assignment was to give the division's battalions actual combat experience in a part of the front known as the East Poperinghe Line.[4] While a part of the division served in the line on a rotation basis, other parts trained in the use of various weapons and practiced wave formations of attack.[5]

It was during this period of time that Pvt. Truesdell writes that his unit has been issued new overseas caps. Like canvas leggings, deemed unsuitable for trench life and replaced by puttees made from the same material as the uniforms and wound around the leg, the wide-brimmed campaign hat or "Montana hat," also incompatible with trench warfare, was replaced by the fore-and-aft style overseas cap.[6] Of course in the front lines, soldiers wore steel helmets.

Because British intelligence had determined that the German armies under Prince Rupprecht of Bavaria were preparing for a major offensive in Flanders with the probable goal of seizing the Channel ports, the 27th Division, as well as the 30th Division, now in reserve positions on the front from Ypres to Scherpenberg (the East Poperinghe Line), faced a severe test in combat conditions. It was at this time, July 14, 1918, that the 107th Regiment of the 27th Division lost its first soldier killed in action. Corporal William Leonard lost his life when the Germans sent heavy artillery fire to the British unit to which he was detailed for observation work.[7] On July 22, 1918, Brigadier Gen. P. E. Pierce, commanding general of the 54th Infantry Brigade of the 27th Division, issued the "Plan for Defense of the East Poperinghe Line" and stressed, "Under all circumstances the East Poperinghe Line is to be held."[8] Combat conditions with further casualties could be expected.

The 107th Regiment of the 54th Brigade, 27th Division, having moved closer to the front, set up headquarters at a British aerodrome near Abeele, Belgium, on July 23. This aerodrome was also the headquarters of many British bombing planes. Also in this area a number of British observation balloons were kept aloft during daylight. These balloons drew intense shelling; in fact, the entire area drew extensive shelling during the time that the division was stationed there.[9]

On August 1, the 107th headquarters moved back from the front to the town of Boisdinghem. Here the regiment, now under the command of Colonel Charles DeBevoise, underwent more—and very intensive—training at a rifle range. Pvt. Truesdell writes, "We are (the whole regiment) some distance back of the lines shooting at a rifle range. It seems a relief not to have to wear our gas-masks over our shoulder and to hear no big guns booming....[R]ight now I am sitting on the ground at the 500 yd line waiting to shoot." He also reports later that while he was at the rifle range, he was promoted to corporal. A nearby large British flying field with three huge canvas hangars not only sent off several bombing planes each evening but also was the setting of a divisional show. Twice during this period of training, one of these hangars was used as a playhouse. The men of the 107th also enjoyed several motion picture shows there, made available by the British.[10] The newly promoted corporal writes that "our division theatre gave a variety vaudeville show last night at the aerodrome which is about 200 yds. away and I went. It really was fine for we have some good talent. Two or three times a week the British fellows at the aerodrome have 'movies' and I went the other night. First class pictures—the first I've seen since I arrived in France."

After a week in the Boisdinghem area, rifle practice and maneuvers came to a close on August 8. The 2nd Battalion left immediately to return to Winnezeele, with the other two battalions and headquarters following two days later. The 2nd Battalion, closely followed by the 1st and 3rd Battalions, moved to the front lines in front of Mont Kemmel, captured by the Germans in mid-April. Moving forward to the frontline trenches of the East Poperinghe Line in small detachments at night, the battalions passed all kinds of debris, the effects of brutal warfare, while enemy shells exploded all around them and pyrotechnic flares of the Very lights lit the sky.[11] The 107th Regiment remained in that part of the Ypres salient, defending the Dickebusch and Kemmel sectors in the front and support lines, for a period of about two weeks.[12] The entire 27th Division, charged with defending a front of approximately 3,000 yards, continued to be on special alert because the anticipated German drive to the coast was expected while the division occupied the front lines.[13] But rather than only standing on defense, the 27th and 30th Divisions began preparations for storming Mont Kemmel. Just as plans had been completed, the Americans discovered that the Germans had left Mont Kemmel. A captured German officer said the evacuation had taken place because the Germans believed that a great many American soldiers were being massed at Kemmel.[14]

The 27th Division's tour of duty in the front line was a severe test of the division's ability to face the reality of warfare, as opposed to the training experienced in previous months. As Jacobson writes, "Mont Kemmel afforded the enemy every advantage. From its heights, Boche observers could view the surrounding country for miles, and it was imperative that the troops occupying the Allied lines remain absolutely quiet during the hours of daylight."[15] Because at this time of year darkness lasted only six hours, much had to be accomplished, aside from nightly raids into No Man's Land, during those few hours: digging, repairing barbed wire, replacing duckboards, bringing up food and ammunition, and carrying back the dead and wounded.[16] Yet the men had to be alert during daylight when they had to keep watch over the parapet or man their guns against the enemy.

Soldiers in the Headquarters Company of the 107th Regiment, along with the rest of the 27th Division, had now been in Europe for more than three months in training and combat conditions. By this point, Cpl. Truesdell reports that some of his personal items need to be replaced and writes that these items can be ordered from an American department store and delivered via its Paris or London branch. Amazingly, London and Paris stores could deliver to the front parcels of not only non-perishable items but also perishables such as cakes, butter, and fresh fruit. Fussell reports that Fortnum and Mason's and Harrod's offered gift assortments designed especially for the front. Fortnum's fruitcake was a favorite. [17]

While the 27th Division was in Belgium, elsewhere on the Western Front, American soldiers were taking part, with their allies, in other offensives. Four companies of the American 33rd Division fought with the British and Australians in a successful attack on July 4 on the village of Hamel.[18] Further, following the last of the German offensives known as the Champagne-Marne or "Friedensturm" Offensive, French and American troops delivered a surprise, devastating counter-offensive on July 18.[19] Following these Allied victories, Foch summoned Haig, Pétain, and Pershing to inform them of his plan for a massive assault on the entire Western Front—the British in the northern part, the Americans in the southern section near Verdun, and the French in the middle.[20] The Allies continued to keep up the pressure. On August 8, the British, Australians, and Canadians launched an attack on the Germans near Amiens. The use of tanks, aircraft, light Lewis guns carried by fast-moving infantry, gas, and high explosives resulted in a triumph.[21] Ludendorff later described August 8 as "the black day of the German Army in the history of this war."[22] Then on August 20, the French attacked the Germans and captured more than 8,000 prisoners in the Battle of Noyon. On August 21, the British pushed forward near the old Somme battlefield and retook Albert. Further attacks at the end of August and beginning of September resulted in the capture of

Mont Saint Quentin and Péronne, forcing the Germans to retreat to the Hindenburg Line.[23]

Back in the United States, in an apparent effort to aid anti-Bolshevik forces in Russia, President Wilson had agreed in early July to send troops to Siberia, and in mid-August, American troops began to arrive in Vladivostok, East Siberia; by early September, American troops would also arrive in Archangel, North Russia. American troops would not be fully withdrawn from North Russia until the summer of 1919; the last American troops in Siberia were withdrawn in the spring of 1920.[24]

About the same time that the 27th Division was completing its tour of duty in the East Poperinghe trenches, the subject of amalgamation arose yet again in the highest levels of Allied military leadership. After a good deal of heated disagreement between Field Marshal Haig and Gen. Pershing regarding the placement of some American divisions under British command, Gen. Pershing compromised and allowed two divisions, the 27th and the 30th, to remain with the British. The 27th and 30th would be with the British permanently, but Pershing was adamant that the two divisions must function under their own commanders."[25]

Amalgamation was a source of contention with the French as well. On August 28, Foch again said that he needed American troops under French command. According to Persico, "Pershing resisted, and a violent argument flared." When Foch persisted, Pershing is said to have replied that the American Army would fight wherever Foch decided, but only as an independent American Army. By September 2, they reached a compromise. Foch approved Pershing's plan for a Saint-Mihiel offensive, but immediately thereafter Pershing was to send his forces northwest to the Argonne Forest.[26] Pershing had formed the American First Army, effective August 10,[27] and presumably felt the First Army was ready for an offensive of significant size.

After moving back out of the front lines in late August, Cpl. Truesdell and the rest of the headquarters of the 107th Infantry Regiment of the 27th Division were again established near the Abeele Aerodrome. Here the regiment underwent daily inspections and practiced various offensive maneuvers for several days. Then on September 1, the regiment was ordered to march to the vicinity of Oudezeele, headquarters of the 27th Division during its service in Belgium.[28] While the regiment was billeted near Oudezeele, Major Gen. O'Ryan issued orders on September 3 that the division would make an imminent move of significant length to a destination some distance away. Organizations within the 27th Division were assigned to quarters in the new area; the Headquarters Company of the 107th Infantry Regiment would be quartered in Beauquesne.[29]

Thus, on September 4 the regiment was again on the move. While some of the men thought they might be headed south to join other American units in the American Sector, they were actually on their way back to Doullens, the town they had left on July 2. From Doullens, the regiment marched about 10 kilometers to Terramesnil and Beauquesne, towns where the men found billets. Although the men were supposedly scheduled for a period of "rest," they actually spent their days in specialty training such as machine gun practice, advancing with tanks, and taking machine gun nests.[30] During this period of time, Cpl. Truesdell was also engaged in specialty training and tells his parents that "we are having Signal school at present, studying ground telegraphy, buzzer, Fuller phones, lamps, etc."

Learning to advance with the support of tanks was extremely important for all the men. This training was conducted by the British in mid-September near St. Pol, where their tank center was located. British officers indicated that training with tanks was a priority because an important mission against the Hindenburg Line, in which the Americans were expected to participate, was in the planning stages.[31] American training in France also emphasized cooperation between infantry and artillery.[32] It was important to practice moving forward behind a creeping or rolling barrage, a wall or curtain of fire, sent by the artillery on a fixed schedule over the advancing infantry as a screen and protection against enemy action.[33]

While the 27th Division was undergoing various types of specialized training, on September 12, under Pershing's command in the American Sector, seven American divisions supported by the French attacked and subsequently cleared the Saint-Mihiel salient. The first major American-led offensive of the war, the operation was considered a great success, with the Americans seizing 460 German guns and 15,000 prisoners.[34] Although the Germans had started to withdraw the day before, the remaining troops put up a stout defense and caused something close to 9,000 casualties.[35]

On September 19, Major General George Read, commanding officer of the American II Corps, composed of the 27th and 30th Divisions, was told about the plans for attacking the Hindenburg Line. He also learned that the two divisions in his II Corps would become attached to the British Fourth Army under General Sir Henry Rawlinson and that the two divisions would be placed facing the outer defenses of the Hindenburg Line west of the St. Quentin Canal tunnel.[36] This was the area in which the 107th Infantry Regiment, including Cpl. Truesdell, would soon be located.

Breaking the Hindenburg Line would clearly be a tremendous undertaking. The Germans, in defending the territory they had captured, began to build, almost as soon as static warfare settled in, deeper and stronger trenches than the Allies did. In general, Allied commanders did not favor such well-fortified defenses because they wanted to encourage the offensive spirit of their soldiers. The Hindenburg Line, known by the Germans as the Siegfried Line, or "Siegfriedstellung," was built in the winter of 1916-1917 by the "forced labor of prisoners of war and conscripted French citizens and consisted of three trench systems protected by heavy barbed-wire entanglements. To strengthen their trench systems, the Germans constructed concrete machine-gun emplacements, concrete observation posts with concrete shelters, and dugouts that were wired for electric lights in some cases." The Germans considered the Hindenburg Line impregnable.[37]

While the Allies were making plans for coordinated attacks on the Germans on the Western Front, important developments were taking place on other fronts. British General Sir Edmund Allenby's forces achieved great success in Palestine in mid-September, forcing the Turkish armies to retreat. In Salonika, a strong Allied offensive would lead the Bulgarians to seek an armistice in the latter part of September.[38]

Meanwhile, the plans for the Western Front took shape in the following way: The first attack, to be made by the Americans and French, would take place in the Meuse-Argonne sector on September 26; on September 27, the British would push toward Cambrai; on September 28, the Belgians, French, and British would attack in Flanders; and on September 29, the British with French support (as well as that of the American 27th and 30th Divisions) would attack the Hindenburg Line near St. Quentin.[39] Thus, on September 26, the Americans under Gen. Pershing, having made a miraculous shift from the St. Mihiel Offensive, undertook a new offensive in the Meuse-Argonne sector.[40]

About the same time, the 27th Division left the area of Beauquesne and traveled by boxcars on September 24 to the town of Tincourt. From Tincourt, the men marched to Allaines and set up camp in an area newly won by the Australians and scarred by the ugly effects of warfare. Cpl. Truesdell writes on September 25, 1918, "This ground...is absolutely pitiable. The little town we are camped near, for we can't find a billet in it, is simply razed to the ground. There isn't a building left standing, not a roof left of any kind, just a wall here and there and great heaps of bricks and stone." Because many dead Germans lay unburied near the area where Americans were bivouacked, the men were warned not to touch these bodies because the Germans had been mining some of their own dead.[41] It was in this area that the Americans linked up with Australian units, which were to be in support during the coming assault.[42]

In "The Battle of the Hindenburg Line," a section within the "History of the 107th Infantry U.S.A." devoted particularly to the 107th's military operations from September 24 to October 1, Jacobson tells us that the Second American Corps was assigned to an area between Cambrai and St. Quentin.[43] Specifically, the 107th was assigned to attack an 1800-yard front facing a part of the St. Quentin Canal, on the left of which was open canal and on the right, the northern section of the St. Quentin Canal tunnel.[44] Jacobson describes the tunnel:

> The tunnel itself afforded splendid shelter and protection for thousands of German reserve troops, and the labyrinth of connecting tunnels rendered all that part of the Hindenburg Line easily accessible to these fresh troops in the event of an emergency.... Some of these tunnels ran to cleverly concealed openings beyond the foremost German positions so that in the event of Allied troops capturing the German frontline trenches, the Boche reserves could readily rise up in No Man's Land, and thus have the assaulting forces between two fires.[45]

Additionally, great belts of barbed wire, in places eight to ten feet high, were a further barrier.[46]

Although each American division was supposed to have a strength of 28,000 officers and men, the 27th Division was significantly under strength by around the middle of September. One reason was that the first major wave of Spanish influenza hit the Western Front around September 15; further, the division was without its artillery regiments, and also the division had taken numerous casualties during training and operations in Belgium. These reasons resulted in a depletion of the ranks. Because the division had not received replacements since it had arrived in France, it had only 16,136 men when it was about to enter the line.[47]

While the 27th Division, along with the 30th Division, was preparing with the British Fourth Army for the upcoming attack on the Hindenburg Line, the main part of the American forces, the American First Army, was pursuing its own offensive, opened on September 26. The Americans fought against an extremely determined German defense in the Meuse-Argonne sector.[48] During the campaign, Pershing created the Second Army under General Robert Bullard and made General Hunter Liggett commander of the First Army.[49] Thus, Gen. Pershing became group commander of both Armies. The re-organization created a much stronger fighting force. Accounts of American participation in World War I have tended to emphasize the progress of the St. Mihiel and Meuse-Argonne campaigns over those of the American II Corps, largely because the First American Army, and in time the Second

American Army as well, were fighting under American command.

The second great Allied attack began on September 27, the main obstacle being the Canal du Nord. The Canadians and British successfully threw back the Germans despite three German defense systems extending back about five miles. In the third major Allied offensive, which began on September 28, the British, French, and Belgians made significant gains in Flanders.[50]

For several days in advance of September 29, the anticipated date of the American II Corps attack on the Hindenburg Line, the British and Australians attempted to push back the Germans in order to establish a favorable jumping-off line. In a report written by Lieut. Col. W. H. Hayes and included in *the History of the 107th Infantry U.S.A.*, we learn that the Australian Corps accomplished its assignment so that, when the 30th American Division moved up to the front lines for the assault, the 30th was positioned on the desired jumping-off line. To the left of the Australians, the Third British Corps, however, did not accomplish its mission, despite three attempts.[51] As Harris points out, this failure "to make any headway against the entrenched enemy would cost the approaching New Yorkers dearly."[52] Consequently, the American 27th Division was ordered to undertake the assignment of gaining its proper jumping-off line. The mission was to be carried out by one regiment (the 106th) of the 27th Division on the morning of September 27. The regiment was successful in gaining its objective but found that German infantrymen appeared in new places to their rear even though the regiment had repeatedly mopped up German holes, dugouts, and tunnels. The entire day of September 27 was spent fighting to retain the objectives already gained.[53]

The 107th was supposed to relieve the 106th, but unfortunately, the location of various units of the 106th was uncertain. Following a conference of officers, the 107th began to move forward to take positions that were virtually the same as those held by the 106th before its morning assault.[54] This movement toward the front on the night of September 27, in itself, was fraught with difficulty because trucks, limbers, wagons, artillery, and ambulances jammed the center of the road so that the regiment had to move forward in single file on the sides of the road.[55] Traffic issues had been considered in the extensive Field Orders issued on September 24, 1918. Regarding "Road Movement," the orders warn that:

> The country over which the attack will pass in its early stages is very much shell-pitted and all roads have been very badly damaged. To enable guns and ammunition wagons and the armored cars to pass across this area the Chief Engineer of the corps has arranged to develop four roads as rapidly as possible…. Every body of troops will be allotted its own definite road and will on no account use any other.[56]

Despite these special preparations, traffic apparently became a significant problem.

When the day dawned the next morning, September 28, the men cautiously tried to get their bearings. All they could see was a wasteland, desolation, and barbed wire that was unusually high and deep. Because German artillery fired all day on the regimental positions, the Americans suffered a number of casualties on September 28. In the meantime, some distance in front of the trenches, the battalions' intelligence sections laid out a white tape to indicate the jumping-off line so that the various units would start the attack the next morning on an even line.[57]

About 4 a.m. on September 29, company commanders were ordered to line up their men on the white tape for the imminent assault, which altogether was along a 40-mile front.[58] At 5:50 a.m., the battle began with the foremost wave of attacking doughboys, moving forward under a creeping barrage. However, that barrage didn't provide the protection that it should have because it was dropped so far ahead—1,200 yards—of the advancing troops. This was done to avoid hitting the units of the 106th Regiment that were cut off by the enemy but still somewhere out in front of the 107th.[59]

While the 30th Division reached its objective on schedule, the advancing doughboys of the 27th soon ran into serious trouble. Just as the 106th Regiment had experienced on September 27, German machine gunners and infantry rose from the maze of tunnels that ran from the St. Quentin Canal tunnel to positions well to the rear of the attacking Americans. Despite horrific fighting, elements of the 27th Division reached their objective and held on while the rear elements of the 27th Division and the Australians, who were to "leapfrog" the Americans and continue the assault, moved forward.[60] The Australians and some of the units of the 27th Division continued over the next two days to clear out the Germans and push them back. After the Australians passed through the Second American Corps, the latter was withdrawn from the line to refit and reorganize.[61]

Yockelson tells us that "in two days of hard fighting, the [27th] division lost 26 officers and 648 men." On September 29, the 27th Division's 107th Infantry, in which Cpl. Truesdell served, "had the greatest number of losses, with 349 officers and men killed. It was the highest number of casualties for an American unit on a single day in the entire war."[62] When the regiment was relieved on October 1 and marched first to an area near Saulcourt and then on to Doingt, the entire Headquarters Company plus other details remained behind to gather and salvage both enemy and American weaponry and also to collect and bury the dead.[63]

Following the four Allied offensives in late September, Germany requested an armistice on October 4, adroitly made to President Wilson, based on his Fourteen Points. The points essentially called for transparency in relations between nations, self-determination by colonial peoples, open seas, free trade, the formation of a league of nations, the relinquishing by Germany of territory it had taken during the war, and the return of Alsace-Lorraine to France.[64] Wilson's response was a request for clarification.[65]

In a letter written to his parents on October 4 directly after his regiment had been withdrawn from the front lines, Cpl. Truesdell writes poignantly of the many casualties in his unit: "I thank God I came out whole for one of our signal corporals was killed, another died of wounds, another was wounded, another is missing, and a couple of our privates are missing." While he understandably feels relief that he has been spared from injury, one senses his shock, sadness, and sorrow for those who had not fared so well.

Lightly wounded men had to make their way back to regimental aid posts located behind the reserve trenches. More seriously wounded men had to wait for stretcher-bearers to come for them. Well behind the regimental aid posts were casualty clearing stations, farther to the rear were field hospitals, and even farther away were base hospitals.[66] Men who had been killed were removed from the battlefield and buried by regimental units. As evidenced by the long lists, in cemeteries in France and Flanders, of soldiers "missing in action," many of the fallen were never found.

Letter #5 written abroad and sent from the continent
Letter received Wednesday, July 31st 1918

Sunday P.M., June 30th 1918

Dear Folks,

Well, I am going to take a long jump and sit on the front porch with you for awhile this afternoon. It is just twenty minutes of three now, and I can imagine that you are all spending part of a hot day on the porch. It is beautiful here today. I am sitting underneath a big tree with the birds singing and a nice cool breeze blowing. The sky is clear except for a few fleecy clouds. As Ede said, when things are so beautiful it is hard to believe that there is any war. I can just shut my eyes and presto—I am sitting under one of the elm trees in front of the porch. It's wonderful to have such an imagination, isn't it?

My last letter to you was dated June 24th. We are still in the same small town that we were when I last wrote, and it is very pleasant to rest up and get over all our hiking we did last week. Since I wrote you last, I have been detailed in the Adjutant's office helping on the pay-rolls. We were paid yesterday A.M. The work is very interesting in the Adj's office, but I expect now that the rush on the pay-roll is over, I will

come back into the company again. Yesterday was a big day for we
were paid (for the month of May, about a month late) and we also rec'd
mail from the States for the second time. I have had plenty of money
all the time so far, needn't worry about that. You can't buy much here
[even] if you have plenty of money, for it isn't here to buy at any price.
Eggs cost about the equivalent of $1.00 a doz in our money. I buy
myself a good meal occasionally, and some sweet chocolate and sweet-
ened crackers at a Y.M.C.A. tent where they have them. Of course I
keep supplied with "smokes." I was talking with a "Tommy" this A.M.
and he was saying it's about the same with all of us. When we were in
civilian life, a pleasant period of entertainment consisted of going to
the theater, taking an auto ride, or visiting with friends, but now when
we march into a town for the night, we consider we have had a perfect
time, where we get some good "eats." You can get potatoes, beef or
pork, eggs, a small amount of bread, butter, a small can of jam (usually bought at a grocery store), coffee, no desserts of any kind and not
much sugar in your coffee. Jam and sweet chocolate are about the only
sweet things one can get. Of course, it has to be a fair-sized town to get
such a feed. Ordinarily, I have a small glass or two of vin blanc with a
meal instead of water. It is so weak that I could drink quarts of it, and
it would not have any effect. However, I don't (drink quarts of it) and
I don't like it well enough to drink it alone, only with a meal instead of
water, for drinking water is scarce. By the way, let me know whether
you are receiving all my letters. You can tell as I number each one.
Also don't worry any more about my arm, as it is all but well, and there
will be but a very small scar.

Monday P.M. [July 1, 1918]

Baths are very scarce, on account of the lack of water. I had a
sponge bath a week ago today and am going to try to get another
tonight, but one has to accustom himself to being quite satisfied
with a bath once a month and with being happily surprised if he gets
more. Capt. Heylman, our Regimental Personnel Officer, told me
to continue to report here in the office. I have been working under

him in the Personnel office which is part of the Adjts. Office, and it looks as though I might be transferred from the Signal Platoon to the Headquarters Platoon. Don't know for sure as yet — hope so anyway. The work is good in here, altho not quite as interesting as the Supply office. Tod is orderly for Capt. Heylman, and is figuring that if I can get in here, he will try, so we will both be together. This is all hot air, so far. Would like to do it. Sat. P.M. an English "Tommy" gave me a good-sized piece of bacon, and with a can of orange marmalade (from canteen) and 3 eggs each (bought from a farmer), a loaf of bread (bought by one of the fellows), and oranges (from British canteen), four of us had a real meal Sunday A.M.

I stopped writing yesterday P.M. to go over to regimental divine service, conducted by the chaplain. It was a short service, several hymns and an address. I understand you can send newspapers over here. Please find out as I would like to get the Republican and the N.Y. Times if you can send them.

Friday, July 5th

Well, I am ashamed to have taken so long to get a letter off to you. You can see that I started this letter last Sunday. Well, I went to sleep while I was writing, and so didn't finish Sunday. Monday I was again busy in the Adj's office; also got a hot sponge bath in during the evening. (Bath, luxury, no longer a necessity.) Tuesday we got ready to move, and Wednesday A.M. we walked about a mile, took to our Pullman trains, rode about eight hours till about 6 P.M. and then started hiking. We stopped about 11 o'clock in a small town, and slept in fairly clean billets.

Saturday P.M., July 6th

More apologies — we have moved again. We hiked about two hours from where we were Wednesday night. We spent Thursday there and yesterday A.M. came on to this larger town. We are now probably 10 miles from the front lines. Not much doing up there now I guess. In the last town, along came an American Y.M.C.A. truck, and believe me, everybody was mighty glad to see it. We were able to buy Little Bobbie cigars, Sweet Caps, Prince Albert, Lowney's sweet chocolate, etc, and it certainly seemed good to get <u>American</u> goods. They expect to travel right along with us from now on. Hope they do. Well, before I go any further, I must tell you about the mail I mentioned in the first part of my letter. They are as follows:

Mother's	postmarked	June 1st
Ede's	"	" 4th
Mother's	"	" 6th
Father's	"	" 6th and duplicate—good idea!
Ed's	"	May 31st
Ed's	"	June 6th
Joe Valentine's	"	" 2nd

I was much interested to know about so many more B. fellows going to Camp W. and particularly about Ed Parsons. I can't tell you how much I appreciate the newspaper clippings and all the similar bits of news, Mother, for I don't get much or very often. You seem to think that only a few of your letters will reach me. I expect they all will, but possibly with some delay. I am interested to hear about Marks B. Sorry about Reed K. However, if he gets over it O.K. he may get to Blighty for a while anyway. Remember me to Helen, also to Dorothy and Sally B. Very nice about Ibbie Farnsworth's new daughter. Ede's letter was very newsy too. Ede, you should see the fine Red Cross trains (U.S.) that run through here and the numerous Red Cross ambulances—saw some Red Cross nurses this A.M. Bill Phelps is certainly a good sport to get into the Red Cross game. How is the Ford working?

And now Father's letter and duplicate, the latter a good idea. You folks must quit worrying about my arm, for it is just about healed up, and from the small scar that will be left, you would never imagine that I had so much trouble with it. The weather is beautiful here, as is the country. I have been able to view considerable landscape as we have hiked about 20,000 miles, more or less, mostly less, but it seems that much. Should like to be remembered to Bob Brooks and Geo. Harris.

We certainly had a good business for May. Hope you get some pleasure and comfort with your new jitney. I've got to insist that you don't overdo, and that you keep in good shape, for when I come home, you've got to dance the one-step with me. Thursday was 4th of July — I didn't realize it till about a day or two before. I worked in the Personnel office, the same as any other day. The rest of the company drilled in the A.M. and had some sports in the P.M. I read in the Daily Mail that the Fourth was celebrated generally throughout all the Allied countries. It now looks as tho I might possibly be detailed permanently in the Personnel office and possibly Tod too. I am getting along well in there and I think the Captain may see the Major about it. Last night I worked on the telephone switch-board as operator. You see we hiked in the A.M. and the Personnel office stuff wasn't unpacked till night, so there wasn't anything doing there. They were short of men, so I went in as operator for the switch-board. Today I have off, so I'm getting this letter finished and doing some errands. Our switch-board is located in a small chapel (vacant), a rather peculiar place, eh? I slept next to the altar, during my off hours. Before we were in it, it was used as an operating-room. The chapel is connected with a very good sized hospital (vacant) in which we are now billeted — a hunky-dory place, clean, light and dry but hard sleeping on the floor. But I'm used to sleeping anywhere now.

Now, about Ed's two letters, both most interesting. He tells about the gas scare at the plant etc. Also about making out the pay-rolls. Well, I can understand about the pay-rolls, for we are working on the whole regiment's in the Personnel office. It's mighty fine, he has his Sgt's stripes now. Will you please send this letter on to Ed, for it will be a terrific job to write another such letter, and this gives all the dope. I'll enclose an envelope addressed to him. Words for Eddie: I appreciate your letters very much. Please don't think I do not, but we are moving around so much, it is very hard to write. This letter is as much for you as the folks at home, and they will send it on to you. Keep on writing to me, and pretty soon you'll find a letter from me. Had a good letter from Joe Valentine. Tell him I'm having a devil of a time trying to write home. But I think of all of the boys at the store and our Saturday

A.M. meetings. Give him some news from this letter and tell him to write again. By the way, I bought a few Little Bobbie cigars from the American Y.M. day before yesterday. One of them got broken in my pocket, and I tried to think of the ones who occasionally chewed a piece of a cigar. I couldn't remember for a minute, but then there arose in the mind the old familiar picture of the boys around the table in the Salesmen's office on Saturday A.M. and Laurie would say to Dewitt: "Dewitt, have you got a piece of a cigar that I can have a chew of?" You might read this to the boys.

Tod and I and a nice chap in the band named Judd from N.Y. City go out occasionally for a good meal. Judd was drafted. He is in the automobile tire business I believe, and is comfortably well off. He is a gentleman and we three have some very pleasant times. We are planning to go out tonight. We have arranged with a woman in a café to French-fry us some potatoes, and give us bread and butter. She will buy some pork at the butcher's and she will cook it for us. Also we may have some salad and a small jar of jam. We'll have a regular feast if nothing turns up to prevent it. Tod is well and is in good spirits. So am I. It's great stuff, touring France on foot. Must close and will try to write sooner next time. Regards to all my friends and love to all of you and the folks on Stuyvesant and Front Sts.

Bob

**Letter #6 written abroad and sent from the continent
Letter received August 3rd 1918**

July 14, Sunday P.M.

Dear Folks,

Well, we are settled here for a few days—maybe for a month or six weeks. We are in the same place we were when I wrote that long drawn out and much delayed letter of a week ago, July 7, Sunday, Letter #5. We are sleeping in our pup tents and on account of the slight chance of an occasional bomb or long-range shell, I am lying here writing to you under my pup tent and in a hole about two feet below the level of the ground. It is raining out but I am quite comfortable—I have a little hay on the ground to make it a bit softer. We are about 12 miles behind the lines and as I lie here, I can hear the distant roar of the big guns together with the patter of the rain on the tent and the mooing of the cows—they occupy the same field we do. The guns don't do much work during the day but as night comes, they begin (it is now 7:45). During the night it isn't unusual to wake up and hear Fritzy's aeroplanes over our heads and then the anti-aircraft guns popping away at him and then our own planes shooting at him with machine guns.

I am thru working in the Personnel office for the present and am back in the Signal Platoon. I told you, I believe, that Lt. Wilson did not wish to transfer me to the Supply Co. so that ended that. As for the Personnel office, I spoke to Capt Hyleman, but he has all the men he is entitled to there now and before he can have any more in there permanently, I believe he has to consult the Colonel. He said he would give me a chance if he could arrange it. Meanwhile as I said, I am working again in the Signal Platoon, the work of which is becoming more interesting. This AM I was out "shooting trouble"—the connection between our control and the 3ʳᵈ Battalion was out and I and another chap went out to locate the trouble. We found that the wire was broken. Then I have been on the switchboard a couple of times, taking care of the different calls that come in—the same as the central at home does.

You folks are mistaken about not being able to send me newspapers for Tod has received a bunch of Presses from his girl and I have about a dozen right here which I am going over <u>very</u> <u>carefully</u>. They are mostly issues of from May 1 to May 15 and altho old, they are most acceptable. From one of them I have cut a letter to the editor and which I enclose—it both aggravates and amuses me. Here is someone quibbling over to whom belongs the "honor?" of being the first draft contingent sent from B. Good Lord, there was the National Guard which left Aug. 18 and which has received the least attention of anybody—no banqueting, no big mass-meeting to "honor" them.

A great many of them, like myself, volunteered, knowing that in a short time, the N.G. would be taken over into Federal service for duty abroad. And now somebody is arguing about to whom the honor belongs for being the first who were compelled to enter the service and leave B. Well, as Shakespeare said, "Such is life in a big city." While speaking upon and pondering about the subject of "enclosures," I will make a few remarks in connection with the other "enclosure I enclose." This one amuses "much." "Cootie" Wright (nickname does <u>not</u> imply he has

Drafted Boys in the First Broome County Contingent

To the Editor The Binghamton Press:

Will you kindly inform me through your valuable paper, why the boys who left Binghamton Sept. 27 are always spoken of as being the first contingent to leave Broome county in answer to the draft call? Where are the 27 lads who left here Sept. 6? Are they to be ignored entirely? Many, if not all of them, have been in France for nearly three months to do their bit.

There were 9 from the county and 18 from the first and second districts. Let us play fair and give honor to whom honor is due.

From one who likes to see fair play.   L. O. T.

Technically, the boys who left Sept. 6 and those who left Sept. 27 belonged to the same, the first, contingent. The detail which left Sept. 6 was sent in advance to prepare the camp for those who came later. Theirs was the honor, however, to be the first selected men to go from Broome county, and your point is well taken.—Editor The Press.

"cooties") who hails from Walton and is a good scout is my tent-mate. He received recently via U.S. mail a copy of "The Christian Statesman," which may be and undoubtedly is a paper full of much virtue. However, I believe that they are a bit far-fetched in their editorial which I tore out and send to you. In fact it amused me immensely, not withstanding the fact that I am trying to lead a decent clean life. Honestly, these goody-goody fellows make me sick. If they could only understand what a comfort a good smoke is after working hard or being out in the rain or probably while in the trenches altho I haven't experienced that yet. Smoking doesn't seem to have hurt me yet nor broken down my morals. I enjoy reading the Bible and keep myself clean and pure—inside all the time and outside when I can get the water—I have the soap. I will say right here that I prefer champagne to cider, white or red wine. The latter statement, please understand, does not mean I am a habitual drunkard.

My next paragraph will deal with Ede. I wish to congratulate you, Ede, upon your birthday. I wish I could be doing it and tickling you under the chin, all at the same time. However, it "cannot was"—maybe next time.

Right next to us is a camp of Canadians, many of whom are from the States. They have a good shower-bath and a week ago just after we got here, they invited us to have a bath. Most of us accepted. Since that time, however, our C.O. has thought it best not to "sponge on them" too much so we are not permitted to enjoy the baths.

We have an American Y.M. canteen nearby where we can get Tuxedo, Prince Albert etc.—sweet chocolate, too. So we are able to get smokes all right. Occasionally Tod, Bill Jude and I scam around and dig up some eggs and chips (French fried potatoes). Eats get more scarce as one gets further "up the line." "Up the line" means toward the trenches and "down the line" means away from the trenches.

We were issued our new overseas caps today and we all present quite a "tony" appearance now.

Tod is out today with the band. They have been busy most every minute playing for church and giving concerts for the different battalions which are nearby.

I bought a pound box of very ordinary chocolates today at a British canteen and paid 5 francs 50 centimes—just about a dollar—but believe me they were a treat—for they are the first I've seen since arriving.

My writing desk consists of a cigar box which contains six hen's eggs—bought at the same British canteen—they set me back just ½ franc each. $1.08 per dozen is rather expensive but they do taste good now and then. If you ever mention corn-willy or hardtack to me upon my return, I shall commit some desperate deed—I can't say just what it will be at present.

Since I wrote last, I have received two batches of mail. Just after mailing my letter a week ago, I received eight letters. All of them were older than the batch which preceded this one, that is—they were post-marked May 9th to May 29th. I had already had some dated around June 1st. However they were very welcome. They were as follows,

Mother—May 9—to Newport News
Bill Hones—May 19—to Spartanburg
Mother—May 27—A.E.F.
Ed—May 27—A.E.F.
Ede—May 27—A.E.F.
Orra & F. Summers—May 27—A.E.F.
Father—May 27—A.E.F.
  " —May 28—Dup.
  " —May 29—Trip.

Tuesday Evening, July 16

Mother's letter written May 9 of course was considerably delayed. I am glad you called up Mrs. Birdsall. Bill Hones' letter was brief. Says he is very busy and not much more. In Mother's letter of May 27, she speaks about the possibility of my not receiving all letters—there is some delay of course, but I get most of them eventually. Right before me I have about 20 letters, received in three different batches of mail. You must have had quite a big Red Cross parade. I'm glad you only had to walk to State Park, Mother, and not about twenty miles with a fifty pound pack on your back. I presume you were just about as tired as I was when we marched that twenty miles—for you hadn't done much hiking.

(I can count twelve or thirteen planes in the air just at present and about eight or nine observation balloons. The guns are booming too.) It is 7:45 PM and I am sitting on a pile of sod and earth which I piled up around my tent—am wearing my "tin-derby"—it is an order but it hardly seems necessary as we are a considerable distance away from the excitement. Ed's letter of May 27 contained much of interest about the big plant. So Hocky is now a corporal. He'll have to cut out some of those visits to Baltimore, now, eh? It's great about your getting your three stripes, Ed. Hope you can get a furlough home, Ed. I know you would enjoy it immensely and so would the folks—and Amy too—eh, Ed? Very nice about Marg. Stoker, Ede. Don't try to climb any telegraph poles, Ede, with the " ? ." Had a very nice letter from Orrie and

Frances—all about what they are doing in the country. Father's letter
of May 27 and the dup. and trip. of the 28 and 29 all came together.
When I first saw them, I said, "Whee, look at all the letters from Father"
but I am "wise" now and when I see two or three letters of consecu-
tive dates, I don't get excited. In regard to where I am, I will give you
the very exact information that I am living at present in France, not
in Italy or the Phillipines. Undoubtedly you have read in the papers,
in fact I read in one of the Presses I have here, where the American
troops were mostly placed—those that were not in the American
sector—and I have told you that we were not in that sector. This
last batch of letters I have been talking about, I received a week ago
Sunday (July 7).

The next batch received about Wed. or Thurs. last week are as
follows,

> Mother—postmarked June 10
> Father—   "   from N.Y.
> Miss Hoag of Yonkers—postmarked June 11
> Father—postmarked June 13
>   "   "   14 (dup. of 13th)
> Ruth Jenkins—   "   17

It is very interesting to know about all the boys getting over here,
Mother. Hope I run in to some of them. I was very sorry to hear
about the Griffiths' little baby. Glad Helen Kellam and Reed Jr. are
progressing so nicely. It would be fine if Reed was on his way home.
Hope his accident wasn't very serious. In regard to the flag Bartlett
Relief Corps presented to me, will you please express my thanks to
them? I believe it's best for you to keep it at home as I have no place
to keep it here. Now, in regard to sending anything to me—it is permissible to send letters, newspapers and magazines to me. In order
to send any other articles, I must first write you, asking you to send
them to me and I must have my request endorsed by my commanding
officer. In sending me these articles, you must display my letter and

endorsement to the postal authorities and also note on the outside
of the package that the conditions for sending have been complied
with. There is really not much that I want. Here is a way you send me
things—Wanamakers and several other N.Y. stores have branches in
Paris—simply order the articles at the N.Y. stores and they will cable
to their Paris branch to mail me the articles from there. This takes no
red tape—you do not have to have any written order. Bill Jude, Tod's
and my friend in the band, is acquainted with the Gen. Agt. of the
American Express Co in Paris and thru him I have sent my watch to
be cleaned and have a crystal put in. It is impossible to have this done
around here in any of the towns altho there are several fair-sized ones
nearby as most of the inhabitants have moved out on account of Fritz's
bombs. The note from Miss Hoag was very nice and I thought it quite
thoughtful of her to write. Father's letter of June 13th was very interesting (as was the duplicate of June 14th) ha, ha. I am glad Charlie Morris
is getting along well. Would like to see him. Fine of you to have him
in to dinner. I supposed Mary did the typing on your letter. Tell [her]
she does excellently—but she had ought to look up in the dictionary
and see how "sargeant" is spelled. That's one on you, Mary. Tell all
the people who signed their names to your letter that their signatures
looked "immense" but not quite as good as they themselves would.
"Sam" Jenkins' letter informs me that "Vint" has joined the Navy after
being turned down several times. She also gave some bits of gossip
about B. young people. She spoke about "Pop" Hotchkiss's being taken
with appendicitis. Hope it is not serious. I certainly must be a "winner"
with the girls when I have married ones and engaged ones writing to
me, eh? I'm some kid, eh? (In a pig's wrist.)

We have had quite a bit of rain the last few days but it has cleared
up again this PM. Yesterday some more mail came in and I received
three epistles as follows,

Mother—postmarked June 16
Ede—   "   17
Walt Hankins— "   20 (announcement of his marriage)

If Walt is as enthusiastic about his girl as he is about his work, he [will] sure have a "wonderful wife." I am glad you finally received my other transport letter. I didn't think we had such a terrible storm coming over—maybe the chap Miss Hoag spoke of, thought so. I hope Father will get some pleasure of the Ford now and ride around a bit—also it is nice to take out Grandma T. and Aunt Sarah.

Hal Murray's engagement is somewhat of a surprise—also his commission as the last I heard he was a sergeant. The picture Mother sent in her letter does remind me of Marsh and yet it isn't exactly like him. Ede's account of the organizing of the canteen is quite amusing. Dave's escapade with his "nursey" is Dave all over. It will probably die out after a while.

I was on the telephone switch board again last night and so had all day off today. Some of the boys are out in the field now playing ball. It is beginning to get twilight. We had a test this PM and had to keep our gas masks on for four hours—however I didn't have to as I was off duty—being on the phone last night.

I am finishing this as you probably noticed on Tuesday evening, July 16. Most of my letters seem to be continued stories, don't they? Do you happen to recall that it is just a year ago yesterday that the Nat. Guard was called into active service. It was on Sunday that we put on our uniforms and from then till we left B. we had to report for drill. We ate at the Y.M.C.A. noons, remember?

Well, here's quite a book. Love to all from

Bob

P.S. Ed, be sure and send this on to the folks. I thought it was about time to send a letter to you. It's pretty hard work to write two "books" like this so I send one for you and the folks together. This one goes to you first. Regards old kid—

Your bro
Bob

Letter #7 written abroad and sent from the continent
Letter postmarked U.S. Army Field Post Office, Aug. 4, 2 PM
Passed by Censor No. 5105
Received August 24th 1918

July 28, 1918, Sunday P.M.

Dear Folks,

I have received mail from you two or three times since I have written last—and my last written to Ed was mailed July 16th—I told Ed to send it on to you. It hardly seems possible that it has been 12 days since I wrote you but again I have moved.

Well, the mail I have before me is as follows:

Mother—June 16
Ede—   "   17
Father—   "   22
Mother—   "   23
Mother—July 1
Ed—   "   1

Mother's June 16 letter—I am glad you finally received my best letter off the transport. I received a note from Miss Hoag and that it was very kind of her to remember me. I'm glad Father can get up to the Forks now with the "jit." as I know he enjoys it. I'd like to be home going with you, Father. Am quite interested to know about Hal Murray's engagement, marriage and commission in the army.

Ede's letter of June 17. Glad to hear all about your canteen. How's music going nowadays, Ede? On my way after a pail of water this PM, I stopped in to listen to a "Tommy" singing. He had a real nice baritone voice and sung nicely. He belongs to a Divisional show which goes around to various hospitals and ambulance companies. I staid an hour and I enjoyed it more than anything I have experienced for some time. A bit of good music is fine.

Father's letter of June 22 was a dup. or triplicate of his June 20 letter and I expect to receive the other two soon. It was very newsy and interesting. Sorry that Frank Marble has left as it throws quite a lot more work on Ad. Who [is] putting in to help him? Is Edna Grover going to stay in B. with you or will she go with Ray? Edg. Hotchkiss does get home pretty often, doesn't he, but Ed's letter I got last night, shows that "sticking to business" pays and I sure am proud that he is a battalion sgt-major, now. There is no reason why he shouldn't do better yet with the help of Major Vaughn. That certainly is fortunate to have a C.O. who knows you and your folks. Hope Ed <u>can</u> get home for a few days for all concerned would enjoy it, eh?

In Mother's letter of July 1, she announces the arrival of my first letter from France. Glad you finally got it. You can see how long it takes for a letter to reach you — about a month. And also about the same for yours to reach me — I received Mother's letter of June 30 last night (July 27). Lieut. Darling who is in the 2nd Batt. (Co H) is at present some five or six miles from here. Haven't seen him for quite a long time. "For the love of Mike," send me some Republicans, do up a bundle of them and send them. The government permits newspapers to be sent, for Tod has received quite a lot of Presses from his girl. Give my best to "Neudge" and tell her to be a "good girl," also my best to the rest at 46 Front. I am going to try to write to "Neudge" soon but I find it pretty hard to write just you.

Ed's letter of June 30 was mighty interesting for he wrote that he is now Batt Sgt Major. It's certainly fine. Please send this on to Ed. Depending on you to do this, I'll address a few remarks to Ed. First off, my congratulations on your promotion — good stuff — I expect you'll soon be reg'tal sgt-major. Major Vaughn ought to help you — and then a commission — I have it all laid out for you. See if you can stir up Tod Corbett. If you write him, you tell him, it's a pity he can't write his old-time pal — answer his letters, since he has time to write other newer friends, as Maj. Vaughn. Put it up strong — I'm tired of trying to get him to answer my letters, in fact I have given [up] some time ago. Hocky certainly fell in soft, in driving down Maj. Vaughn's car, didn't he?

Sunday Evening [July 28, 1918]

Well, I stopped to get mess and after that, sewed a button on my shirt.
Tonight and the past day or two, I have itched to a certain degree.
So — I also hunted a bit before finishing my letter to you. The result
of the contest (we compete with each other — quantity counts 50% and
size 50%) was that I found about 6 to 10 cooties [lice]. I've felt them
playing tag on me as I said. I'm now more of a soldier — having had
them play leap frog on me. I expect I'll have some on me occasionally
till I retire from the army over here — it's impossible to keep them
off me — it gets worse, the farther up the line one goes. I also got the
original of Father's June 20th letter, tonight.

As I said in the first part of my letter, I have moved — and
twice — since I wrote last. The Signal Platoon left the old camp last
Monday and went up the line about 5 or 6 miles — we went in such
a hurry that I didn't have time to hardly see Tod. We pitched pup-
tents and dug in, two feet and then as usual got orders to move again.
Meanwhile the rest of the company had moved up about 3½ or 4 miles
to where we all are now, and our orders were to come back here and
join the rest of the company so we are altogether again. — Jerry is
overhead and I have just been out to see our anti-aircraft gun shells
burst around him. We were up above the other morning, doing
"physical-torture" when Jerry [Germans] started sending "iron-rations"
(shells) over about 200 yds away so we were dismissed. I was lucky on
these last two hikes as I was on the loading detail and rode each time.
When we came back here again, I struck it lucky. Eight of us have a
dandy billet — a shack made of corrugated iron. Whoever was here
before us had built a stove, also a good table. I built myself a cot and
sleep O.K. We cook quite a little stuff for ourselves and have a regular
private room. Four of us, including myself, are telephone operators on
the regimental exchange — we work six hours and rest 18 hours, — not
bad, eh? It is very interesting and there is lots to learn. I have been on
from midnight to 6 AM for two days and am now on from six AM to
noon every day. I have my PMs off and all night to sleep. Night work
is not quite so good but not at all bad. The other four work on the

lines, making repairs when there are breaks. So at present I am living high — have a good job and good eats. Today for dinner I had fried potatoes, rice croquets and jam, fried eggs, bread and coffee — not bad eh? Hope we stay here for some time.

Be sure and send me some papers. I am feeling OK and so is Tod. He sends his regards. He is busy playing these days as the band is giving numerous concerts around the country. This AM the chaplain held a service just outside the telephone office. I couldn't go out but I hummed over the hymns as the band played them and I wished I could be with you in church.

Well, it is time for taps and I must close. With love from

Bob

Letter #8 written abroad and sent from the continent
Letter postmarked U.S. Army Field Post Office, Aug. 7, 1918
Envelope marked "Opened by Censor 3341"
Received Sept. 4th 1918

Monday A.M., August 5, 1918

Dear Folks,

It hardly seems possible that a week and a day have passed since I wrote to you last.

Three or four days ago we left the place from which I last wrote you and after a hike and a railroad trip and then some more hiking we arrived close to where I am now. We are (the whole regiment) some distance back of the lines shooting at a rifle range. It seems a relief not to have to wear our gas-masks over our shoulder and to hear no big guns booming. Our camp is about three or four miles from the range and right now I am sitting on the ground at the 500 yd line waiting to shoot. We hiked over from our camp this AM, brought our dinner with us and will hike back tonight. We are sleeping in our pup-tents at this camp and I am quite comfortable. I and another chap in the Signal Platoon have charge of the telephone exchange and spell each other off — except for today when we came to the range. We expect to be here for seven or eight days, I believe. I don't know where we go from here.

As I wrote you, our last camp was a fine one as I had a good comfortable billet to sleep in and a cot and an interesting job on the telephone switchboard. I hated to leave it.

Tod is well and feeling fine and "me too." The country is beautiful and the weather nice except a bit too much rain at present. Yesterday morning I attended the regimental church service and also a communion service afterwards. It was the first communion service I have attended since I have been in France, and sometime before. It seemed good to be able to attend one again. The table was an old box and the floor, the green sod, — the roof, a cloudy sky, but I closed my eyes and I was with you all at home. From what I have read and heard, it looks like the French and Americans are doing great work down around Rheims — that they have driven Jerry back considerable distance and taken many prisoners. Things look very favorable.

Haven't had any mail from you since I wrote last altho some of the boys have received letters. I enclose a field postcard to show you what they look like. I may send one now and then if I am too busy to write.

Send me some newspapers. It is permissible to send them. I will finish later. It is raining now.

There really isn't much more to write. I may add something more before I mail this. With love to you all.

Oh, yesterday, you will recall, was the fourth anniversary of the beginning of the war. The talk the chaplain gave us was on this subject.

Tuesday P.M. [Aug. 6, 1918]

Well, now I have some more to tell you.

We finished up at the range yesterday PM — in the rain — and hiked back — in the rain. When we got back, we were pretty wet but no harm came from it and our reward was a good supper and best of all — some mail from home. I received ten letters as follows –

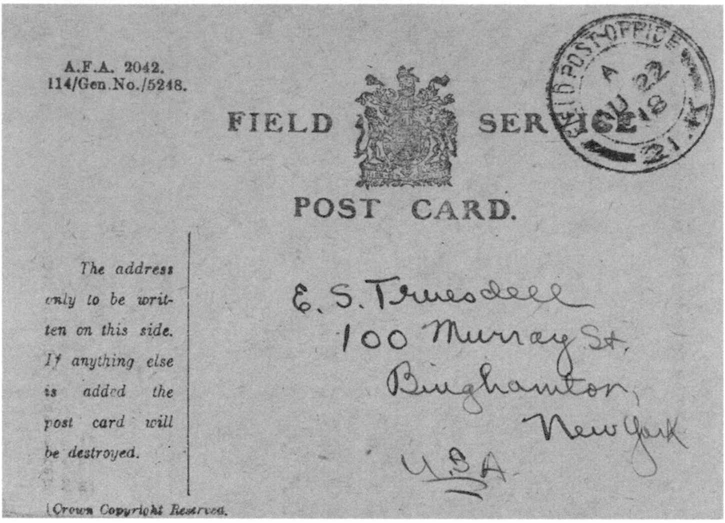

A.F.A. 2042.
114/Gen.No./5248.

FIELD SERVICE

POST CARD.

The address only to be written on this side. If anything else is added the post card will be destroyed.

E. S. Truesdell
100 Murray St.
Binghamton,
New York
U.S.A.

Crown Copyright Reserved.

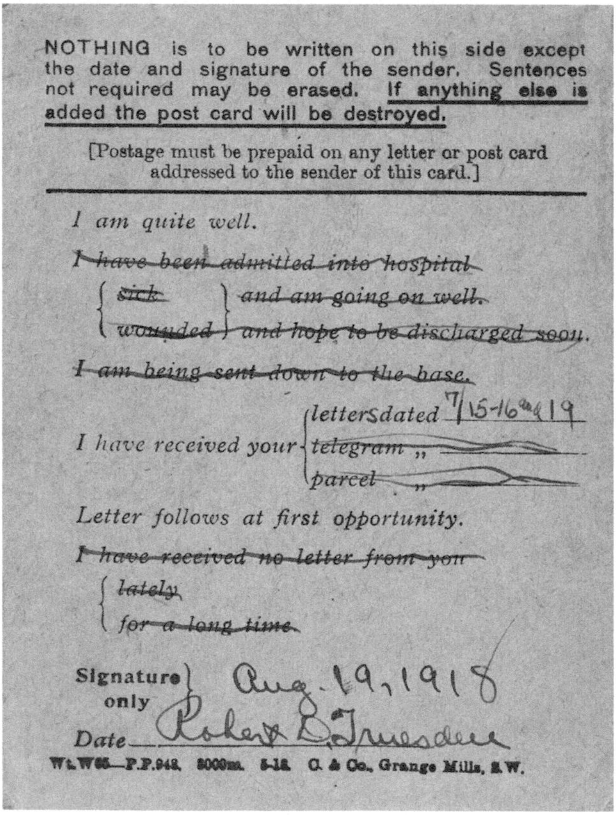

NOTHING is to be written on this side except the date and signature of the sender. Sentences not required may be erased. **If anything else is added the post card will be destroyed.**

[Postage must be prepaid on any letter or post card addressed to the sender of this card.]

I am quite well.

~~*I have been admitted into hospital*~~

~~*sick*~~ ~~*and am going on well.*~~

~~*wounded*~~ ~~*and hope to be discharged soon.*~~

~~*I am being sent down to the base.*~~

I have received your *letters dated* 7/15-16 and 19
~~*telegram*~~ ,,
~~*parcel*~~ ,,

Letter follows at first opportunity.

~~*I have received no letter from you*~~

~~*lately*~~

~~*for a long time.*~~

Signature only Aug. 19, 1918

Date Robert D. Truesdell

Wt.W65—P.P.948. 8000m. 5-18. C. & Co., Grange Mills, S.W.

```
Father—   July 2
Father—    "  3 (dup)
Edith—     "  4
Father—    "  5 (NY)
Edith—     "  7
Pete Jenkins—July 6 (forwarded by Mother)
Mother—July 8
Walt Hankins—July 8
Ed—             "  11
Mother—         "  14
```

I hear that there is some more mail yet. That's the way it comes—in batches. In regard to where I am or was, I'll take a chance and say that my first letter (the one you have received) was written from Rue. I'm some distance from there now. Our last camp was in Belgium. Yes, we were up pretty well towards the front—about 4 or 5 miles and in range of Jerry's big guns. Give my very kindest regards to Mrs. Corbett when you drive up to Conklin again and tell her I shall look forward to having a meal with her. Glad to hear about Roy and the N.Y.G. Mother tells me that Henry Hopkins had an attack of appendicitis and was operated on. Write me how he is, please. Now dad, keep well and don't let the future price of canned beets or the affect of the war on the quality of New and True coffee worry you too much, for you and I have many chats and confabs coming—with Mother, Ede and Ed on the sidelines, to see who wins. In regard to the cherries, you and Mother went up and got from Miss St. Clair—I beg Mother to set one jar aside for the royal banquet when I <u>return</u>—um—yum!!

Important—I think you must have been misinformed about not being able to send over newspapers, for Tod has received several bundles of Presses and other fellows have received N.Y. Times—all of which I got hold of and read. Call up Tod's folks or his girl, Miss Parker, and ask them about it. I should very much like to get some Republicans and the Sunday edition of the N.Y. Times and maybe the daily edition if possible.

In regard to "cooties"—the report is short—"I have them" and expect to keep them for the duration of the war for it is impossible to get rid of them with the facilities for keeping clean we have over here. You would understand why I have them and the other fellows too, if you could see some of the places I have slept in. Don't be shocked or too overcome with worry when I tell you I am sitting in a "re-modeled" pig-pen at present. For all this, I am fairly clean and by hunting, I can keep fairly clean of "cooties." You ought to see me—just like a monkey—take off my shirt and undershirt and look them over. This kind of talk is not very elevating but such things are a common occurrence with all of us. To relieve your mind, I'll say that this pig-pen is clean with cement floor and brick walls—built on one side of a barn and we have our telephone exchange in it. Two of us, who have charge of it, built a cot and swept it out and every other night, we sleep in it—taking turns—as some one must be at the exchange all the time. The pig-pen has just been built and has never had any other occupants besides us. But this is the kind of quarters we are in most all the time—barns, shacks etc and with all kinds of men in them before (for four years) you cannot help getting the "cooties." I have my clothes washed by farmer-women and so far have been able to have them done every week or so. When we get way up the line—of course—I'll have to do it myself and it may not be done at all if the shells are too thick. As to baths, I have taken the words, "bath-tub" "hot tub bath" and like words out of my dictionary and dismissed them from my mind. They are a thing of the past and of the future but not of the present. My bath, which I try hard to be a weekly affair, consists of a pail or less of "aqua" not always absolutely "pura"—which liquid is either begged, borrowed or stolen—for water is not plentiful—nearly always cold and a quiet spot in a corner of a field. There I disrobe and take a cold sponge bath, not awfully cleansing, but the best I can do. I had one this AM and feel the better for it. So much for the subject of "cooties" and baths.

Wednesday A.M. 7:30 [Aug. 7, 1918]

Well, here's another day and still I'm writing my letter. I wrote yesterday PM while I was on duty and supper-time came before I finished. I was relieved at supper-time for the evening. Our division theatre gave a variety vaudeville show last night at the aerodrome which is about 200 yds away and I went. It really was fine for we have some good talent. Two or three times a week the British fellows at the aerodrome have "movies" and I went the other night. First-class pictures—the first I've seen since I arrived in France. Today I am on duty in the AM—tomorrow in the PM again and so on.

Ede's little description of the Kilmers' tea for Mrs. Whitman was very amusing. Ede, do please take some pictures of the jitney with you all in it and some of the house and of the neighbors—and of Sally and Dorothy etc etc—some of the folks at the store, too if possible and send me. They certainly will look good. Does Father drive the "jitney" any? Send me a picture of him at the wheel. Now, you had better stay at home, Ede, and do your Red Cross work as long as you can feel satisfied.—I just stopped to buy a "Daily Express" and read the news. I see the Germans have made a stand. The little French boy who sells the papers sounds just like an American kid when he yells—he speaks English—I could shut my eyes, listen to him yell and believe I was on Dean's corner, waiting for a Leroy Street car.—To go on with my sage advice. Ede, as long as you can do good service and valuable work and stay home, do that. And I think you are doing that, now.

Pete wrote me a fine letter and I was pleasantly surprised for he is not any too good a correspondent. He has made one flight already—about 2400 feet and stayed in the air for half an hour. He says the weather is very hot but dry.

I was sorry that I had to give away my Red Cross knitted goods, Mother, but just stop and think how you would feel with about 60 or 75 lbs. of equipment hung on you, marching anywhere from 10 to 25 miles a day for a week or so and for that matter intermittently all the time. A man just takes his pack off at the end of a day like that and lies down anywhere and goes to sleep. I have thrown my pack off and lay in the dirty road or on a pile of rocks—you don't care where only to get off your feet—and gone to sleep. However, don't think I am in bad physical shape for I never felt better in my life and am fat as a pig. But you can do just so much hiking in one day and if you have too much on your back or it is excessively warm, then it is so much the harder. I know that I shall need some knitted things for the coming winter but I'll have to get them later.

Ed's letter was interesting. Glad you have a little more time to yourself now, Ed. Yes, I had a card from Walt Hankins announcing his marriage. So Hank Lehrbach has also set sail. When you're writing him, give him my regards. I remember him well. He is a good scout. Has Ed Parsons received a non-com's warrant yet or is he still a "bum" private. Keep your gas mask at the alert position my boy and don't let your nose get a sniff of chlorine, for it's deadly stuff. Send over lots of bombs and grenades and we'll see that Jerry gets his "iron rations" O.K. You know the English have to carry iron rations as part of their equipment—it consists of one can of corn-willy, one can sealed air-tight containing tea and sugar in two separate compartments, and some hardtack for use in case of emergency. Well, when we are sending over lots of shells and bombs, we say we are sending over "iron-rations" for Jerry. There is one unique feature of your last letter dated June 10. You mentioned Miss Moore's name. Don't think that I don't like to know the condition of her health and happiness, my boy—and don't "get your wind up" as the English say on account of above kidding. I wish I was fortunate enough to get a N.Y. Times every AM.

So you saw Bill Powell and "Man" Ford at the Red Cross, Mother. When does Bill expect to get "tied up"? And "Man," too? Marion is a fine girl. I will omit any statements regarding what she said about me. I suppose all of the girls are getting home from school and college, now. But, ahem, with none of us men there, it must be very quiet. Glad Tod Corbett came in to see you and hope he does write me. He spoke the truth about being a "bum" correspondent. So Bob Harris and Dave Murray have sailed and by this time are over here—well, I hope to see them some time but you never can tell. Very sorry to hear about Billy Phelps.

I'm a bit ashamed I didn't remember about Grandma Truesdell's birthday being the same day as Ede's but I hope you fixed things up all right. I remembered Ede's, sure thing.

The planes here at the aerodrome are very interesting. There are lots of them and they make frequent flights, of course.

I have plenty of time now and will give you a little idea of what an average French farmhouse looks like. A fairly well-to-do farmer usually has a two-story brick house with gable roof and the barn built on one end of it, altho the one here hasn't. This one in front of me has a large room on each side of the front door and the rooms are two deep. The hall runs right thru to the back of the house. There is an "L" built on the left side where the people live, for our offices take up the rooms in the house proper. I'll take back what I said about the barn being a separate building. Beyond the "L" and built on to it, is the barn and it is at right angles to the "L." It looks thus—

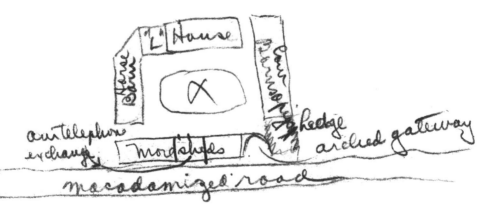

There are several little nice green trees in front of the house—but the worst feature of all is what I have marked X and it is usually found in front of every farmhouse. It is a small artificial pond, sunk in and lined with stone and brick walls into which is thrown the manure from the barns. It is a very stinking place to use punk language, and also most unsanitary, I believe. I don't see how the people can stand it but I suppose they are hardened to it. The women are all hard workers, driving the horses and going into the fields and of course are dressed for it.

Water is scarce here, I believe, war or no war, and the French are used to going some time without a bath. However they look fairly clean, and their houses, especially their kitchens are scrupolously (can't think how to spell it) clean.

Tod and Bill Jude and I have finally got a woman to promise us a fried chicken for dinner today — so we are looking forward to a good dinner this noon as we haven't tasted chicken since we left the States.

Well, I must close. I hear there is still more mail come in. Will tell you about it in my next [letter]. With love to all

                                                        Bob

P.S. Be sure and send this on to Ed.

                                        RDT

P.S.S. Ed, what is your proper address now?

    Batt Sgt Major EST jr
    Ordnance Det. "E" ?
    US Gunpowder Reserv.
    Edgwood Md

Letter #9 written abroad and sent from the continent
Letter postmarked Field Post Office, AU 15 18
Exterior envelope postmarked Field Post Office, AU 28 18
and marked "Passed by Censor No. 6461" Signed "Lt. HS Nielson"
Received Sept. 6th, 1918 (although exterior envelope
shows that it was received Sept. 25th, 1918)

                                    August 11, 1918, Sunday A.M.
Dear Folks,

Back up again where we were before we went "down the line" to the rifle range. I enclose a corporal's warrant. It looks as tho I am a corporal now, doesn't it? A detail of us Signal Platoon men including myself go into the lines tonight—leave this AM shortly to start up. Don't know just where we go, but I presume in the reserve trenches. Some of the fellows have already been up and back. Were getting experience. It's beautiful here this AM—clear, sunny and warm, green grass and trees and fields—the oats partly cut—it's a wonderful AM—one might think he was in the States except for an occasional shell bursting in the distance—and now and then an aeroplane flying overhead. Looking toward the lines, I can see here and there an observation balloon.

The band is playing for regimental church service and I am going over. I am with you in heart and spirit. Will write again in a few days or a week when we expect to come out again. With love from

Bob

P.S. Feel finer than silk and so does Tod. He sends regards.

Letter #10 written abroad and sent from the continent
Letter postmarked Field Post Office, AU 27 18

Sat, August 24, 1918

Dear Folks,

Well, here goes—I will start my letter and try to finish it as soon as I possibly can.

First off, I will mention over what mail I have received from you all. It is as follows –

Father—	July	15
" —	July	16
Ede—	"	17
Father—	"	19
Father—	"	24
Mother—	"	24
Ed—	"	22

I might say right here that all of this was received while I was up in the lines. A week ago Sunday PM our Signal Platoon was split up in details to go with the different battalions of our regiment and I was assigned to the 3rd Battalion. I sent you my corporal's warrant. I was made [corporal] while we were back at the rifle-range. Two or three days afterwards, we moved back to about where we were—from there we went to the 3rd Battalion in a day or so and the following day went up to the front.

Monday P.M. [Aug. 26, 1918]

Will go on with my letter, now. This A.M. we got more mail—as follows,

Ede—	July 29
Father—	" 29
"	" 30
"	" 31
Ed	" 28

Glad to hear that Henry Hopkins is better and the Hotchkiss[es] too. Glad you got my June 25th letter. Send me some snapshots of you all. Send me newspapers. Edith Parker sends them to Tod and Stuart Donley a Bing. boy with me gets them. I have finished looking over about 2 dozen from June 15th to July 25. I forgot to say that I was at 3rd Batt. Hdqrs when I started this letter. We came back to Hdqrs Co. yesterday where I am writing now. It's about a mile from here to 3rd Batt Hdrs. I saw in the papers that Montrose had quite a fire. Also that "Ren" Holcomb had volunteered for YMCA work. Am sorry that Cousin Hattie is sick. I can't remember what I wrote you in my #3 letter or just where I wrote it from—couldn't tell you the latter anyway—but anyway, you are all doing great work in sending me letters and I surely do appreciate it. In regard to Marsh Williams, I'm darned if I can think just who Marsh is engaged to—he's had so many girls. Hope I'll see Dave and Bob and Ed Parsons—but I haven't the slightest idea where they are, of course. If you see Marian Edwards Grant, Mother, give

her my kindest regards, please, and wish her many years of happiness for me. I note what you say about cablegrams and will keep it in
mind. I have plenty of money. My pay, now, as corporal, is a bit over
$40 per month which is quite sufficient as my needs are small. I have
no surplus to speak of, but I never run out of money from one payday
to another. It's fine that Ede could go up to Rocky Point [a resort in
the Adirondacks]. Can't Father and Mother get away [for] a vacation?
Better do it, folks. It'll do you good. Yes, Ede, you can knit up a helmet,
sweater or two, wristlets, muffler, etc. and have them ready to send
me when winter comes, if you will. Father, we are just over the line in
Belgium. Wish Ed could get home for a few days but his hard work
seems to be getting him results. Why don't you and Mother take a
week or ten days and go down to see Ed? Could he get any time off?
It's great that Ed may get a commission—he deserves it and I hope
he gets it. He can handle himself in first class shape as an officer, I
know and he should take all legitimate help from Col. Vaughn. I don't
know whether he has mentioned it to you or not. Tod's girl wrote him
that she heard from Elizabeth that Hocky had to wear his gas mask
all the time he was at work. Ha, ha, I guess Hocky has something
uncomfortable to do, now. Father, look up Poperinghe on the map.
Ed's letters are both most interesting and I thank you, Ed, for them.
This letter will come to you after it goes to the folks. Folks, how about
a little box of candy and a small sized toilet kit to hold comb, no hair-
brush, tooth brush in case, safety razor, shaving brush, shaving stick,
tube of tooth paste and soap-box and a pocket to hold wash cloth and
hand towel. You can order it at Gimbel's or Wanamaker's in N.Y. and
they will deliver it from their London or Paris branch. I have bought a
Gillette safety razor—their khaki model, a very handy thin box—as
my Gem junior is getting worn. My comb is O.K. If you could put in a
new shaving stick, a new tooth brush and case, a new soap box and a
new Rubberset shaving-brush, it would fix me up in good shape. My
Rubberset is going all to pieces since I used salt water on it on the
boat coming over. Be sure and get a case with a pocket in it for a towel
and wash cloth. All this, of course, providing you can do it without too

much trouble. It isn't necessary to have an officer's signature on this request if the shipment is made from London or Paris.

Father, write how things are coming along at the store. I'm interested to know. Also how things look for you on working out our proposition on the stock etc.

Well, I also have letters from –

> Pete Jenkins
> Walt Hankins
> Bob Brooks
> Ruth Safford (her mother forwarded)
> Ruth Jenkins (round-robin from the lake)
> "Neudge"

I enjoyed Pete's, Ruth Safford's, Sam's from the lake and "Neudge's" especially. ["Neudge," Marion Newell, was Cpl. Truesdell's first cousin.] "Sam's" was a round robin from Lake Ontario and it surely did remind me of the many good times I have had up there. There were notes from Mrs. F.W., Mrs. Matthews, Marian Matthews, George Jenkins, Mrs. J.J. and Bob Douglas, Ethel Leighton and others. Ruth Safford wrote a fine letter, too. Will answer as soon as I can. "Nuedgey" writes such a good letter, too. She is a fine girl and I think a lot of her. She is unaffected and sincere and a good sport. Give my best to the folks at 46 Front.

The last time I wrote we had just returned from the rifle range. It was there that I was made corporal. Then the details were made for the different battalions the next day or two and a couple of days afterward we went into the trenches—each battalion as a unit. For six days the English were with us, then we took over the sector by ourselves for four days. I stayed at Batt Hdqrs. all the time. We were in a quiet sector, of course, but it was lively enough—there was a certain amount of shelling. Jerry strafed us usually about 1 PM and intermittently all night. We fired 10 shots at Jerry to one of his at us. I slept in a partly knocked-down barn. Of course our only danger was from the shells as we were about 3000 yds in back of the front trenches. A few shells landed close to us and we got just a little sneezing gas from shelling. Naturally there were some casualties of which you no doubt have read by this time. Now, don't worry anymore than absolutely necessary about me—you know why I came over at the start and naturally I will have to be in the trenches every now and then. If God wills that I come out O.K., it will be so. Just keep up your spirits, pray as I will, and do your "darndest" to help win the war over there. Remember there are thousands of other fellows over here who have mothers and fathers at home and we're only a drop in [the] bucket. I figure that Jerry hasn't got my number and isn't going to get it, either. Meanwhile, I'll go ahead with signal work. Don't know when we'll go in again. My job was to take charge of the usual signaling from the forward companies to batt. hdqrs. I had a detail of 4 men. It is an easy job as long as communication is OK by wire. When the wires go "dis" (disconnected) or brake, then all messages come back by lamp. We didn't have much doing. We came out last Friday AM before daylight. It was a beautiful night—full moon—and a wonderful sunrise—great morning to come out. Took a good hot sponge bath yesterday and cleaned up—picked off all the cooties I could find. They're like the poor—always with us. Tod didn't go up to the line as the band doesn't ordinarily except in emergencies. I've had a good visit with him and compared our letters. Father, we are considerably further north than you figure. Am feeling fine and so is Tod. Be sure and send this on to Ed. The news from down south is very encouraging, isn't it? By the way, I heard that Lieut. Darling was severely wounded while the 2nd Battalion was in the line. I do not know this to be absolutely true, so do not spread it around. If it is so, you will have heard about it before this reaches you.

Well, I will write you soon again. With love to all of you from

Bob

**Letter #11 written abroad and sent from the continent
Letter postmarked ? Bordeaux, date unclear
Envelope marked "Passed by Censor No. 5077"
Received Sept. 27ᵗʰ 1918**

Friday, Sept. 6, 1918

Dear Folks,

Well, here I am in a new place—sitting in an old French house (our billet) smoking a Murad cigarette, with United Cigar Store Ricoro cigars in my pocket and an Everybody magazine as a writing pad—not very bad, eh? Somebody got a package from Paris with some Murads in it and I got a package and the cigars came from the Y.M. canteen which we have along with us.

Well, I'll start off from where I left off in my last letter which was written August 27ᵗʰ—a week ago last Tuesday. As I wrote after coming back from the trenches, we had a rest and we all thought we'd be going up for another trick but new orders came and we packed up, hiked a couple of hours, rode about 10 hours and then hiked two or three more coming back down again to where we were, some time ago. We are still not as far down as the American sector, but it is warmer here than where we came from. The weather is fine and the country, beautiful. The crops seem to be plentiful here this year—lot of oats, hay, corn, potatoes, hops, etc. It is a beautiful evening tonight—the sun is just going down and the band is playing outside—it isn't at all like war for we are some distance behind the lines and there is not a sound of a gun—but there, I hear an aeroplane going over, high up,—it's just a faint hum—but that is all. Otherwise I might be sitting in any little village, in the good old U.S.A. of a few hundred population—for that is the size of this place—I am on the second floor looking out the window at the green trees and blue sky—and thinking of you. All the boys in this room are band fellows except me. Tod and Bill Jude got me in here. More of the fellows are up and down stairs and some have their pup tents in the back yard below. This is the first time since the days of the old 1ˢᵗ in Camp W. that Tod and I have slept together as we usually bunk up with our own platoon fellows. Tod is fine, the band is being enlarged and the boys are all in good spirits. Give my kindest regards to Mr Mulford when you see him next time. You might look up Doullens on the map, too. Compre?

The Allies are certainly doing great work, aren't they? We get the Daily Mail most every day and today's issue continues the good news of further advances by the Allies who have pushed the Germans back over the ground which it took them three great offenses to gain. I hope the good work continues and we are soon home again.

Had a letter from Russell Tuttle whose father is a harnessmaker on Hawley Street. You remember him, Father, he was one of our original 1ˢᵗ boys. The 105ᵗʰ F.A. are over here — I don't know where, have had the necessary training and are ready to do business, I guess. Haven't heard from any of the 1ˢᵗ Pioneer boys yet.

Don't know when we'll go up to the lines again. I'm feeling fine — except I'll say if you will pardon me — damn the "cooties." You see the British who stay in one certain sector for some time, have their division baths (showers), but we, traveling about, don't have any and a shower-bath (not even thinking of a tub-bath — wonder of wonders — luxury of luxuries) is a rare thing. Today I got hold of an old hard tack tin, heated some water and had a hot sponge bath and it sure was a relief. My last was about two weeks ago. Ordinarily I have my clothes washed by some French woman and am having this done today. Costs a couple of francs which it is worth for the job is better done.

Had a very delicious dinner this noon — the first "feed" we have indulged in for some time — French-fried potatoes, fried eggs, a can of French peas, bread and butter, coffee and jam. De-licious — cost us each about 1½ francs (85 cents or 90 cents).

The mail I have received from you since I wrote last is as follows,

Father — Aug. 7th
Ed — Aug. 7th
Ede — Aug. 7th (Rocky Point Inn)

It all came about a week ago so it took only three weeks to get here. Mail service is improving for me. Hope you are getting all my letters in proper time. Thank you, Father, very much for ordering the home papers for me. Several of the boys receive the Binghamton Press, and as I see it frequently, I think the Republican would be quite enough to send me—also it would save space in the mails and you, money. You certainly had some hot weather, didn't you? The conclusions you drew from what Moss McLean wrote and sent home were quite correct. By the way, what is Naumbourg's proper firm name and has he a Paris office? If so, what is the address? It is going on four months now since we arrived in France and tho I expected that it would be some time before we get a leave, I'd like to know where I could get a little money if I needed it, when I do get a chance to go to Paris. As corporal, I get $40.20 per month or 217.08 francs at 5.40 exchange less my insurance which $6.60 per month and my Liberty Bond which is $5.00 per month. This leaves $28.60 or 154.44 francs. Last month's pay (July) finished the payments on the Liberty Loan Bond, so for August I'll receive $5.00 more. We'll get August pay in about a week. This makes my pay from now on $33.60 or 181.44 francs per month which is quite sufficient for all present needs, in fact I expect I could send home $10. per month in a voluntary allotment, but I'd like to have a little money in my pocket to get a "feed" now and then, buy a few crackers at the canteen and get the few necessary toilet articles and small things the government does not furnish, get my clothes washed, get some oranges once in a while when I can etc. etc. I have no surplus money at present but I really don't need it. I forgot to mention smokes in the above list—they're important. In a few days I'll receive $33.60 and also about $10. I have loaned out to some of the boys this last month, so I'll have plenty. By the way, you wrote something about sending me some snapshots of you all and home and the store and the new jitney etc. Please send them as they will look almighty good to me. It's been seven months since I've seen Ede and good old Binghamton and four since I've seen the rest of you.

N.B. You can send me photos, but I can't send you any except por-
traits, I hear. Maybe I can send you my picture if I can get it taken
somewhere.

Also, here's something Mary McMahon can do for me if she will,
please. When the calendars come in for next year, send me a little one
like I have now. It's a playing card with the whole year on the face of
it—just fits my pocket book. Rather early to speak about it but it will
be October by the time you receive this and I would like it very much.
Ede's letter from the Adirondacks was most welcome, too. It's fine you
could have a good vacation and I believe Mother and Father should by
all means take one, too. You both need it, for the times are strenuous
and Father is so busy all the time at the store that I know he needs one.
I will now take out my family "album" and look at you all. Doggone
you, you've all got to keep well and happy so when I return we can
have a grand reunion. Your faces are before me and I carry them in
my left upper coat pocket all over France. Every now and then when I
get "visiting" (a chip off the old block, eh) with some French people, I
take out my pictures proudly and show them what my folks look like.
As ordnance sergeant, Ed, I now congratulate you—next comes your
commission—just keep humming—you can do it, I know.
You know I asked you in my last letter to send me a toilet kit from
London or Paris just a medium-sized one with a new soap box, tooth
[brush] and shaving brush—I have the rest of the articles O.K.—well,
I have been able to get a shaving brush—the really important thing is
the case. Also as I said a little candy and in addition some cigars and if
it were possible, a few Ramesis cig'ts would be <u>most</u> acceptable.
Well, nine pages will have to do for this letter. With love

> Bob

P.S. Please send this on to Ed. RDT

Letter #12 written abroad and sent from the continent
Letter with unclear postmark
Envelope with unclear censor stamp
Received Oct. 8ᵗʰ 1918

Wed., Sept. 11, 1918

Dear Folks,

Am still in the same place where I was when I wrote Letter #11. I expect you can keep track of where I am, better, now that Gen. March is publishing the locations of the various American units every little while in the newspapers. We were in Flanders but are now a bit further south quite a ways behind the lines. So everything is quite peaceful. We have an extra good billet here. I am with seven other band boys including Tod and Bill Jude in a room on the second floor of a pretty respectable house. There is a fireplace in the room and we have "scrounged" up enough to have quite a cheerful blaze.

Yesterday was a great day for I received fifteen letters in all. Heard from Ed, Ede (Rocky Point Inn), Father, Mother, Aunt Nell, Frank Summers, Orra Summers, Marian Ford, "Sam" Jenkins and somewhat to my surprise Harriette Waters. Haven't heard from her since Camp Wadsworth, that is, we haven't corresponded since then. The best news of all was Ed's commission.[67] I have written him. I certainly am proud and very much pleased for he surely deserves it and he will surely feel fine about it, too. I have two letters from him, one dated Aug.1ˢᵗ and the other dated Aug 17ᵗʰ, the latter telling me of his commission, but not giving many details. Your letters are as follows:

Father—Aug 2
    "   " 5
Mother " 5
Father " 9
Ede   " 16 (Rocky Point Inn)
Mother " 14
Father " 14

Father's letter of Aug 5 was very interesting with all the news. Very pleased to hear that Henry Hopkins is improving satisfactorily. Ditto—Pop Hotchkiss. I should like to be remembered to Mr. and Mrs. Birdsall very especially. Tod has an extra sleeveless sweater he is giving me. He is able to put some extra stuff in the case he carries his horn in and so carries it in that manner. If you should send me any money, send it in the form of an American Xpress money order as Bill Jude will cash it for me and send it on to his friend, who is manager of the American Xpress Co branch in Paris. Oh, yes, Father, we all have maps of the country and follow out our travels on them. You must know by this time that Lieut. Darling was wounded while we were up the line. He was attached to the Supply train and while they were bringing up rations one night a shrapnel shell burst and a piece went thru his neck coming close to the jugular vein. I understand he is coming along well in the hospital. This is not official but what I heard from a Co H boy. Please remember me to Mr. Moon. Nice that Ede can visit Marg. West, besides her trip to Fourth Lake. Glad to hear Ed Parsons has arrived over here safely. The coming generation is certainly coming all right by the announcements Mother made in her letter. There are lots of new arrivals. Had a very nice letter from "Man" Ford also one from "Sam" Jenkins at the lake. The letters from Franklin Forks were full of good local news. Glad to hear from them.

Bill Jude sent my wrist watch to Paris for a new crystal and strap and I have just got it back. It runs fine and is a great convenience, tell the boys at the store. I certainly do appreciate their gift very much.

Well, there really isn't much more to write about. Look up Doullens on the map. Sleep tight and look out for the horsecars as our local comedienne says. With love from

Bob

Letter #13 written abroad and sent from the continent
Letter postmarked Recd from Army, Bordeaux,
Sep 24, 1918, 6 PM
Received Oct. 16th, 1918

Wed., Sept. 18, 1918

Dear Folks,

Still in the same town as when I wrote Letter #12 but have changed billets. Had to leave the good house with the fireplace in it as I had to get my squad together. They were all scattered around and the sergeant wanted the squads together. I have a fair billet, tho—upstairs in a barn—clean but not much light. I got hold of a cot, a frame with burlap stretched over it and with some straw in my shelter half as a mattress, I sleep O.K. The Signal Platoon and the platoon from the Signal Corps attached to the 107th are messing separate from the HQ Co. The company is so big that they are trying out this scheme. We are having a Signal school at present, studying ground telegraphy, buzzer, Fuller phones, lamps, etc. We start at 8 in the AM, finish at 11:30 and start at 1 in the PM and finish at 5. Then we have retreat at 5:30. Keeps us pretty busy. Reveille in the AM is at 7:00. As I wrote you, we are some distance behind the lines. Don't know how long we'll be here. We are in the vicinity of Doullens. The town we are in is about 4 or 500 in population and has a couple of stores and lots of estaminets (cafes) as usual. Tod and Bill Jude and I had about the best feed we have had, the other night—two small chickens, French fries, lettuce and tomato salad, canned peas, bread, butter, jam, and coffee. Chicken is a rarity and so are fresh vegetables, so they tasted very good. It cost us 6 francs apiece. About $1. We were paid a couple of days ago for August and I received 185.50 francs or $40.20 less my $6.50 insurance—$33.70.

As I have had to change my billet and also am more busy with our school, I don't see Tod quite so much at present, still I see him every day. He is well and busy with the band and sends his best regards. You remember young Payne of Co H, Father—the chap you gave a box of

Penns to, when he was home on furlough—well, Tod has gotten him the job of orderly to Capt. Hyleman. Tod gave it up as the Capt. is going away to school somewhere and Tod didn't want to leave the band.

The only mail I have received since I wrote last is a letter from Father dated Aug. 19 and enclosing the snapshots the girls took at the store. They <u>certainly</u> <u>are</u> <u>dandy</u> and especially the one of you, Father. Of course, they are all fine of the boys and girls and they make me a bit homesick but yours is the best. Send me some more—and add some of the salesmen and the other boys who weren't in the first batch. Also I would like some of home and Mother and Father and Ede and Agnes if she is still with you. Also of some of the neighbors. Tell Ede to snap a few sort of "promiscuously." They are "tre bon." Oh boy, it will be a great day when I hit Binghamton again. You spoke in your letter of Mr. Mulford's letter from Tod in which the latter wrote that I was going into the trenches and about a farewell party. Well, Tod was mistaken. We went up the line a little way but not up to the trenches and came back shortly and joined the company again. Our trip to the trenches wasn't until about the middle of August. Ed Hotchkiss certainly gets his share of furloughs, eh?

Also had a letter from Frank and Ethel Summers.

Have no surplus of money now but my pay runs me thru pretty well from pay day to pay day.

After dinner

Another manouever—spelled wrong? Must hurry and pack up. Will be back here in a day or two. Love to all

Bob

Letter #14 written abroad and sent from the continent
Letter postmarked Recd from Army, Bordeaux, Oct. 4, 1918, 6 PM
Envelope marked "Passed by Censor No. 5086"
Received Oct. 19th 1918

Saturday, Sept. 21, 1918

N.B. I enclose a few stamps which are of no use to me.

Dear Folks,

More mail yesterday — three letters as follows –

Ed—	Aug	25
Mother—	"	26
Ede—	"	27

Ed hadn't received my letter #7 of July 28 from you when he wrote. Said he had had a letter from Rollin Harrington who is now a 2nd Lieut. in Waco, Texas. Please send this letter on to Ed, as usual. By the way, Tod got a letter from his girl yesterday in which she wrote that Hocky had been made top sergeant. What the devil (please excuse) do you know about that? [One] is just speaking very soft and weak. I can see Hocky — Company attention — Report — All present or accounted for — Open ranks — March — Front — Prepare for inspection — Close ranks — March — Right by squads — March — and so on — I can just see Hocky pulling off that stuff.

Mother's letter was most "instructive," interesting and newsy. Glad you see the Mulfords occasionally. Give my best regards to Bill and Cretia. Hope Bill comes along O.K. Have not heard from Tod Corbett as yet. Glad to hear of Hal Murray's progress. Ede's letter contains the best news really, for I am very glad that Ed can be home for just a short time, even. I know you'll be glad to see him and he'll be mighty glad to be home. Ede's letter is also full of other news — it's an exceptionally good one. I had heard that Moss McLean was going back on some special duty but didn't know he was a captain. By all means, send me some pictures, Ede, as you suggested. You don't know how welcome they are. Some of the girls at the store took some and Father sent them to me. They were fine. You take some of the folks, of the house, of the "jit," of the Newells, of the folks on Stuyvesant St. and of the neighbors and send me. Then I would like some more of the store—including the girls and boys who weren't in the first batch. Am pleased to know of the good work the canteen is doing. I have plenty of socks so far, Ede.

There is a message for Ed. I thought about this three or four times but don't think I have written him about it. I send you "large" greetings for your birthday. Of course they will reach you late but they are multiplying in this letter every day until they reach you. Your commission is a fine and a just present for you. My present will be the greeting and the fact that I will be thinking of you especially that day.

I closed my letter #13 written last Wed. Sept. 18 rather hurriedly as the division was going out on a manouever. Well, we manouevered—started Friday at 1:30 PM, hiked 10 or 12 miles, stayed all night in pup tents, arose at 5 and began manouevering in the direction of "home." The advance took place so fast that Signals couldn't keep up. I and two other chaps were left behind on a telephone and about 5:30 we got word to start back and so we loaded our property into a limber, arriving "home" at 10 o'clock. All I can figure out about a manouever is that we hike anywhere from 2 to 20 miles, rush around trying to maintain communication and locate the different units as they advance or retreat, get lost and then hike back arriving any time from 6 o'clock to midnight and the next day, the officers say it was either a success or a failure. The band including Tod stayed back and loafed.

Our Y.M.C.A. has some "real American chocolate bon-bons" and they are delicious—my first since we arrived in France. They also have Murad cigarettes which are a great treat. As I wrote you before, cigars would be most welcome if you want to send me something.

I have begun to receive the Republican and the Press and they are most welcome. I pass them around to the other Binghamton fellows.

There seem to be a few signs pointing toward another move for us. Don't know where we may go.

The war news is certainly most encouraging and I hope by another year we will be home.

Tod and I are both well and feeling fine. Tod has been promoted to 2nd class musician. Will close for this time, with love to all of you, from

Bob

Monday P.M. [Sept. 23, 1918]

N.B. We are moving tomorrow a little bit further south and up into reserve. On ground held until recently by Jerry. Will write you when I get there. It's about a day's journey, partly by train and partly by foot. I am unable to mail this until we arrive at our new destination as the mail sergeant has packed up.

RDT

Wed. P.M., Sept. 25, 1918

P.S. Here we are, in some very barren looking country, in our new location, after traveling some 40 or 50 miles in a roundabout and slow fashion by train and a short hike. This country until recently was held by Jerry and there is lots of German clothing and equipment and shells etc. lying around on the ground. This ground, as I understand it, has been fought over two or three times and it is absolutely pitiable. The little town we are camped near, for we can't find a billet in it, is simply razed to the ground. There isn't a building left standing, not a roof left of any kind, just a wall here and there and great heaps of bricks and stone. Half the trees are dead and the ground covered with litter. We are about 13 or 14 miles from the front lines yet and can just hear the faint rumblings of the big guns and see the observation balloons in the distance. Now and then you can see a squadron of aeroplanes go by. Just saw one of fifteen like mere specks in the sky. It is now about six-thirty PM and the sky is beautiful—the sun is just setting. Nothing can change the beauty of the heavens. On our way here, I got my first view of German prisoners. These were captured quite recently — about the first of Sept. and they surely were a rather poor lot, small ones and big ones and pretty dumb looking. Well I must close and get this off. With love,

Bob

Letter #15 written abroad and sent from the continent
Letter postmarked Field Post Office, date unclear
Received Nov. 1ˢᵗ1918

Friday, Oct. 4, 1918

Dear Folks,

Well, I'll have to apologize again for it has been two weeks since I have written you. Letter #14 was dated Sept. 21. But I have passed thru a new experience. We have just come out of the trenches near Tincourt and are in a rest camp near Perrone for a few days. We were used as shock troops to start an attack and our casualties were heavy. However we reached our objective and were successful in our attack. I thank God I came out whole for one of our signal corporals was killed, another died of wounds, another was wounded, another is missing, and a couple of our privates are missing. Of course our casualties in the Signals and HQ Co, generally, are slight in comparison to those in the line companies as their danger is greater — going over the top. We left the place where I wrote Letter #14 a few days after I wrote it, a short ride and a hike and into the line in a day or two. Our brave fellows did splendidly but being new to the game, lost heavily. Before you receive this letter, you will no doubt have seen the casualty list published. We were in the line about 5 days. The regiment went over the top about 5:30 in the morning after a terrific barrage of 20 or 30 minutes by our artillery. Then the Australians came up and helped us hold the new line and they advanced further. You should have seen all the tanks. They are a wonderful thing — they'll go anywhere. I was detailed and am permanently, unless changed, to regimental HQ in charge of visual

signaling so was safe from rifle and machine gun fire but subject of
course to considerable strafing by HE and gas shells and shrapnel.
You remember the boy I wrote you about in Camp W. who used to talk
about himself so much because he didn't know any better—in my
tent down there—Glenn Kelso by name. He was up with one of the
battalions in charge of lines and was killed instantly by machine gun
fire. He was a corporal. Then Stuart Donley whom Father may remember for he is a Binghamton boy and has an uncle who is connected
with one of the big Endicott concerns was wounded in the neck. He
came by regimental HQ and I talked with him. He did not seem to be
badly wounded and it doesn't seem possible that he died from wounds
later—in the hospital. From internal bleeding I hear. If Father could
look up his mother I wish he would and tell her that Stuart did his
duty like a man. I believe a word of sympathy would do her good altho
she will be feeling very badly. Then another corporal from Brooklyn,
Clinton Prouty, was wounded in the flesh of the arm—a slight one
and another corporal is missing in action. I was not up where the dead
and the wounded were lying about but it was terrible enough to see
stretcher after stretcher of wounded come back home on the shoul-
ders of four stretcher bearers and then the walking wounded besides.
Americans, Australians and a few Germans scattered in our HQ Co.
stayed in the line one day extra to help gather the dead and salvage
equipment. I believe the Germans are licked—their infantry haven't
much pep—it's their artillery and machine guns that are their main-
stay. When they cry for peace, then I say give them double hell and
make them grovel in the dirt for you folks at home can't realize what
desolation and ruins this country is in. It is pathetic and fills one with
a feeling that the Allies and especially the French must have absolute
reprision. When their towns and territory have been ruined, then they
will realize what they have done to France. They should receive no
easy terms of peace but be forced to an absolutely favorable peace for
the Allies. I haven't heard about the casualties in the Binghamton Co
H boys but I know there are some. The band stayed behind the lines at
a detail camp and I found Tod well and happy and glad to see me back

on my return yesterday.

A big batch of mail was distributed last night and my share was 12 letters and a couple of Presses. The letters were as following,

Father—Aug 1st—Delayed on account of mistake in
                reading address
Father—Aug 28
Henry Hopkins—Aug 29
Father—Aug 30
Mother—Sept 1
Ede—   " 2
Father—   " 6
Ede—   " 8
Mother—   " 8
Ed—   " 3

There was a mistake about Slackford being wounded for he is absolutely well here with us. I haven't made many new friends here, Father. There are two Walton boys, old Co F 1st Inf. boys whom I chum a bit with—Harold White and Malcolm Wright—respectively called Pinny and Peanut. They are good scouts. Then Tod and Bill Jude and I chum around together, too. I am satisfied—for I'll have my old friends when I return home. Your news of the store and the prices of goods is most interesting—please write me about them often. Also I can tell you how much I appreciate the picture of the boys and Mr. Birdsall. Remember me to the boys and ask them why the devil they can't find a spare minute to write me a short letter. It's fine to have friends who on your departure present you with a wrist watch—which by the way is running fine and giving much satisfaction—but who never write me—Joe and Henry excluded. Please remember me most especially to Mr and Mrs. Birdsall, too.

Most interested to hear of K Niles and Mainy Wilson's wedding. Am very glad to hear of Clevey's receiving his commission. The description of that Sunday in Ede's Sept 1st letter sounds so good. I can just see the beautiful clear cool crisp day with the sun shining. I hope Ede will surely take some pictures for you don't know how I appreciate them. They make me a bit homesick but they do look good. Those of Ede and Glad and Helen's baby were fine and I have placed them on file to look at every little while with the rest of my pictures. Ede's letter was most interesting, too — about her trip to Syracuse.

Saturday A.M. [Oct. 5, 1918]

Am finishing this AM. Weather pretty chilly and hard to write. Cold sleeping in pup-tent last night with one blanket and overcoat. Slept as issued — in other words, removed only shoes and leggings. Reminded me of Camp Wadsworth.

More mail last night. Letter dated Sept 9 from Father and one from Ed dated Sept 9. Father wants to know whether I am now on telephone exchange work. No, since I was made corporal, I have been taken off and as I have written, I am in charge of visual signaling at Regimental HQ. Visual signaling consists of signaling by flags, shutter and lamp. The first two we use very little — depend mostly on the lamps for both day and night work. Usually signaling is used only in cases of emergency i.e. when the wires are dis. (disconnected) from any cause — usually on account of shell-fire. We use an English lamp which is very compact and handy and does good work. It is called the Lucas lamp. It is small — about five or six inches in diameter but with a strong bulb and good reflector and throws a beam of light for a mile or a mile and a half. It is my job to establish communication with the forward battalions and with brigades and then in case the wires go dis all messages go over the visual until the wires are mended again. We use the international Morse code. Of course, it is only possible to communicate from front to rear on the front line as the enemy could read our messages if we signaled the other way. We see quite a lot of the British Tommies and lately of the Australians.

In regard to money, I am not broke — neither am I flush. If you wish to send me a little for a Xmas present, it will be most acceptable (by postal money order or Amer. Xpress M. order). I still have some money in the bank. Send me some of that. I have my bank-book here but it is with some extra junk which Tod is taking care of with the band stuff and is not accessible just now. I feel fine—am in excellent health. My feelings, Father, are still deeper than yours—if that is possible—in regard to my affection for you and my greatest desire is that you continue in good health, so that when I return, I can again have that greatest help and pleasure of association with you. I am not homesick for I know it is of no use, but I long for the day when I shall return home again, for I have had a house which could not have been improved on. We hear that Bulgaria and Turkey have surrendered and that certainly is fine news. Also it is stated that official news has been received at the Adj. office that Austria has given Germany seven days to bring about peace. Otherwise Austria will break with Germany and make a separate peace. How true this latter statement is, I don't know—but I surely hope it's authentic.

I also received letters from—Neudge, Margaret Harrington and Ruth Jenkins, all giving me interesting news.

Please don't forget about sending me a small calendar for 1919—the size of a playing card.

Well, I don't know much more to write about this time. I expect it will be some time before we go into the line again.

Our Y.M. has some stick candy in stock in #1 tins which certainly tastes good, although it costs 2.15 francs a can (40 cents).

I will go over and mail this at once.

With love to all from

                                        Bob

Here is a letter from Edwin Summers Truesdell, Sr.
to his son Robert Truesdell:[68]

Dear Bob,

Your letter of Sept. 18th rec'd yesterday just 4 weeks to a day after written. As usual we devoured it completely several times over. When I
see your familiar writing I look a little further and picture you as you
penned the lines and I am near you again for the moment. We are glad
to have all the news of your daily life as far as you can give it and to
know you are well and keep in good spirits. We know your div. went
into action soon after you wrote and were in heavy work for some days
and now for some 10 days I am unable to locate them at all and am
thinking you are having a rest again and we hope and pray you are
safe and well. I know we cannot hear from you about your experience
for some 2 weeks yet so we will wait and trust all is well. Bob you are
the nearest and dearest I have and I am proud of the splendid spirit in
which you have always met duty in every spot and place in life. How
we shall enjoy life together when you return. We are well altho there is
a great epidemic of Spanish Influenza here which is now abating a little.
There is such a lack of nurses that Edith has volunteered today and is
at the City Hospital helping. We have been fortunate in the office and
store. Frank Marble is just recovering. Abe is back from a few days
struggle with it. Bill Cline has a twist but no one very bad. There are
many cases of pneumonia in the city and 15 funerals today. Churches
and theaters closed and no public meetings allowed.

We are about thru with the loan and have our quota raised. Geo.
Rick's (shoe store) has not subscribed to any issue and would not do
so this time. As he is worth at least $200,000, the workers did not like
it much. This morning his store front was painted yellow and the word
"slacker" was printed all over his windows. A great crowd was watching
him try to clean up all this AM and everybody giving him the laugh.
Everybody must go their limit now and most people do and do it gladly.
We have great news every day now and I believe the end of the war is

in sight and not later than 1919 and by a miracle almost it may be over sooner. The Germans have been outwitted and out-fought all summer since July 15th and are certainly in the toboggan. They seem to lack men and material both and may crumble at any time but may be strong enough to go through another winter yet. I see a member of your company was awarded the Medal of Honor by Gen. Pershing for work in Flanders—and I see the 106 reports quite a number of casualties. Mr. Phelps had a letter from Jack yesterday. He was on the line and hard at work. Well and in fine spirits. Business good and no special news at the office. Ed expects to sail in 3 or 4 weeks. He is very busy helping to get in shape. He writes often. Well Bob good bye for a day or two. Keep your spirits high. With love and affection

Father

Notes

1   Jacobson, *History of the 107th Infantry U.S.A.,* 34.

2   Ibid., 35.

3   Ibid., 36.

4   Harris, *Duty, Honor, Privilege: New York's Silk Stocking Regiment and the Breaking of the Hindenburg Line,* 138.

5   Ibid., 139-140.

6   Sheffield, *War on the Western Front in the Trenches of World War I,* 141.

7   Jacobson, *History of the 107th Infantry U.S.A.,* 38.

8   O'Ryan, *The Story of the 27th Division, Vol. II,* 631.

9   Jacobson, *History of the 107th Infantry U.S.A.,* 40.

10   Ibid., 42.

11   Ibid., 42-44.

12   Ibid., 46.

13   Seward, *Binghamton and Broome County, New York, A History,* 578.

14   Ibid., 579-580.

15   Jacobson, *History of the 107th Infantry U.S.A.,* 93.

16   Ibid., 94.

17   Fussell, *The Great War and Modern Memory,* 66.

18   Simkins, Jukes, and Hickey, *The First World War: The War to End All Wars,* 165-166.

19   Ibid., 166-167.

20   Persico, *Eleventh Month, Eleventh Day, Eleventh Hour,* 266.

21   Stone, *World War One,* 171-172.

22   Simkins, Jukes, and Hickey, *The First World War: The War to End All Wars,* 168.

23   Ibid., 170-171.

24   Keene, *World War I: The American Soldier Experience,* xiv-xv.

25   Yockelson, *Borrowed Soldiers: Americans under British Command, 1918,* 92-93.

26   Persico, *Eleventh Month, Eleventh Day, Eleventh Hour,* 268.

27   Lacey, *Pershing,* 148.

28 Jacobson, *History of the 107*th *Infantry U.S.A.*, 46-47.

29 O'Ryan, *The Story of the 27th Division, Vol. II*, 694.

30 Jacobson, *History of the 107*th *Infantry U.S.A.*, 47.

31 Yockelson, *Borrowed Soldiers: Americans under British Command, 1918*, 111-112.

32 Sheffield, *War on the Western Front in the Trenches of World War I*, 152.

33 Smith, *Lingo of No Man's Land: A World War I Slang Dictionary*, 5-6.

34 Simkins, Jukes, and Hickey, *The First World War: The War to End All Wars*, 175.

35 Persico, *Eleventh Month, Eleventh Day, Eleventh Hour*, 273-274.

36 Yockelson, *Borrowed Soldiers: Americans under British Command, 1918*, 115-117.

37 Ibid., 112-113.

38 Simkins, Jukes, and Hickey, *The First World War: The War to End All Wars,* 176.

39 Ibid.

40 Stevens, *The Great War Explained*, 137.

41 Jacobson, *History of the 107*th *Infantry U.S.A.*, 48-49.

42 Seward, *Binghamton and Broome County, New York, A History*, 581.

43 Jacobson, *History of the 107*th *Infantry U.S.A.*, 97.

44 Ibid., 99.

45 Ibid., 98.

46 Ibid.

47 Yockelson, *Borrowed Soldiers: Americans under British Command, 1918*, 127.

48 Matloff, *World War I: A Concise Military History of "The War to End All Wars" and The Road to the War, 108-109.*

49 Ibid., 111.

50 Hart, Peter, *The Great War: A Combat History of the First World War*, 458-459.

51 Hayes quoted in Jacobson, *History of the 107*th *Infantry U.S.A.*, 114.

52 Harris, *Duty, Honor, Privilege: New York's Silk Stocking Regiment and the Breaking of the Hindenburg Line*, 2.

53 Hayes quoted in Jacobson, *History of the 107th Infantry U.S.A.*, 114.

54 Jacobson, *History of the 107th Infantry U.S.A.*, 52.

55 Ibid.

56 O'Ryan, *The Story of the 27th Division*, 701.

57 Jacobson, *History of the 107th Infantry U.S.A.*, 54-55.

58 Ibid.., 55.

59 Ibid., 56.

60 Hayes quoted in Jacobson, *History of the 107th Infantry U.S.A.*, 116-117.

61 Ibid., 118-119.

62 Yockelson, *Borrowed Soldiers: Americans under British Command, 1918*, 176.

63 Jacobson, *History of the 107th Infantry U.S.A.*, 112.

64 Persico, *Eleventh Month, Eleventh Day, Eleventh Hour*, 290-291.

65 Matloff, *World War I: A Concise Military History of "The War to End All Wars" and The Road to the War*, 110.

66 Sheffield, *War on the Western Front in the Trenches of World War I*, 122.

67 Cpl. Truesdell notes that he has received the news that his older brother has been commissioned. His brother, a college graduate, seemed to be quite deliberate in his search for a situation in which he knew an officer. That officer was apparently very helpful as Cpl. Truesdell's brother received several promotions within a fairly short period of time, although he never served abroad.

68 Robert Truesdell received this letter from his father. The exact date of the letter is unclear, but the month is clearly October; it is probably the letter dated Oct. 7, acknowledged in Robert's letter dated Nov. 6. His father's letter is written on Newell & Truesdell Co. stationery. The letterhead includes the following:

Importers and Wholesale Grocers

Teas, Coffees, Molasses, Canned Goods

POST-BATTLE SERVICE
AND RETURN TO THE U.S.

Following the battle, Cpl. Truesdell reports that he was ordered to gas school in Châtillon-sur-Seine and was away from the regiment for about three weeks. He left the regiment on October 7 and, with a sergeant and two other corporals, made his way by train to the school in Châtillon-sur-Seine, via Paris. He clearly enjoys seeing Paris and mentions the "cafes aplenty with their little tables out in front." After a week of "tedious" sessions on gas warfare, he had to pass through Paris again on his return trip and writes in some detail about attending a performance at the Follies Bergère. Paris certainly seemed to be a pleasant interlude.

On the same day that Cpl. Truesdell left for gas school, the regiment, now similar in size to a battalion, moved back toward the lines and in succeeding days chased the rapidly retreating Germans. The 107th drove the enemy from its position along the Selle River, Jonc de Mer Ridge, St. Maurice River, and the vicinity of St. Souplet, from which the regiment, along with other parts of the 27th Division, was ordered to withdraw from the line for a period of rest.[1] "The remnants of the division" were taken in boxcars to towns close to Amiens.[2] The 107th regiment relocated to Glisy and Blangy-Tronville, near Amiens. While the men were billeted in these small towns, they took the opportunity to visit Amiens, once a large, flourishing city. As fighting had drawn close to the city, its inhabitants had fled, but by this time, the Germans had retreated, and refugees were now returning to the city and re-establishing their lives. Thus, soldiers could go to Amiens for a meal and a hot bath, which cost two francs.[3]

By the time that President Wilson responded to Germany regarding its request for an armistice and Germany in turn replied on October 12 to Wilson and agreed to all Fourteen Points, the French and British heard about the peace feeler but were not in a mood to allow Wilson to take unilateral action.[4] Wilson soon replied that the Allied military leaders would set the terms of the armistice.[5] At this point, Germany's military leaders were facing disaster; on October 26, 1918, Gen. Ludendorff, out of favor, resigned and, wearing a false beard and dark glasses, fled Germany and crossed the border into Denmark.[6]

By the latter part of October, Cpl. Truesdell had returned from gas school and was back with his regiment, now billeted in the town of Glisy, near Amiens. Also during the latter part of October, influenza and pneumonia were spreading rapidly, causing many of the men in the regiment to become extremely ill, some fatally.[7] The fatality rate in the A.E.F. from influenza was appalling. Influenza caused the death of roughly one out of every three American soldiers who contracted the disease.[8] Back in the United States, the deadly disease was taking its toll there as well. In the last week of October, approximately 21,000 people died of influenza, while 2,700 doughboys in France died from all causes.[9] Ultimately, the pandemic killed some 600,000 Americans and an estimated 20 to 50 million people worldwide.[10]

Despite the many cases of influenza, the Americans and their Allies were wearing down the Central Powers. On October 29, Bulgaria surrendered to the Allies. The next day, October 30, the Ottoman Empire surrendered to the Allies, and on November 4, following a defeat in the Battle of Vittorio Veneto, Austria-Hungary also signed an armistice with the Allies.[11] At the same time, sailors in the German navy mutinied, and revolution spread throughout Germany.[12]

Allied success on the battlefield was moving toward victory, but men of the 27th Division whose valor had helped to make victory possible and who had given their lives in the recent battles were not to be forgotten. On November 5, 1918, Major Gen. O'Ryan issued Field

Orders regarding a parade, to take place on Sunday, November 10, 1918. According to the orders,

> The parade will be in honor of the memory of our comrades who died in the recent series of battles. Their bodies have been buried in cemeteries organized on the fields where they fell. Their graves have been marked and appropriate religious services have been held. Nevertheless the Division Commander believes that the soldiers of the division would express by some ceremony, in which all may share, our admiration for their valor and our loyalty for their memory. It is fitting that the ceremony should be military in character, for no soldiers were ever animated by higher military ideals or were more responsive to the requirements of military discipline.... Always shall we honor them. Never shall we forget their devotion and splendid courage.[13]

Victory did indeed appear to be imminent. Early in the morning of November 8, a group of German delegates, whom Marshal Foch had agreed to see, arrived by train at a siding in the Forest of Compiègne. It was here, in Foch's railway car, that the German delegation heard the Allied conditions for surrender: German evacuation of all occupied lands in Belgium, Luxembourg, and France as well as Alsace and Lorraine; Allied occupation in Germany west of the Rhine; withdrawal of German forces from Austria-Hungary, Romania, and Turkey; the surrender of 10 battleships as well as numerous other parts of their naval squadrons; and well over 30 more conditions, including taking blame for the war and paying reparations for all damages they had caused. Foch gave the German delegation 72 hours to gain their government's consent to the Allied terms.[14]

On November 9, Kaiser Wilhelm II was forced to abdicate. He escaped to neutral Holland, and Germany was proclaimed a republic.[15]

At last bringing an end to the hostilities, the Armistice between the Allies and Germany was signed about 5 a.m. on November 11 in Foch's railway coach in the Forest of Compiègne. The Armistice went into effect that day at 11 a.m. after 1,568 days of conflict.[16] Thus, hostilities ceased at the eleventh hour of the eleventh day of the eleventh month of 1918. Many of the men in the 107th regiment had leave that day in Amiens. "Soldiery and citizenry alike joined in a mad revel of lifting joy—French, Americans, English, Australians, and Canadians marching arm in arm up and down the streets of ancient Amiens, shouting and singing themselves hoarse."[17] Cpl. Truesdell writes, "Talk about your excitement when the armistice was signed—Amiens was full of drunk civilians and soldiers running and shouting thru the streets, fireworks were shot off and flags everywhere." Almost immediately after the Armistice, a week's leave to London was made available to doughboys who were fortunate enough to get a furlough. Cpl. Truesdell applied and quickly received the good news that he could be on his way. He left Glisy on Monday, November 18, was in transit for three days, and arrived in London on Wednesday night, November 20. In his first letter from London, Cpl. Truesdell tells about crossing the English Channel by boat. He was lucky that the trip was smooth because the English Channel has long been known for its rough seas. He writes at length about seeing the famous sights in London and attending several good musicals.

Many a soldier on leave from the trenches, particularly British soldiers, had found the proximity to London hard to believe. Just 70 miles from terrible trench life was "the rich plush of London theater seats and the perfume, alcohol, and cigar smoke of the Café Royal."[18] Away from the trenches, apparently life went on as usual so that soldiers on leave in London often felt estranged and even angered by uncomprehending civilians. However, civilians could not know the terrible conditions of the front because soldiers tended to avoid the truth in the letters they wrote to loved ones at home. If a soldier did write about terrible combat conditions, the words were excised by company officers, who were assigned duties as censors for outgoing mail.[19]

Not all fighting came to an end on November 11. News of the armistice reached Germany's colony in Africa slowly. Thus, General Paul Emil von Lettow-Vorbeck in German East Africa continued to fight until he learned, on November 23, of Germany's surrender. He was the last German commander to cease fighting in the war.[20]

While Cpl. Truesdell was on leave in London, his regiment moved to a new location southwest of Paris. On November 24, the 107th left the towns near Amiens where they had billeted and entrained in Corbie for an overnight ride southward to the area of Le Mans.[21] Thus, when Cpl. Truesdell returned from his leave at the end of November, he had to find his regiment in its new location.

Cpl. Truesdell, like many other soldiers in the 27th Division, was hoping for an imminent return to the United States, but that was not to be. He does express a mild desire to have been in the Army of Occupation, but going home wins out. He tells his parents, "It's a wonderful experience for a fellow if he goes into Germany—I kind of wish we had gone and yet—it's 50/50 for I want to come home toute suit." The American occupation troops knew they would not be returning home any time soon and, as occupation soldiers with responsibilities for maintaining peace, entered Germany on December 1.[22]

Working on a lasting peace was of course the responsibility of leaders of the U.S. and its allies. Accordingly, on December 4, President Wilson sailed on the *George Washington* from New York City for France. In so doing, he was setting a precedent for future sitting presidents because he was the first American president to go to Europe while in office.[23] Arriving in Brest on December 13, the *George Washington* "steamed slowly in through a great avenue of battleships from the British, French and American navies," and huge numbers of Bretons hailed the president with "Vive Wilson."[24] However, Wilson soon began to sense the difficulties that lay ahead. The Peace Conference was not scheduled to start until mid-January, but the maneuvering had begun.[25] Later in the month, President and Mrs. Wilson joined Gen. Pershing on Christmas Day and thereafter left for a visit to London to meet with British leaders. Although Wilson was greeted enthusiastically, his initial talks with British leaders were somewhat restrained.[26]

Peace negotiations officially opened on January 18, 1919 at the Quai d'Orsay in Paris.[27] Cpl. Truesdell writes to his parents that he is "watching the news of the Peace Conference with much interest" and tries to get a newspaper every day. One of the many Peace Conference meetings dealt with the establishment of the League of Nations. The work of the Commission on the League of Nations proceeded quickly.[28] After a draft of the covenant had been written, President Wilson sailed back to the United States for a short stay before returning to Paris.[29]

Meanwhile, the 27th Division continued to train during the months directly following the Armistice. Drills and maneuvers continued with a tedious series of reviews and inspections.[30] One such inspection took place on December 30, when Major Gen. O'Ryan and his staff reviewed the four infantry regiments of the 27th in a competition based on appearance and discipline. The winning regiment was the 107th with a score of 90.9. Not only was Major Gen. O'Ryan determined to keep his division fit and disciplined, but he also was attentive to the men in his division who had been wounded. He visited every hospital in which soldiers of the 27th Division were being treated for wounds sustained in the fighting in September and October. He also made it possible for many of those men to rejoin their old unit in the division when they were discharged from the various hospitals in France and England.[31]

Another important inspection took place on January 22, 1919, when Gen. John J. Pershing, Commander-in-Chief of the A.E.F., reviewed the 27th Division.[32] Gen. Pershing, Gen. Read, Gen. O'Ryan, and all their respective staffs slowly walked past each line of the troops—25,000 men, all at attention—spread out in a huge field. "Gen. Pershing inspected every man with an all-apprising look from the top of his steel helmet to the toes of his shoes."[33] Cpl. Truesdell writes about this inspection but reports that, unfortunately, he had to "stay behind" because he was in charge of the Message Center.

While the troops continued to wait for their return to the U.S., French and Belgian civilians whose homes had been along the Western Front made their way back home to learn what remained of their houses, villages, and farms, many of which had been ruined by shelling, tunneling, and trenches. The French government sought reparations from Germany, partly to pay for the massive work of reconstruction. Unexploded shells, grenades, and mines were a particularly serious problem for those trying to return to fields and farmland where there had been combat. "Farmers were often killed when this ordnance exploded."[34] Incredibly, even today someone loses his life while plowing his fields.

The weeks of weary waiting continued. Cpl. Truesdell writes that "it's enough to try the patience of Job—this everlasting, eternal waiting, waiting." But finally, the waiting came to a close, and the 1st and 2nd Battalions of the regiment were shipped in boxcars—larger American-made boxcars—to Brest on February 21, with the 3rd Battalion and Regimental Headquarters following the next day. After a ride of about 24 hours, the men arrived at their destination and marched through the city to a field beyond the old Pontanezen Barracks, just as they had done when they first arrived in France. However, the field was now a great camp, "a veritable city of tents and barracks." Happily for the doughboys, the stay at Brest was short. On February 25, Regimental Headquarters and the 1st and 2nd Battalions boarded the U.S.S. *Leviathan,* which had once been the German ship *Vaterland*, and sailed for home. The Regiment's 3rd Battalion followed three days later on the Dutch liner *Nieuw Amsterdam*.[35] On March 6, the *Leviathan*, with the 107th Infantry Regiment aboard, steamed into New York harbor.[36] At last Cpl. Truesdell and other members of his regiment were back in the U.S. Upon arriving at Hoboken, N.J. and docking at a government pier, the men went by ferry to Weehawken and then marched to trains bound for Camp Merritt at Tenafly, N.J. At Camp Merritt, the doughboys were thoroughly deloused. Uniforms were steamed in huge boilers while each man took a medical bath to be rid of any remaining lice.[37]

On March 24, the 107th left Camp Merritt and went by ferry to the foot of West 23rd Street. From a public playground at 30th Street and Tenth Avenue, where the men had assembled, the Regiment marched up Fifth Avenue and across 67th Street to the Seventh Regiment Armory on Park Avenue where they spent the night. The official parade of the entire 27th Division took place the following day. Early in the morning of March 25, 1919, the Regiment marched to Washington Square and lined up on a side street for the divisional parade to begin at 10 o'clock.[38] The day was beautiful with clear blue sky, and the five-mile parade route along Fifth Avenue from Washington Square to 110th

Street was decorated with thousands of flags, banners, and pennants.[39] Millions of people lined Fifth Avenue and "kept up a constant roar of cheering."[40] Cpl. Truesdell writes, "The day was magnificent and, folks, you never have seen such a gigantic crowd and decorations galore."[41] Tickets to welcome-home dinners at many of the large hotels and restaurants were made available to the division's men who wanted them, and leave for the night was also given to those who wished to be "free" for the evening. The next morning, the men who had been replacements and who had come from other parts of the country were returned to Camp Merritt, then to camps near their homes, and later demobilized. The remaining members of the 107th were taken, by ferry and train, to Camp Upton at Yaphank, Long Island, where they prepared for demobilization.[42]

Letter #16 written abroad and sent from the continent
Letter received Oct. 30ᵗʰ 1918

Wed., Oct. 9, 1918

Dear Folks,

Just a short note this time. Since writing you Letter #15, I received orders to go to Chattillon-sur-Seine for a week's course in gas school, along with a sergeant and two other corporals from our regiment. So Monday we left the regiment, went to a replacement camp nearby and after spending a night there, started on our way. Rode part way with some Australians in side-door Pullmans and at Amiens, got in a second-class passenger coach. Arrived in Paris, where I now am, last evening, stayed overnight, sleeping in a regular honest-to-goodness bed and having some "bon" meals.

Chattillon-sur-Seine, Friday, Oct 11

Regulations are pretty strict for the fellows who want to stay in Paris. We arrived at 7 o'clock in the evening and stayed until noon the next day. The Provost Marshal didn't want us to stop at all, but go right out again at 8 that evening. Of course, it's very easy for men coming in to overstay and be A.W.O.L. and we could understand that all right. But we were given eight days to get here and it only took us three days so we hoped we might be able to stay in Paris for a couple of days. Well, we got a look around anyway and I rode in the subway, by heck. It is a beautiful city—somewhat like New York, but no high buildings. Lots of taxis around and surface-cars. Cafes aplenty with their little tables out in front. We had a good meal on our arrival at a Red Cross canteen which was absolutely free. Then Sgt. Farrington (Sgt. Roswell Farrington of Co E—lives in New York City), a good scout, and I went to a French play for the fun of it. Of course we couldn't understand what was said but the characters were funny and the music and songs good—it was evidently a musical comedy—and we enjoyed it, together with looking at the audience which was composed entirely of French people including many French soldiers. Then we found a good comfortable-looking hotel and had a wonderful snooze. The next morning we found a restaurant where we had real American oatmeal and ham and eggs. After walking around a bit, it was time to catch the noon train to Troyes. Arrived there about five and found that on account of very strict regulations, no soldiers were allowed out of the station. Result—we slept on benches in the waiting room that night—not however before we ate a very delicious dinner in the station restaurant, consisting of soup, roast beef and beans, bread and grapes for dessert. The next morning, after getting a cup of hot water from the French fireman on a locomotive and shaving and then having a bite to eat, we entrained, via 1ˢᵗ class accommodations to Chattillon-sur-Seine, arriving about 11 o'clock. Reported to gas school commandant, had mess, had a hot shower bath, got a new uniform and went to the barracks with our packs. Bunks are two-deckers, made of wood with straw ticks on them—very comfortable. Farrington and I went to the movies at the Y.M. in the evening. This morning we slept until eight-thirty, for we don't have to start the school until next Sunday or Monday and therefore have nothing to do until then except to amuse ourselves and see the town. This morning, I am devoting to writing letters—hence this book.

This is a very pretty place—of moderate size—lots of pretty streets and quaint alleys and lanes and pleasant little parks with streams and ponds. Of course I haven't had much time to look around yet. Will write you more about it later. The gas course starts next week and continues till Saturday. Then I expect we will rejoin our regiment. It is a wonderful vacation getting back into such beautiful country again. The other boys in our party are Cpl. Strong from Co. C and Cpl. Engle from Co. K. both agreeable chaps. The war news certainly does look good, altho President Wilson will not talk business until Germany has retired from France and Belgium, for our troops are steadily driving the Germans back and giving them no rest. The morning after the night we stayed at the replacement camp after leaving our regiment, we heard a barrage and heard that our boys were going over again but

don't know for sure. Some outfit hopped over anyway from the sound
of the barrage.

Before leaving the regiment, Bill Jude obliged me by cashing a
check for $40. I found upon looking over my check book that I had a
balance of around $125. in the Peoples Trust Co. yet. We hadn't been
paid for September so I had to get some money somewhere for I didn't
want to make this trip without some "dough." Bill fixed me up fine. By
the way, the address of the concern he is interested in is—

> The Hudson Rubber Co.
> 1906 Broadway
> 63 and 64 St.
> New York City

of which Mr. C.L. Tilley is the manager. Bill says to call in and see Mr.
Tilley who will be very glad to see you. Bill's folks live a little way out
of New York and he said you probably wouldn't want his home address.

Tod was well when I left and I expect he'll be the same when I
return.

Mail came in, in great quantities before I left the regiment and
besides, many Presses and Republicans. I received,

> Father—Sept 5
>   "   " 5
>   "   " 11
>   "   " 12
>   "   " 16
> Mother   " 16

Thanks for your congratulations on my being made corporal.
Don't feel any different than I did before—the cooties bite me just the
same—by the way—here is a joke about cooties I just heard—one
of the boys said he never understood until now why Napoleon always
stood with his hand under his coat.

Please tell Henry Hopkins I received his good letter and was mighty glad to hear that he is recovering in nice shape. Tell him, I have at last been able to step off a train and gazing about, say — <u>So this is Paris</u>. Also please give him and the people in the office as much news as possible from this letter.

I am writing this in the Y.M. here. There is a nice place to write and also a canteen where you can buy American tobacco, cigts, cigars, gum, hot chocolate, sandwiches, etc. besides innumerable other little necessities in the way of toilet articles etc.

Well, I will write again in two or three days. Love to all of you.

Bob

PS I enclose subway ticket, theatre ticket and pass that I got in Paris.

Letter #17 written abroad and sent from the continent
Letter postmarked US Army Postal Service, Oct. 24, 1918, 4 PM
Envelope marked "Passed by Base Censor 15"

Sunday, Oct. 20, 1918
<u>Paris</u>, <u>France</u>

Dear Folks,

Well, I had planned to write you again before I left Chattillon-sur-Seine but found that school took all my time. We rose each morning at 5:30, washed if we were lucky to have time and down to school. We slept in barracks up on the hill above the town. Had breakfast at six and started school at 7. At 11:45 we finished for the morning and fell in for mess. At one o'clock we fell in again and worked and heard lectures till 4:30. We then had until 5:40 to do <u>just</u> what we wanted to — which wasn't much. At the latter time we fell in for mess and then from 7-9 in the evening we were supposed to study. But after such strenuous days most of us went to bed for we were pretty sleepy. It was a course for N.C.O.s to take who weren't expected to be Gas N.C.O.s — ie — who drill the company in adjusting gas masks, who inspect them etc. Since

I am a Signalman, I don't expect there'll be much more to it, but at least it was a change and I have seen Paris. The food was "rotten," and the hours so long and the school so tedious that I am glad to be thru with it and on my way back to the company. I am at present in Paris and had a fine nights rest in a good bed. We will undoubtedly start on some time today to find the company.

I did get time to do one thing while in Chattillon-sur-Seine, which I imagine will please you. I had my picture taken. I will send you one as soon as I get back to the company for there wasn't time for them to be finished before I left, so I had them mailed to me to the company. They will be there when I get back.

Expect I will find some mail from you when I return to the company. The weather is somewhat rainy here and was most all the week at school but didn't bother us very much.

Will write again soon. With love—

Bob

**Letter #18 written abroad and sent from the continent
Letter postmarked Army P.O. 3, Oct. 27, 1918
Received Nov. 25th, 1918**

Wed., Oct. 23, 1918

Dear Folks,

Letter #17 was mailed from Paris and I forgot to number it. I wrote it last Sunday.

I forgot to tell you about the concert which the Y.M.C.A. arranged to have given for us while we were at gas school. There was a company of French musicians who have traveled extensively throughout France including Paris. The company included a pianist, violinist, cellist and vocalist—mezzo-soprano. They were fine. The man who played the cello has been in the States, sent there by the French government, and has played in the Metropolitan Opera House in New York.

Well, we did several other interesting things after I wrote you from

Paris on Sunday morning. Sunday isn't much different from any other day in Paris and as we only had that one day to spend there, we had to make the best of it. We transgressed by going to the "Follies Bergere" which was very much like the Hippodrome. Between the lobby and the theatre there is an immense big room filled with little tables and chairs where one can buy all kinds of drinks. Around the edge is a wide balcony where one can promenade and watch the crowd below and listen to a pippin of a jazz band which plays before the show and during the intermission. We had a little box for four in the front of the balcony. The show was fine, the scenic effects and costumes were fine and the music full of "pep." The actors and chorus were English and American and most of the talking was done in English. We certainly enjoyed ourselves immensely. Again we slept in a regular bed. We left on Monday morning and came up to this reinforcement camp from which we will be sent back to our regiment which is in this vicinity, in a few days. I forgot to tell you about the parade I saw Sunday afternoon. It was given by the class of 1920 French youths in celebration of the French soil recently won back. It was most interesting as there were many different troops marching and lots of music.

I am anxious to get back to the company and see Tod and find out what the casualties have been in the stunts I have missed while I have been away to school. Also to get my mail for there must be quite a bit as it has been nearly three weeks since I left. And then there is my September pay, too. As I told you, Bill Jude cashed a check on the Peoples Trust Co. for me before I started for school. It was for $40. but that is about gone, for besides stopping in Paris, I spent some in Chattillon-sur-Seine for grapes and apples which one doesn't get very often and other nick-nacks, as cigars etc.

Well, there isn't much more news. Will write as soon as I get back to the company. With love from

Bob

Letter #19 written abroad and sent from the continent
Letter postmarked Field Post Office, Oct. 30, 1918
Received Nov. 29th 1918

Monday, Oct. 28, 1918

Dear Folks,

Back again with the regiment and my company. Left the reinforcement camp from which I wrote Letter #18, last Saturday morning and after a train ride of four or five hours, detrained near the regiment which was just coming out of the lines. We had to hike about three hours to find them and arrived in this small village where we are [Glisy] about 10 o'clock in the evening. The town is in pretty fair shape and the civilians are beginning to move back in. We have a good billet—an old French house. I am sitting on a home made cot I made of old boards and canvas and burlap. On the other side of the room about 25 or 30 feet away is a tremendous fireplace—the regular French style—in which there is a nice fire burning. The wall paper is peeling off, a few panes of glass are broken in the window and door and they are covered with tar paper and burlap, so we are quite comfortable. The nights are fairly cool and it gets dark about 5:30. This is really a pretty "cushy" billet, in fact so good that the billeting sergeant has been around trying to put us out but so far we have talked him out of it. There isn't much in the town—one store which has not much of anything in stock. But we can get passes for a day to go to Amiens so we can get some things there. Am going to try to get down in a few days.

I found Tod feeling pretty well except for a cold which has settled in his eyes. However he is getting along well—has some eyewash he is using. Most all the fellows have colds due partially to getting some gas and also to sleeping on wet ground in the rain when they were up in the line. You see after our Sept. 29 stunt on the Hindenburg line of which I wrote you and our coming out for a short rest, at which time I left to go to gas school, the regiment went back in again and there were more casualties until now our regiment is pretty small. I missed this trick and I guess I missed no vacation. Some of the boys were gassed and most all have colds or coughs. I have a slight cold which I got down at school but it is improving rapidly. It seems pretty tough to see our division shot to pieces so—but it's in the game of war I suppose and I count myself fortunate to be on hand in good health. We are getting a bunch of replacement troops in to fill us up again but I believe it will be some little time before we go into the line again.

I want a new picture of Ed for my "album"—in his new uniform. Do you get me, Ed? It takes a month for this letter to get across and another month for the picture to come back. That's long enough to wait. Don't make me keep asking for it, but have it taken right away. About 4" by 6"—is the size. I had mine taken while at school and just as soon as they arrive by mail, I will send you one.

Haven't got our pay for September yet. It looks as tho we will get two months pay at one time for it's most time to get October pay.

I enclose my Christmas package coupon. They have just been given out and somewhat late, too, I think for I understand that your package must be in at the post office by Nov. 20, however I hope the P.O. will accept it if you do present it a few days late. The coupon must be pasted on the package. Put in some good home-made fudge or hard candy if you can, a few Ramesis cigts, sweet chocolate, gum, money (U.S. in bills, Amer. Xpress Co money order), one pair of socks, a helmet, a box of Hess candy—any of the above will be most acceptable. It's hard to think just what to send me. I guess a little money is as good as anything.

War news is good. We're driving Jerry back every day. Peace talk doesn't seem to bring much results as yet.

Received nine letters when I returned here. More mail in and will probably get more in a day or so. Letters received as follows:

> Mother—Sept. 23
> Ede—   "   24
> Father—   "   25
> Ed—   "   25

"—   " 27
Ede—   " 30
Mother— " 30
Orra & Francis Summers—Sept 30
Eliz. Spaulding—Oct. 1

The picture from the NY Times which Mother sent me does
look like me but it is not for I don't remember of ever seeing the map.
You must have had a very pleasant visit with Mr. DuBois. As I said, I
can use one pair of socks, but I am pretty well fixed on them. I can't
carry too many pairs on my back, you know. Tod gave me a sleeveless sweater and the Red Cross have just sent the regiment five or six
gross which will be given out soon. We will be issued heavy underwear
soon. Am well fixed for clothes now as I got a new uniform at school.
Have a good overcoat and the pair of gloves I bought when I was home
on my furlough from Camp W. last February. As for money, it is always
acceptable. As we haven't yet received our September pay, I am out but
Bill Jude has lent me some and will lend me more if I need it.

Father wants more particulars about my experiences in the
trenches. Well, I wrote more fully about the Sept 29 stunt than I did
about our time in Flanders. I guess he has enough dope on it now. It's
work, work, work for us on our wires, visual and [other] means of
signaling with not much sleep and cold food mostly. Wondering when
a shell may get you, ducking when you hear one whistling your way,
getting up and going on, smelling gas, putting on your mask which
gets most uncomfortable after [a] while, seeing the dead lying about
and the wounded coming back, hearing the machine gun bullets
whizzing thru the air and desolation everywhere. I was standing in
the trench just outside the Signal HQ dugout when an H.E. landed
fairly close and threw up a big bunch of earth. I had come up for a
minute and didn't have on my helmet. I ducked when I heard the
shell coming and after it exploded straightened right up again, looked
around and said, "Well, I guess it's all over but the shouting" when
"blingo" down comes a big hunk of dirt on my crown. It was funny for

I hollered just a little too soon. Haven't seen anything of our divisional artillery or ammunition train or sanitary train. Wrote Bud Sheak the other day. Also Bob Harris. Yes, I see a good deal of the Tommies as our division is attached to the 4th British Army. They are pretty good fellows but do not seem to be quite as well thought of as fighters as do the French, Australians, New Zealanders. Yes, I have seen lots of Jerry prisoners, but mostly at a distance. There is a prison camp right here of about 500. The country where we have been fighting is all shot "to hell"—to speak most plainly. One can hardly realize what it looks like unless one sees it. You wouldn't know that some towns had ever been in existence—not a brick left standing and shell holes everywhere—trees, nothing left of them except a bit of trunk. You ask whether any men in our company have been wounded. I can tell you about the Signal Platoon. Our full strength is 76. Our present strength is 32. This 44 includes all casualties, dead, wounded, missing in action. I forgot to mention that I received 17 papers yesterday—Presses and Republicans dated from Aug 20th to Sept 25. Very welcome, they were. Ede's letters were very interesting with its news. So were Ed's. Sorry to hear about Bob Harris but expect he'll come out OK. Give my love to Grandma T. and Aunt S. Also to Madamoselle Agnes. Stay home, Ede, and do your work there. "Oh Lord, send me some stuffed dates and a cake." I don't know how I'll act when I get home. I think I'll most always be on the mess line for seconds. The roll of honor Mother sent me from the church was most interesting. Thank you. Give my kindest regards to old Mrs. Norton.

Eliz. Spaulding wrote me a nice letter and enclosed a few sticks of gum in it. I've heard of the boys getting a bar of sweet chocolate inside a package of newspapers or magazines, too. She also enclosed a snapshot of Father which she took a couple of years ago at the fair. And it looked almighty good to me, dad. I'd give most anything to see you for a while. Orra & Frances sent me a letter full of news from the Forks. Always glad to hear from them.

I enclose a pass I got in Paris. Also a movie ticket and my boat ticket which I have carried around for the last six months.

Don't forget to send me a 1919 calendar all on one card about the size of a playing card.

By the way, if you can put in a pack of playing cards in my Xmas box, do it please.

Love to all. Will write again soon.

Bob

Haven't received my pictures yet. Will send you one just as soon as they come.

Letter #20 written abroad and sent from the continent
Letter postmarked Recd from Army, Bordeaux, Nov. 6, 1918, 6 PM
Received Nov. 25ᵗʰ 1918

Letter #20 was written on the back of the stationery of a letter Robert Truesdell had just received from his mother. The letter was written by his "mother," who was, as his biological mother's sister, also his aunt and who became his stepmother. Because his biological mother, Aline Root Truesdell, had died when he was 4 years old, Robert, the youngest of three children not much more than a year apart, said he could not remember her and thus called his stepmother, Lillian Root Truesdell, "Mother" because she had, at the request of his father, Edwin Summers Truesdell, Sr., taken on the role of mother for the three very young children in the family. Lillian became Edwin's second wife. This is the letter:

100 Murray Street
Sunday P.M. 6/10/18
[Oct. 6, 1918]

Dearest Bobby:

Since my last letter, written last Sunday, the 29ᵗʰ Sept. (your mother's birthday) we hear that your Division was engaged that day in very hard fighting, and more or less, this past week. No reports have been sent out yet from Washington, and of course, we are very anxious, but hoping for the best. Your last letter (written Sept 6th, No. 11) reached us on Sept. 27th, and I sent it on to Edwin [Jr.] who still has it. We had great news from him this last week. He has transferred from Edgewood to the "Gas and Flame" and is awaiting orders to go to Camp Sherman, at Chillicothe, Ohio, where they will train a regiment for service "overseas." Washington sent a call to Edgewood for ten 2nd Lieuts. to volunteer for that service. Edwin was accepted. He thinks he should be in active service. He thinks they will be sent over after from six weeks to two months' training. We hoped he was more contented since he got his commission, but I can see his point of view, and I cannot blame him, though it is hard to let both our boys, all we have, go over there. But the cause is great, Robert, you know that, by this time, better than we do, even. Though it is an awful sacrifice, it must be gone through with. We can't go back now. These devils must not be let to rule the world—but it is hard.

Just heard that Mr. Hotchkiss has received a telegram from Edgewood that Edgar is very sick. Father has gone up to the train to see Mr. H. off. He left at once, and is very anxious about Edgar. Don't know what the trouble is, though there are about a thousand cases of Spanish influenza there, it is said. You know there is an epidemic of it here in some parts of the country, and in many of the camps. It has caused many deaths. I do hope poor Edgar is not awfully sick. I am sorry for them, they have had so many operations etc. in the family this last summer.

Saw Paul Titchener on the way to church this morning. He is here for his grandfather's funeral. Going back tonight. He enquired all about you. Edwin saw him in Washington last week when Edwin was sent for to be interviewed in regard to his transfer. Paul said Edwin was looking fine. Well, my dear dear Bobby, we shall be anxiously waiting to hear from you. You cannot realize our feelings, but you surely know we love you and are praying for you.

Faithfully,
Mother

And now, Letter #20:

Tuesday, Oct. 29, 1918

Dear Folks,

Paper is a bit scarce tonight so will write back on one of Mother's letters, just received tonight—good service—Oct. 6 to 29—about three weeks.

Wrote you yesterday—Letter #19—and dated it the 29th I guess—a mistake. But having received 18 more papers and 13 more letters, thought I had better keep up on my correspondence. More mail tomorrow, too.

First I was to say that thru an error Stuart Donley was reported "dead from wounds." I wrote you about it and then afterwards found that it was an error and that he is in a hospital getting along O.K. Am sorry I misinformed you but it was given to me as official information. I am glad that he is coming out of it O.K.

Next—about Ed. I understand how he feels—but Lordy, when he gets over here, that will be something more for me to worry over. I don't worry over myself. I hope to come out O.K. and I must take things as they come but I do hate to think of Ed over here for I know what a hell it is, if he gets into the fighting. However we will just have to pray for the best and keep smiling. Have a new job for a while. Have to go to the ration dump every day to draw the rations for the HQ Co. A "cushy" job as it relieves me of all the other duties.

Am sitting here on my bunk with a candle stuck in an old wine bottle, for a light. It's a great life if you don't weaken.

Tod Mulford had a letter from Art Gale tonight, who is a sgt major in the 1st Pioneer Infantry, same as Bob Harris. He writes that he don't think that Bob had to be operated on.

Letters received as follows:

Ede—	Sept 17
Father—	" 17
Father—	" 18
Father—	" 20

Father—   "   23
Father—   "   28
Mother—Oct. 6
Mary McM—Sept 10
Frank and Ethel Summers—Sept 18
Joe V.—Sept 18
Aunt Nell—Sept 27
Myron Kipp—Sept 27
Bill Hones—Sept 23

Think I still have some more mail of yours coming dated around the first part of September as Ede mentions some pictures that I haven't received as yet. As I was away for three weeks, and the regiment in the line, the mail is a bit mixed up. Hope Ede's pictures get here. Didn't hear anything about King George visiting us. Don't worry too much about my being in the "mud and cold and lice," Father. Of course when we are in the trenches we get a dose but we're not in the trenches all the time. When we're out, we're fairly clean. (My last bath was two weeks ago last Thursday—down at school—time for another one, eh?)

You guessed pretty well where we were on Sept. 29. Our boys went over the top on Sunday the 29th on the St. Quentin Cambrai front. We were hard at it on my own mother's birthday. Sunday doesn't mean so much over here in the Army—of course we have services if it's possible. The money you are sending will come in quite handy. If you wish, I can mail you a check for it for I still have a balance in the Peoples Trust Co. I will have plenty of money, for we are still waiting for September pay and October is also due. That will bring me about $66.00. Things are pretty high over here, but a little something out of the ordinary does taste good now and then.

Tell Aunt Nell that I did receive all her letters and that I mentioned it in my letters to you. I have also written her. Will write her again soon. Can't get any paper for a day or two. Mary McMahon wrote me a fine letter as did Joe and they were most welcome. I shall answer as soon as possible. It's pretty hard to tend to so much correspondence. Myron Kipp sent me one of his store papers and a note. Still at it in Cal.

Well, it's after ten and taps, must stop and go to bed. Love to all.

Bob

Letter #21 written abroad and sent from the continent
Letter postmarked Recd from Army, date unclear
Envelope marked "Passed by Censor No. 5086"
Received Nov. 25ᵗʰ 1918

Sat., Nov. 2, 1918

Dear Folks,

A short one this time as there isn't very much to talk about.

"Beaucoup" mail coming in. Received four more letters last evening as follows,

Father—Oct 4
Ed—   " 12 <u>good</u> <u>service</u>—from Camp Sherman
Mother— " 13 good service—18 days

I forgot to say much about what Father wrote in regard to sending me $50. I think I wrote that I still had a balance in the Peoples Trust and he could deduct said $50. from it—or if he wishes it on me gratis, it will do very nicely. I spoke about my money for a Xmas present. The above $50. would naturally more than fill the bill so don't think any more about a gift of money. I will feel O.K. if you wish to take the 50. out of my balance—just as long as I get the money. I wrote you that Bill Jude cashed a check of $40. for me to take on my trip to gas school—and Paris.

I sometimes think that you are worrying about me more than necessary and also more than I deserve. Of course you can't tell just when to worry and when not to. At present I am living "the life of Riley," so to speak. Have a comfortable home-made cot, sleep well, am well, eat three wholesome (tho not luxurious) meals per day upon which I seem to

thrive wonderfully well and do a small amount of work for we are getting
a good rest after our hard work. I hardly got started on my job going
to the ration dump each day for Hdqrs Co. rations when I was changed
and am now in charge of all the Signal property of our Signal Platoon.
Good job. I am looking and feeling fine. If you could see me, you would
say that I look no different than if I were at home. I expect to receive
those pictures I had taken in Chattillon-sur-Seine in a day or two and will
mail you one just as soon as they come. Then you see for yourselves.

There are two things which are quite plentiful here in
France—pommes-de-terre fri (otherwise known as French fried potatoes or chips) and "cooties." You can get some chips and eggs most
anywhere and <u>they</u> <u>are</u> <u>good</u>. There is one place where you can get
chips here and it's crowded most of the time. I help crowd it every
now and then, for "chips" are a nice change from "corn-willy" and
"McConnauchie"—the latter a British ration containing meat and vegetables and put up in tins. In regard to "cooties," I thought I was free
from them but while hunting this PM, I bagged a few. It seems impossible to get rid of them entirely. It is hardly to be wondered at when
you stop to think that I haven't had a decent bath since I've been over
here and have slept in every kind of place.

I am also in charge of the Signal Platoon mail now. Some in tonight
and I will get it in the morning. I get my share of it, all right—so
there'll probably be some for me.

The war news looks very good, doesn't it? Today's "Daily Mail"
tells of the Turks' absolute surrender and of Austria's near approach
to it. It looks as tho the Germans will have to give in, pretty soon. "The
sooner, the quicker" for me.

I'm over with Tod and Bill Jude in their billet tonight. They have a
good one with a big fireplace in it and a nice fire going. The days are
getting pretty short now. It gets dark about 5 or 5:30 so the days seem
quite short. It isn't very cold at night, tho—a little cool.

Our division is now starting to give seven-day leaves to the men.
Eight men from the regiment can go every day. I don't know what the name
of the leave area is. I shan't try to get one until I find out about Ed's

coming over. Maybe he and I can spend Xmas or New Years together.

Haven't got our pay for September or October yet. Will probably be getting both months together in a few days.

Ed's letter was short—just gave me his address and a bit of news. Will write him tomorrow. Ed's and Mother's letters certainly made good time—about 18 days to get across. That's the best yet. There is quite a lot of Spanish "flu" over here but so far I have escaped it. Hope all of you keep well. Take good care of yourselves. You can do it much easier and better than I can.

This was going to be a short letter. It has developed into a book. Tod sends his best. My love to all of you and best regards to my friends.

Your young and sprightly son,
Bob

Letter # 22 written abroad and sent from the continent
Letter postmarked Field Post Office, date unclear
Received Nov. 26th 1918

Wed., Nov. 6, 1918

Dear Folks,

My pictures came at last and I enclose one. How do you like the grin? I will send one or two more at different times in a few days so you will be sure and get one.

Not much news except that we got paid last night for September and I suppose we'll get our October pay in a week or ten days.

Have two more letters as follows –

      Father—Oct 7
      Ede—   " 10

Father, your many words of love and advice are as dear to me as anything in the world. Just sit tight, don't worry any more than you have to and I'll soon be home again, safe and sound, and we'll figure out how the war might have been brought to a close much sooner if we could have had a word in.

I'm glad you're not forgetting me, Ede, on the pictures. I'm waiting for that Xmas surprise.

Reading material is somewhat scarce. Could you send me a Youth's Companion and a McClures or American now and then? Once in three or four weeks? The postal authorities allow it. I like to read a little light fiction once in a while.

Joe Valentine wrote me that he had to register. What other of our boys had to and what are the possibilities of their being called?

Will close for this time.

With love

Bob

Letter #23 written abroad and sent from the continent
Letter postmarked Recd from Army, Nov. 20, 1918
Received Dec.

Monday, Nov. 11, 1918

Dear Folks,

Still in the same little town, but I don't mind it very much, as it looks as tho the war would be over pretty quick. The news certainly does look fine. The latest we have heard is that the German commission has accepted the terms of Marshall Foch's armistice and that hostilities would stop today. "Tres bon," eh? "Finis la guerre." And also that the Kaiser has abdicated, the Crown Prince has refused to take the throne and that a new government would be formed. I hope it is all true, for if it is, we'll soon be marching down Fifth Avenue again.

Received some mail this morning including one from Mrs. Mary Leverett Gates, who among other things spoke very favorably of Ede's singing at the Civic Club. She also told me that the wedding I took part in, at her house some time ago, is having a most successful run — that she and Mr. Gates are most happy. Other letters as follows:

Cousin Carrie Adams — Oct 13
Father —   " 14 <u>contents missing</u>
Father —   15

Cousin Carrie wrote me a very nice letter and I shall try to write back to her and Mrs. Gates. Father's letter or rather envelope of Oct 14 contained nothing. It had never been sealed by the looks. It was postmarked B., Oct. 14, 8 PM. It was marked "Received without contents at Chelsea Terminal R.P.O."

Have lots of money now. We were paid for October the other day so we have September and October pay almost at the same time. Have about 275 francs or $50. But how the "froggies" (French) do take it away from you. I ate my first banana in France a couple of mornings ago and how much do you suppose I paid for it? One franc and it was a very small one at that. Pears cost 1½ francs a piece — 30 cents is some price for a pear, eh? Eggs cost 12 or 13 cents a piece.

Everybody has plenty of money at present and with the peace talk going and our rest in full swing, quite a lot of the fellows are getting liquored up. I can't see it — It makes me sick. Of course I have drunk some over here, white wine and rarely champagne, but don't worry. I don't drink much of it or very often and when I come home, it's "finis" for me. If you shut your eyes, you'd think you were drinking vinegar sometimes, for that's about what some of the vin blanc tastes like. When Bill and Tod and I have a "feed," we sometimes have a bottle of champagne. Our last feed was about six weeks ago, before we went into the lines.

Tod has gone to the hospital. Nothing alarming in the least, and I wish you would reassure his folks. He has a cold and a slight fever. The cold settled in his eyelids, which became enflamed and swollen. He could receive better and quicker treatment at the hospital, so he went. Understand his eyes are OK — it's just his eyelids and he will soon be back. However he may get a chance at a blighty[43] to England. It would be "tres bon" if he could go, for it would be a dandy trip. He wrote me from the hospital that he was feeling fine.

I enclose another picture. Will send still another in a few days. Am going to try to have some more taken down in Amiens. Want some taken with Bill and Tod, but we have to wait till Tod comes back again.

Have some good heavy winter underwear. Was issued a few days ago. Nights are beginning to be cool and days are short. Hope the war stops pretty quick. Everybody is feeling happy for things look good.

Have received several Presses since I last wrote.

Yours for a mince pie,
Bob

Letter #23 enclosed a copy of a letter of commendation, dated October 22, 1918. The letter of commendation was sent to members of the 27th Division from Major Gen. John F. O'Ryan, commanding officer of the division. It is as follows:

HEADQUARTERS 27TH DIVISION U.S.A.
American E. F., France.

October 22, 1918.

FROM: Commanding General,

TO: Commanding Officer, 107th Infantry, U.S.A.

SUBJECT: Commendation.

1. I write to express my admiration and respect for the valor and endurance of the officers and men of the 107th Infantry, so continuously demonstrated during the past 30 days.

2. Since the great battle for the breaking of the Hindenburg Line, our advance has given opportunity to inspect the defenses of that system. Our attack of September 29th was directed against what was probably the most highly organized system of field defenses ever constructed. In that battle the 107th Infantry attacked on the left half of the divisional sector of 4000 yards, and during its advance had to defend its flank against heavy forces of the enemy operating from VANDHUILLE and holding back the division on our left. In the face of veritable hurricanes of fire from weapons of every calibre and class, the regiment by the leadership of its officers and the gallantry and determination of its men broke the back of the main defense line resistance, and at the same time shattered all counter attacks directed upon its flank.

3. Almost continuously since that time, the division has been fighting and marching, and the 107th Infantry has continued its inspiring record for discipline and cheerful endurance in battle. Lying in shell holes at night, attacking at dawn, fighting all day against the most determined and cunning machine gun resistance supported by artillery - repeating this the following day until the enemy which meant lying in other shell holes and pits in a position of close support - to experience these privations with confidence and cheerfulness unimpaired, requires physical fitness and spirit in superlative degree, and well indeed have you demonstrated their possession.

4. In the ten days of operations in which you played so prominent a part the division forced the crossing of the LE SELLE RIVER, captured BANDIVAL FARM, the town of ARBRE GUERNON and in co-operation with flanking divisions compelled the enemy to retire to the CANAL DE LA SAMBRE. It also captured many hundreds of prisoners, and a great amount of war material. In the operations of the past month the regiment has written some brilliant pages of regimental history. All honor to the memory of those gallant comrades who died in the accomplishment of what was achieved.

John F. O'Ryan

JOHN F. O'RYAN,
Major General.

This is a copy of a letter from Maj. Gen. O'Ryan to our C.O. Each man received one. It may interest you.

RDJ

**Letter #24 written abroad and sent from the continent
Letter postmarked Recd from Army, Bordeaux, Nov. 20, 1918
Envelope marked "Passed by Censor No. 6077"
Received Dec.**

Nov. 13, 1918, Wed. P.M.

Dear Folks,

Well, there isn't a great deal to write about, but the peace news is so
good that I must jot down a line to you. Today's "Daily Mail" says that
the Germans desire an immediate peace, now that the armistice is
signed, as there is a possibility of there being a famine in Germany.
Also that the Kaiser having fled, is interned in Holland, that the report
is current that the Crown Prince has been asassinated and that repub-
lics are being formed in Germany. The terms of the armistice are so
drastic that when they are complied with, it will be about impossible
for Germany to resume hostilities, if she wants to. Everybody is feeling
happy and we are all hoping to be home in a few months. I don't dare
hope how soon it will be.

I will enclose a third post card picture, so you will be sure to get one.

We are now able to get leaves to England, most likely to London,
and I have half a mind to try for one. You get seven days at the leave
area, that is, time taken in traveling is not counted in the seven days. I
have seen quite a lot of France including Paris and should we not come
home by way of England, tho there is quite a strong rumor that we will,
I would feel as tho I had not taken a good chance at seeing more of
Europe, when I now have the opportunity.

Tod is in the hospital and I wouldn't be surprised if he is lucky
enough to get a blighty to England. So I think Bill Jude and I will try
our luck at getting a leave to London. Haven't heard from Tod, except
the once, so far, tho I expect it is hardly time, when he said he was feeling fine. I imagine it will be a short job to cure his eyelids.

Went down to Amiens yesterday afternoon. It was shelled but
not very badly damaged by the Germans and the civilians are now

returning in great numbers and things are quite lively. It had a population of 100,000. Talk about your excitement when the armistice was signed — Amiens was full of drunk civilians and soldiers running and shouting thru the streets, fireworks were shot off and flags everywhere. It's a great time over here.

Will Ed come over, just the same?

Will close for there isn't much news. With love to all

Bob

Letter #25 written abroad and sent from the continen
Letter postmarked Recd from Army, Bordeaux, Nov. 24, 1918 6 PM
Envelope marked "Passed by Censor No. 5105"
Received Dec. 11th 1918

Sunday, Nov. 17, 1918

Dear Folks,

Received two more letters from home yesterday — one from Father dated Oct. 25th and one from Mother dated Oct. 27th. In Father's letter was an Amer. Xpress money-order for $25. of which he had written in a previous letter. Thank you very much. You know it makes me feel a little ashamed to have you sending me money for I get a good bit from the government anyway — I get about $33 now and have about no expenses. Here I am, 24 years old and dad still giving me money. Well, when I get home again you won't have to. And all I use the most of my money for, is to buy extras, such as something to eat, etc. Just now I am having a very "soft" time, getting pretty good eats, having good sleeps and doing only a very limited amount of drill. For heaven's sake, don't worry about warm clothing one minute — it's absolutely unnecessary for you. I have two good suits of heavy issued underwear, a sleeveless sweater which Tod gave me, an issue coat-sweater (British issue and a mighty good one), a big fleece-lined sleeveless leather vest (British issue), an overcoat, plenty of warm socks, good uniform — everything is O.K. "possilutely." Am fixed up in fine shape and the best of it is, that the war is over and we fellows won't have to do any fighting in cold weather. "You should worry"—"Ich Kabibble."

I read in the "Daily Mail" today that the censorship on press, wire and post is abolished so I'll take a chance and tell you that I am in Glisy a small town near Amiens where I have been since I wrote you Letter #19 on Oct. 28. It was here that I joined the regiment upon returning from gas-school and it is here that the regiment has been resting since it came out of the line after our stunt at the end of Sept. and the first two weeks of October.

As I wrote you, I have applied for a leave to London, England along with Bill Jude and I hope to get it in a few days. There are strong rumors around that we will soon move, our destination being London to parade before the King, the 27th and 30th Divisions being the only two American units attached to the British (4th British Army). Now this has given way to another rumor which is to the effect that we are going to Le Manes (think this is the correct way to spell it) which is between St. Nazaire and Brest, on the seacoast. They all point to the beginning of our return towards home and which one to believe, it is hard to decide. It seems probable anyway that the troops which have been in the front lines will be the first to get home and that we will not be called on to do garrison-duty in Germany. However, we don't know. At any rate, the fighting is over, tres bien, finis la guerre. If I get my leave to London (for seven days, excluding traveling time) the $25. Father sent me will come especially handy. I also have about 150 francs left from last month's pay making my total about $55.

There are pretty sure indications that we will move next Tuesday—day after tomorrow but where to, is the mystery. Hope my leave comes thru tomorrow before we move.

Tod is still at the hospital and I have had no further word from him except the one letter of which I wrote you.[44] It is nothing to worry about, in my estimation, for his people—I wouldn't be surprised if he "rang in" in a trip to England. In his letter, he said he was feeling fine, so I guess he's not having a very tough time in the hospital. Hope to hear from him again shortly.

Also had a letter from Ruth Jenkins and one from Orra Summers.

Since this will probably reach you about the 15th or 20th of December, I'll wish you a very Merry Xmas and it will be for both you and me, I think, as the "bloody" war is over, even if the peace terms aren't signed.

A few suggestions to you—the last being most important:

1. Bring the fatted calf in from the pasture in the back yard and tie him handy—by the collar.
2. Start a night shift for Agnes [the Truesdells' cook]—to bake up pies and make chocolate cakes and cookies.
3. Don't worry about your boy who is seeing France via steerage, and feeling A No. 1.
4. Keep well so you will be feeling fit to play in the brass band when the Mayor welcomes Cpl. R.D. Truesdell back home again.

Yours on arrival home, after eliminating the "cooties"—Bob

**Letter #26 written abroad and sent from England
Letter postmarked London WC, Nov. 21, 1918, 3:15 PM
Envelope marked "Examined by L 34"
Received Dec 18th 1918**

Thursday, Nov. 21, 1918

Dear Folks,

Well, here I am in the Y.M.C.A. Eagle Hut on Aldych Street, London. I guess the old boy isn't seeing the world, eh? My leave of seven days came thru in good shape, but Bill Jude's didn't. I expect his will in a day or two and am hoping to meet him here tomorrow or the next day.

I left Glisy (near Amiens—as I wrote you) on Monday, went to Corbie (Division HQ) where I stayed overnight. Tuesday we (about 100 27th Division men) left for Amiens by lorry and took the leave-train for Bologne. Here we stayed Tuesday night in a rest camp. I had a little look around the town Wednesday AM and it is a most interesting place. About 60,000 population, narrow streets, lots of fishermen and sailing

boats down at the waterfront. We left about three o'clock by boat and
had a pleasant trip across the Channel—beautiful day and the water
quiet. Took us about an hour and a half to cross. We landed at Folkstone.
From there it took us until about 9 o'clock to get into London. We slept
in the King's Riding School last night. Fine place, good comfortable
cots with sheets and pillow cases. Got my French money changed into
English and am having a great time trying to learn the value of the different coins. I received Father's letter containing check for $25. and
it surely came just at the right time. You see I have to pay for my own
board and lodging but my transportation over here and return is taken
care of by the army. I can get a good cot here for the rest of my stay for
six pence a night—very reasonable and there is an excellent restaurant
here where we can buy real pancakes, also a soda fountain, billiard
rooms, reading and writing rooms, lounging rooms, toilets and bath-
rooms. Wonder of wonders—I had a real tub-bath this morning before
breakfast—my first in seven months and it was "tres bon."

Haven't had much opportunity to look around yet, but am going
to take a sight-seeing trip on Saturday and see some of the famous
spots here, such as Westminster Abbey, etc. Also expect to see some
good plays and musical comedies. Have been on the Strand and seen
Trafalgar Square. Am going to see a good musical comedy this PM
called the "Maid of the Mountains."

Our division is going to move the latter part of this week down to
the American sector, I understand. Our review before the King here
is not going to materialize, evidently, but now we are going down
between St. Nazaire and Paris, so rumor says, and as we are not occupation troops it looks as tho we might be on our first lap towards home.
Here's hoping. I will probably rejoin the regiment, therefore, at their
new location next week. I must close and go out to get some dinner.
Will write again soon. With love

Bob

P.S. This is a very poor looking letter. Please excuse it.

RDT

Letter #27 written abroad and sent from England
Letter postmarked London WC, Nov. 25, 1918, 1:15 AM
Received Dec. 13th 1918

Sunday, Nov. 24, 1918

Dear Folks,

Well, I'll tell you a little more about my visit to London. Thursday evening I saw "Box o' Tricks" at the Hippodrome which was considerably like the Hippodrome in New York but not as large a theatre. It was very good. Friday afternoon I went to the Apollo to see "The Soldier Boy." This was a good farce with some bright music and songs. No, I went to see Box o' Tricks on Friday evening—my mistake. Yesterday, I went on a sight-seeing trip and altho it was a somewhat hurried trip, I enjoyed it nevertheless. We first went to see St. Paul's Cathedral. You know this country is so different from America for it is much older and has many old traditions and customs and historical places of much interest. The cathedral was wonderful. I went to church there this morning and there was a boy choir and some fine music. The next place we visited on our S.S. trip was the Tower of London. This also is very old and full of many interesting nooks and corners. We saw where kings and queens were imprisoned in olden days, where they were so often beheaded, where Sir Walter Raleigh was imprisoned. Also the fighting weapons of the old English kings, armor, etc. Next, we had lunch and then to Westminster Abbey where we saw the tombs of many kings and queens and memorials to England's great men and women. The architecture here is also most beautiful with its mosaic work and carved stone and leaded windows of stained glass. I am thinking [of] going there to hear the music this afternoon. We then went to the House of Parliament where we saw the House of Lords and House of Commons. We saw the coat-room where all the lords leave their hats and coats. The racks are numbered and the name of each lord appears above his hook. Kitchener's name was still there as well as other great Englishmen who are now dead. There were some very fine paintings too, such as the death of Nelson on his ship, the meeting of Blucher and Wellington. Our next stop was at the King's Stables where we looked over his horses which of course are fine animals and also saw his coaches among them, the coronation coach, also the harnesses which really are worth seeing. This ended the trip and tho we naturally could have spent a week going over it instead of a day, still I got quite a lot out of it. I have seen London Bridge, Buckingham Palace, and have strolled down the Strand to Trafalgar Square, up Haymarket to Piccadilly Circus and have given the double eye [?] to Leicester Square, so you see my trip has been most interesting and instructive and I still have two days more after today. I expect to see Elsie Jarvis in "Hullo, America" at the Palace and Joseph Coyne in "Going Up" at the Gaiety both of which plays are comedies—I seem to run to comedies, eh? I forgot to tell you that I went to "Chu-Chew-Chow" last evening. This is an oriental musical comedy and you really should have seen the costumes and scenery. They were great and so was the music. There was a fine orchestra.

Bill Jude hasn't turned up yet and so I have been going the rounds mostly by myself, for it doesn't seem to be very easy to pick up another fellow on short notice who has the same standards and principles as I have and who has the same likings. That is the only regrettable thing about my trip. The streets are crowded at night with disreputable women, the same as in Paris and I do wish I could get acquainted with some decent respectable folks. But of course a week is a short time to do much. The Y.M. people are fine. There is a large staff here at the Hut, mostly men, a few nice American girls and they all do their best to be pleasant and helpful to the boys, and they succeed. All sorts of trips are arranged and your time is mapped out if you wish. The English women of which there are a number helping in the Hut are also very pleasant and are surely doing fine work. The rates are very reasonable here—my bed—a nice clean comfortable cot with sheets costs me 9 d. (18 cents) for the whole time I am here & meals cost around a shilling depending on what you have—there are fine shower-baths and lavatories, barber shop, and boot-blacks, billiard and pool tables, reading

and writing rooms, lots of cozy corners with fireplaces, a concert
hall, places to buy toilet articles, candies, smokes and magazines and
plenty of entertainment at all times. The restaurant serves delicious
meals especially so, after being in the army for seventeen months. The
Y.M.C.A. certainly deserves great credit for the work it is doing.

The great criticism I should make of our boys is their everlasting
"hot-air" and I can't blame the English for disliking it. We all know that
the United States of America is a wonderful country of great oppor-
tunities, of immense wealth and resources and a great power but the
English know it too without being told how much better America is
than England and being criticized about the royalty. So many of our
boys have never seen anything like this and have not read much about
it either so they make many thoughtless as well as some thoughtful
remarks and also can't stop telling about the superiority of America
over the world. All we have to do is to show by actions what we can do
and cut out some of the hot-air.

Well, if I write much more, I shall begin to think that I am starting
a book. There is a good concert starting out in the hall and I believe I'll
forego the trip to Westminster Abbey for this afternoon and hear the
orchestra.

There are soldiers here of every race and color, lots of our sailors
as well as soldiers, all taking a look at London, and I, for sure, am
enjoying it to the fullest extent.

Love to all. Will write again short[ly]. With love,

Au revoir

Bob

PS. Have sent you some postcards.

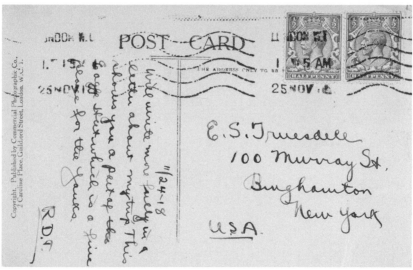

LONDON – ST. PAUL'S CATHEDRAL – West Front

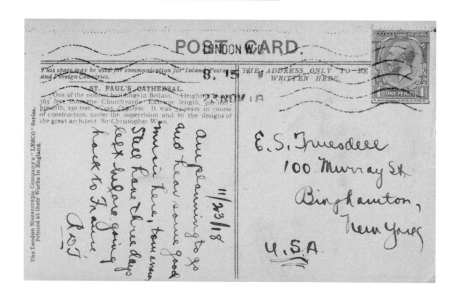

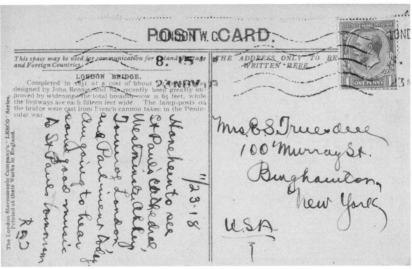

Letter #28 written abroad and sent from England
Letter postmarked Folkestone, Nov. 27, 1918, 11 PM
Envelope marked "Examined by Base Censor"
Received Dec. 23rd 1918

Wednesday, Nov. 27, 1918

Dear Folks,

Well, here I am at Folkestone, having just come from London. My good time is over and this afternoon I take the boat back to Bologne and France. I am writing at a British Y.M. Hut. Have been here taking a look at this town. There isn't much to tell you about it. Just a small place.

My last letter was written Nov. 24. That was Sunday. Mornings didn't count much on my leave as I usually slept till 8:30 or 9 and by the time I had breakfasted, it was too late to do much. Monday afternoon I went to the London Opera House which is now called the Stoll Picture Theatre. They show some very good movies and also have a fine orchestra. In the evening I went to see Joseph Coyne in "Going Up" at the Gaiety. Tuesday evening (last evening) I saw Elsie Jarvis in "Hullo, America." And now I must return to "the wilds"—the day before Thanksgiving and they're going to have turkey and venison at Eagle Hut. Tough luck, eh? Well, I don't mind—I've had a fine time—frittered it away seeing plays and sleeping and seeing London but it certainly was a good "loaf."

If I had known a little more about things, I would have applied to any of the Y. men and gone to a private house, for there are many London people who are opening their homes to the Yanks, taking one or two of them for the week. One of our boys did go and he told me he had had a wonderful time, fine people, very well-to-do, nice home, silk pajamas every night, sleep as long as you wish, dandy breakfast, and so on. They were fine to him and there was a very nice young daughter. "Tres bien." The lady had had a son aged 22, an officer in the Air Force who was killed in 1916, I think, and there was nothing she wouldn't do for the boys. "Live and learn" says I—maybe I'll get another leave to London before I come home. I had a good time but I missed the home environment, altho the Y. was fine.

Bill Jude never showed up so I conclude that his leave didn't come thru.[45]

I expect that I'll find the division further south when I rejoin them. Will write you as soon as I get there.

By the way, have you read about the abolishing of most of the censorship rules? You will notice that I put the company and regiment on the envelope. I am now permitted to do this. Also I can tell you just where I am located and what fights I have been in — in fact everything except statements criticizing the government or Allies or that kind of thing. So I will keep you well informed from now on.

I might tell you that we were first in the line up in Belgium in front of Mt. Kimmel near Dickybush (spelled incorrectly) Lake. Then we moved a bit further south and took part in the big drive on the Hindenburg line near Le Catelet, going over the top on Sunday morning September 29th. We were in the line (St. Quentin — Cambrai front) from September 27 to October 2nd. This is where we had our severest losses. We then had a three or four day rest out of the lines and it was at this time I was ordered to gas school, which saved me from going in the line again with the division which went over the top three or four times more along with the 30th Division, the first two weeks of October. Since that time the division has been resting at Glisy near Amiens, it being this place where I rejoined the regiment upon my return from gas school. I left the regiment at Glisy to go on my leave and expect to find the division down in the American sector somewhere between St. Nazaire and Paris (rumor). At any rate, they are moving or have moved. You see up until this time, we (the 27th and 30th Divisions) have been attached to the 4th British Army but are now detached and moving to the American sector where we have never been. We landed at Brest when we came over, as you probably have figured out long ago coming over on the Susquehanna, an old German boat.

Have you read about Dad's Christmas letter. Well, you might take this for it. Will it do? And every dad is supposed to write his soldier boy a Christmas letter, too. I'll be looking for it. But then I know I'll be getting one anyway whether there were any special arrangements or not. Cheero, righto.

Met a young fellow day before yesterday whose uncle I used to call on in Unadilla, Aitken and Son. His name is Ralph, well I can't think of it now. Anyway he's the first chap I've seen over here whom I used to know in business. He's in the Navy.

Merry Christmas and Happy New Year to all of you. Hope to see you soon. Will probably find some mail from home when I get back to the company. Wish I could have stayed over Thanksgiving in London. But my money is all gone and it wouldn't have been much use. Righto, cheero. Pay day pretty soon.

Love to all.

Bob

Letter #29 written abroad and sent from the continent
Letter postmarked but unclear
Envelope marked "Passed by censor No. 7124"
Received Dec 18th 1918

Friday, Nov. 29, 1918
Rouen, France

Dear Folks,

Well, I'm a step nearer the regiment. Crossed the Channel, coming back to Bologne again, after writing you at Folkestone. Stayed there night before last at a rest camp. Yesterday afternoon we left by train coming here to Rouen arriving at six this morning. Rather tiresome trip altho we traveled third class. Altho yesterday was Thanksgiving Day, I celebrated it no more than any other day. It was quite rainy and foggy. I ate the usual army dinner as did everyone else. Of course they had special doings at the Y. in London as I wrote you and in Paris they had a big time so I read in the "Daily Mail." The visit of King George to Paris was especially appropriate for the Americans as he came on

Thanksgiving Day and there was an immense reception for him.

I understand we leave here tomorrow morning. The name of the district to which we are going is LeMans and as I wrote it is southwest of Paris toward St. Nazaire, so we still have quite a trip to get back to the regiment.

According to the papers, the terms of the armistice are being carried out in proper shape and things continue to look good. I see that the preliminaries of the Peace Conference will soon begin and that President Wilson is expecting to come over the first part of December. There seems to be considerable criticism of his coming over in the States as it is contrary to the general custom that our President does not leave the U.S.A. during his administration. What do you think about it?

I took a walk up the main streets of Rouen this AM. It is a big city but not much different from other French cities. Five big cathedrals.

Well, this is the second time over here I've been broke. Don't worry about it—I'll soon have some money—just as soon as I get back to the company. I was broke when I came back from gas school (and Paris) and now on my return from London I am again strapped. I was foolish not to have saved 20 or 40 francs out of my money to keep until my return to the company. But I didn't, so at present my total wealth is three and half pence. You know it's good experience to find out what it is to have no money and be one of a bunch of dough-boys. Nobody knows you "quite" well enough to lend you any money. But then the situation is far from bad, for being in the Army, you are always furnished with food and lodging and transportation. It's only not being able to buy cigarettes and tobacco and eats and having the feeling that you have no money in your britches.

Well, I am saving the best news till last. The Stars and Stripes, the official newspaper of the American Forces in France which is published each Friday, stated this morning that the 76th, 27th and 30th Divisions would be the first to go home and would soon leave for the States. The 76th is now in St. Nazaire all ready to embark and the 27th and 30th will follow them. So maybe I'll be home for Christmas or New Years, soon after that, anyway. The "Stars and S." praised the 27th and

30th Divisions highly. Altho they did not take part in the big battle of Argonne in the American sector and have never seen that sector, still they broke thru the Hindenburg line near Bellicourt and did great work with the British, for which they have been highly commended. It seems almost too good to be true that we will be home around New Years but it seems to be official.[46]

Well, I must close. There is no more news. With love. Cheero.

Bob

Letter #30 written abroad and sent from the continent
Letter postmarked U.S.Army, M.P.F.S. 702, Dec. 6, 1918, 4 PM
Received Jan. 3rd 1919

Sunday, Dec. 1, 1918

Dear Folks,

Back to the regiment again. Arrived here about six o'clock last night. Everything about the same. Tod isn't back from the hospital yet and I don't understand why we haven't heard from him. Maybe his letters have gone astray. There is a possibility that he may be sent home without coming back to the regiment as we are slated to come home pretty soon.

While the regiment was on its way down here, a wagon fell off a flat car and some mail was lost off. So maybe I'll miss some letters unless the mail is recovered.

I can't understand why the censorship rules aren't altered here the same as they were in London. You know I wrote you about it, having read it as an official announcement in the "Stars and Stripes." Everyone wrote what they wished in London and now I come back here and there is no change in the rules. Well, the change will come here soon, I expect, as the notice was official from G.H.Q. in the "S. and S."

I'll take a chance, anyway and tell you we're located in Connerre near LaMans. It is a nice town and of course has not been touched by shells.

Our important topic of conversation is now—when we are going home and it looks very much like we would be home around Jan. 1ˢᵗ. It's most too good to be true.

The only mail I've received since I got back is one letter from Ruth Safford and three newspapers. May get some more tomorrow.

Monday, Dec. 2

Well, folks, I guess it's a good thing I waited till today to see what mail came in. My share is 19 letters. Fair enough, eh? They are as follows:

Father—	Oct. 28
" —	" 30
Ede—	" 31
Harriette W. -	Nov. 1
Father—	Nov. 2
Walt Hankins—	" 2
Joe V. and Larry O.—	" 2
"Sam" J.—	" 3
Father—	" 4
Mother—	" 4
Father—	" 5
Father—	" 6
Father—	" 8—New York
Mother—	" 9
Father—	" 12
Father—	" 13
Father—	" 14
Father—	" 15
Ford Mulford—	" 20

Believe me, that's a great list of them, isn't it? And they surely were welcome. It's great to get lots of mail.

Father asks whether I have learned to speak much French. No, I haven't, I speak a few phrases. You must understand that altho we <u>are</u>

in France still we have but little time to spare to chat with the French people for we are busy among ourselves. But I hope I may learn to speak and write French later. I like the French people very well. They are much like us. Of course, we have been among the poorer classes and the country people and haven't seen much chance to see the more respectable and well-to-do classes. For that reason, some of us are a little prejudiced. But the poor and uneducated people of America are just the same. If we could stay among the better classes for a while, some of us would soon find our general opinion of the French improved. They're all right.

Thanks for your assurances about my checks. When I left for Paris, Bill Jude gave me a letter to mail, which contained my check which he cashed for me. He was sending it to his friend the manager of the Amer. Xpress Co. who takes care of Bill's account in Paris. In my excitement of visiting Paris, I forgot to mail it until I was about to leave the city, so I asked an M.P. to mail it for me. Evidently he forgot about it and mislaid the letter for Bill's friend has never acknowledged receipt of it. So will you please call at the Peoples Trust and ask them to stop payment on the check if it has not already come thru and somebody gotten away with the money? It is check #88 drawn to the order of William Jude dated Oct. 8 to the amount of $40.00. I enclose another check for same amount in his favor. Will you please mail to his partner, Mr. C.L. Tilley c/o Hudson Rubber Co., 1906 Broadway, NY City and just state the circumstances? Bill and I both thought this would be a little more simple than bothering with putting the check thru Paris, again.

Ede's letter of Oct 31 was full of home news and most interesting.

Hope Aunt Sarah's eyes aren't troubling her much. Give my best to her and Grandma.

It's fine about Ede going down to help Miss Drown. It will be very pleasant for her as well as give her an opportunity to do something to help the boys along. She's been hankering to do something like this, eh? Well, she'll be nicely situated. You must have had a great [time] in N.Y. when you and Ede went down at the time of the armistice. Am glad you went in to see Mr. Tilley as Bill Jude is a fine fellow and also he has been very nice about advancing me money several times.

So Pete and Alma were home. I sent them a card from London and hope to hear from them.

Am sorry I didn't try to cable you that I was O.K. when the armistice was signed so to relieve your mind at once, but to be quite honest, it never occurred to me.

Still have lots of rumors and fairly well-founded reports that we will start for home soon.

Joe Valentine and Larry Olmstead wrote me a fine letter which I was most pleased to get, especially from Larry as he has neglected me somewhat. They also enclosed a money order for $10. as a Xmas present which came in quite handy as I was broke when I landed here from my leave. Also had a letter from Walt Hankins. The boys said something about the rest of the traveling men writing me but haven't received their letter as yet.

Have at last heard from Tod who writes his eyes are about well and that he is feeling fine. He is in a hospital in France—evidently won't go to England for a blighty. Expects to get back with us soon, he says.

I enclose a souvenir for Mother. There are loads of these little handkerchiefs and such over here and some of them are kind of pretty. I'll send [one] to Edith, too and will you forward it to her. They don't amount to much but they're just something to wish you a Merry Xmas. Let me know Ede's address or more likely she'll write me herself.

Must close. With love to all.

Bob

P.S. Stuart Donley has just come back from the hospital, well and healthy as ever. Stop in and tell his mother.

RDT

Letter #31 written abroad and sent from the continent
Letter postmarked U.S. Army unclear, Dec. 11, 1918, 4:30 PM
Envelope marked "Examined by Base Censor"
Received Dec. 30ᵗʰ 1918

Sunday, Dec. 8, 1918

Dear Folks,

No more mail since I wrote #30 letter except some newspapers. These were very interesting, of course, but not so good as letters. The latest one was dated Nov. 2, so I am still waiting to see the Nov. 11 or 12 with its big headlines.

I am enclosing a few postcard views of the town so you'll have an idea how it looks. Explanations on each.

Not much doing this past week. Some drill, guard duty and details and then all over again, the same thing. This morning, I took a detail of eight men down to the R.R. station and unloaded a car of 400 bags of oats for the regiment.

Oh, the important thing which happened this week was Tod's return. He is O.K. again, eyes all well and his slight attack of the "flu" entirely over. We have talked things over "pro and con" and the war is progressing satisfactorily, we have concluded.

The weather is very comfortable here now—a little rain now and then—and no cold spells at all—just cool.

There are so many rumors floating around about our going home very soon and about our staying here for a couple of months yet and about everything in general, that one hardly dares listen to them all. I still believe we may be home soon, altho we have no definite orders to that effect. We'll just have to keep cool and wait, that's all.

Connerré (Sarthe). — Hôtel de Ville

Photo -Edition J. Bouveret Le Mans - Châteaudun

Carte Postale

Tous les pays étrangers n'acceptent pas la correspondance au recto (Se renseigner à la Poste)

CORREPONDANCE   ADRESSE

The town-hall where
the sheriff and constable
hang out. Our regimental
headquarters are located
here.

Connerré. — Rue Nationale"

Photo-Coul. J. Bouveret, Le Mans

Carte Postale

Tous les pays étrangers n'acceptent pas la correspondance au recto.   *(Se renseigner à la poste)*

CORRESPONDANCE

ADRESSE

A view of one of the
"main thoroughfares".
Note the congested traffic.

M

Carte Postale

Tous les pays étrangers n'acceptent pas la correspondance au recto (Se renseigner à la Poste)

CORRESPONDANCE   ADRESSE

Every Wednesday, the
country folk hold a
market on the square. You
can buy anything from
scrub brushes and wooden
shoes to picture post cards
We stand retreat every P.M.
here while the band plays
the national anthem

Sunday Evening [Dec. 8, 1918]

Mail just in. Four letters for me as follows:

Ede—Nov. 15—Atlanta
Father—Nov. 16
Mother—Nov. 18
Al Gilmore—Nov. 18

Ede wrote a most interesting letter about her new work. She
seems to be very much pleased with her job and quite satisfied.
She has already seen several Binghamton boys including Carlton
Cleveland and young Carrington. I think it's good work for her and I'm
pretty sure it's what she's wanted for some time. Will write her at once.

Father's letter was short, just contained the sad news of Alex
Wilson's death and newspaper clipping in regard to it. I tell you,
folks, no honor is too great for the boys who have died on the field
of battle. Any fellow who has been in action and knows what a chap
goes thru—the mental strain, the mastery of self, and moral courage
besides physical courage, the agony of wounds, the dread of death
for we all want to live—can't help but honor a man who has gone all
thru these things and then has given his life. I have seen some pretty
severe action but have been spared some of these things for which I
am most thankful. And it's doubly hard when death comes so near the
end of the war. I thought a good deal about the boys in the front lines
who had to fight right up to the hour of the beginning of the armistice
and who knew all about it. It must have taken more than the ordinary
courage to stick to it until the last minute.

Will you please tell both the Phelpses and the Wilsons how sorry
I am to hear of the death of Jack and Alex and that I know that every
friend of theirs including me holds them in their very highest regard
for giving their lives for such a cause.

Am very sorry to hear of Clarence Hotchkiss' trouble. It's a
strange world—here we are 1,500,000 strong over here—all for the
express purpose of killing Huns—men—and Clarence by accident,

kills one and he is in trouble. Rather a peculiar way for me to look at
it, but one can't help but think of it. Clarence is a good young fellow
and even tho it is proved that it was due to his carelessness, I hope he
doesn't get too severe punishment for the fact that he took a man's life
is enough punishment. Let me know how it turns out.

I was a good deal surprised to hear from Al Gilmore. He wrote a
newsy letter, giving considerable space to describing his efforts, numerous in number, in helping win the war at home. The letter was mimeo-
graphed — I expect he sent out a number reading the same. It's great to
find you can be of so much help in winning the war with a "back area"
job as we call it. Of course this work must be done by someone but why
advertise so much — it's much safer than going over the top.

The terms of the armistice are being carried out pretty satisfactorily according to the papers. The armies are advancing to the Rhine
with no hostile acts toward them. And President Wilson will arrive
in England in a few days to begin the peace parleys. I see England is
going to ask $40,000,000,000 indemnity. France ought to get two or
three times that. I expect it will be March or April before peace is officially declared.

I suppose Ed may be mustered out now most any time. Haven't
heard from him lately and am anxious to hear from him. I suppose
he is disappointed that he didn't get over here, but he didn't miss any
picnic. It's all right if a fellow comes over and gets thru it safely but
every fellow doesn't.

Best regards to all, and love to you. I'm glad your days of worry
are over. It's simply a matter of curbing your impatience, now. It's still
quite difficult to get a bath but at least there are no more whiz-bangs
[shells with a distinctive entry sound]. Cheerio.

Bob

Letter #32 written abroad and sent from the continent
Letter postmarked U.S. Army M.P.E.S., date unclear, 1918
Envelope marked "Base Censor"
Received Jan. 27ᵗʰ 1919

Connerre, France
Monday, Dec. 16, 1918

Dear Folks,

Wrote letter #31 a week ago yesterday and should have written again yesterday at the latest but I was "elected" corporal of the prison guard and was on duty all day so didn't have time to do any writing. We have four prisoners in the regiment and the H.Q. Co. has to furnish the guards.

I received the book of letters [a collection of letters from friends wishing him a merry Christmas] which Edith and Mother invented and, believe me, folks, I can't tell you how much I appreciate it. It was wonderful and I can't thank you enough—especially the pictures I enjoyed. It surely must have taken a lot of time and trouble to do it. I think so much of it that I may send it home again after I have completely digested it, as I may not have a very good place to carry it and I want to keep it always—to look at when I get gray hairs. I sat up until one o'clock Saturday night reading it down at the guard house and all the fellows are anxious to look it over. I could keep telling you how fine it is for a week.

We have had lots of mail lately. Some nearly every other day. Have had a lot of newspapers come, too. Letters as follows:

Father— Nov. 21
Mother— Nov. 24
Father— Nov. 25
  " —   Nov. 26
  " —   Nov. 27
Ed —   Nov. 25 Camp Sherman
Ede —   " 25 Fort McPherson

Eliz. Spaulding
Mr. J.J. Lawrence (church)
Edith Parker (Xmas card)

Glad to get all the letters. I hadn't heard from Ed for about a month. I wrote and jacked him up several days ago. Ede's letter was also interesting—full of her doings and work which she seems to enjoy very much.

Bill Jude was kind enough to cash another check for me amounting to $20. I had used up all I had on my leave to London as I wrote you and I wanted a little extra. That is—he gave me the equivalent of $20. in francs and I hereby authorize you to draw $20. from my account at the bank. Now it happens that a chap in the band wants to send $20. home, so Bill asked me if you would send the check of $20. to this chap's father instead of to Bill at his office in N.Y. and this chap would pay Bill. So please send the $20. check to C.E. Scott, Deposit, N.Y. and draw the money from my account. It saves sending a check across. I know that it is not exactly businesslike for me to write you to draw $20. from my account so if it is not possible to draw the money in that manner, please let me know and I will send you a check. I don't want you to give me the money for you have already sent me "beaucoup."

We had a division manouever last Friday in which the 107th was in support of the 108th in an assimilated attack. It didn't amount to much for us. It was staged over the other side of Montfort where division H.Q. is located and we rode there by lorry.

Bill, Scotty (spoken of, on opposite page), Tod and I had a "tremendous" feed the other night. We have been taking turns treating with a feed. Scotty and Bill had done their turn so I did mine. As Tod has been to the hospital, he has missed a couple months' pay so he is planning on a Xmas dinner for us, for he expects to have his pay by that time. Well, we had soup, salad, chicken, potatoes, celery, peas, bread and butter, tea, jam and cheese. It was "immense" and how we did enjoy it. Then we each had a cigar (Y.M.C.A.) to top it off.

We keep hearing rumors pro and con about leaving for the embarkation port and I still believe we'll see it soon. On the other hand I believe there were definite orders when we first arrived here, to leave for an embarkation port and that they were afterwards cancelled. But the reason of this was the fact that the division paper work was way behind and also that transportation was lacking. I believe that when the paper work is caught up and we get new uniforms (issued tomorrow, I believe) and barracks bags (on the way) we'll be heading (?) for Brest and I think this will be sometime this month. Hope so, anyway.

Our artillery is now down here with us, that is, it is about forty miles from here. I wish it was a bit closer so I could look up Bud and Bill. They are somewhere the other side of LaMans. It is the first time our artillery has been with the division. I believe they have been down on the American sector.

Did I write you that Stuart Donley is back again with us? Wounds are all healed up.

Did you receive the Gas Attack I sent you? It was printed in Paris and it's the first issue since we left the States, I think. It gives you a good idea of our travels.

Had some movies on the square last night. Were pretty good. Also some of the band boys put on a show Saturday PM and evening that was pretty good.

Each division of the A.E.F. is getting a division insignia which is worn on the left sleeve close up to the shoulder. Ours is as follows:

All officers and non-coms will wear them and about 50% of the privates—that is—all privates whom the captain thinks are good soldiers. I presume that everybody will wear them later.

We are now wearing a service stripe on our left sleeve. A gold one below the elbow.

Not much more news. Will write again in a few days. With love.

Bob

Letter #33 written abroad and sent from the continent
Envelope marked "Passed by Base Censor"
Received Jan. 27ᵗʰ 1919

Sunday, Dec. 22, 1918
Connerre, France

Dear Folks,

More mail yesterday as follows:

    Father—Nov. 29
       "   —Nov. 30
    Ed —Nov. 30

I guess rumors were flying around the States more than they were over here about our coming home in a few days—and that's saying a good deal for rumors are thicker than cooties over here. And still we are here. But we don't give up hope—we believe we'll see home by the last of January. We continue to do a little drill each day, lots of details, and manouvers till we can't see straight. I was corporal of the prison guard again on Wednesday & Thursday, four squads of the Signal Platoon including myself had to go to the division railhead at Montfort by lorry, and unload ten days rations for the 54ᵗʰ Brigade. We get this job every now and then. Then on Friday we had more manouvers with about two or three hours of hiking. Yesterday morning was the regular inspection of equipment. Today we have had off.

We are getting an extra uniform issued to us, also our old barracks bags, which we brought over with us and turned in, have arrived.

We are also getting an extra pair of shoes issued to us. Things really point to our coming home before long but just when, nobody knows.

By the way, I just received the November 28th issue of the Republican Herald and was quite surprised to find my picture in it along with quite a line of "bull." I'm better known in Binghamton than I thought. You didn't write anything about putting my picture in.[47] What's the idea?

I saw Lieut. Darling Friday on the manouvers. He is back with the regiment and looks O.K. again. I stopped and had a little chat with him. He said he heard from Ray quite regularly.

Haven't received my Xmas package yet but am looking for it most any day. What do [you] suppose one of the fellows got in his package yesterday? A couple of little ear plugs to put in his ears when he was up near the big guns. I hope you didn't send any thread, soap, tooth-paste, O.D. pills, or iodine in mine.

Glad Ed has made some nice friends. He didn't give me much news in his letter, but the "old skate" enclosed a check for $25. to me for Christmas. It's fine — I'm just wondering whether he's really "flush" enough to send me so much.

We are making preparations to celebrate Christmas in the company the best we can. I hear it's impossible to get turkeys, so we may have chicken and plenty of extras.

I hear we have more manouvers this week — one tomorrow and one next Thursday and Friday. I don't know what the idea is but I guess it's just to keep the boys busy. I'd hate to tell you what I think of them.

Did I tell you we have turned in our English rifles and now have the U.S. Enfields?

Well, folks, I'll be thinking of you on Christmas, of the many merry Christmases you've provided for me in the past and of the many we'll enjoy in the future. I'll try and write you on that day, too. With love

Bob

Letter #34 written abroad and sent from the continent
Letter postmarked U.S. Army M.P.E.S., Jan. 3, 1919, 12 M
Envelope marked "Base Censor"
Received Jan. 27th 1919

Thursday, Dec. 26, 1918

Dear Folks,

Didn't take time, to be honest about it, to write you yesterday, but I
thought of you, nevertheless. I spent my day in the following manner:
got up about 8:30 and hurried down to breakfast. Was lucky enough to
get three pancakes and some prunes—altho I was a bit late. Then Tod
and I got busy on our Christmas dinner which he and I and Bill Jude and
Scotty pulled off at seven in the evening. We bought two chickens, some
celery, and some small oranges at the public market held weekly each
Wednesday AM on the square. Then we bought a can of peas (No. 3 can
cost us 3.50 francs [75 cents]—some price, eh, Father?) at a store and
a can of jam and some cigars at the canteen. Took all these things down
to an estaminet where we have eaten beef steak and pom-de-terre several times and where the Madame consented to cook our dinner for us.
Then we went back up to Tod's billet and played "rummy" for a while. At
2:30, the company had a Xmas dinner consisting of tomato soup, roast
pork, mashed potatoes, salmon salad, bread, coffee, cake, cigars, and a
Y.M. package for each man (besides a barrel of white wine). The Y.M.
package contained a tin of Prince Albert, a pack of Fatimas and a bar of
French sweet chocolate (Chocolat Menier). Just before I sat down with
the boys, I heard my Christmas package had arrived so I beat it up to
my billet to get it. It arrived just at the proper moment. The Rameses
cigarettes and candy were <u>fine</u>, Mother, and I thank you <u>very</u> much. I'll
forgive you for sending the soap and toothpaste. I have to laugh, for in
my letter Sunday, I told you I hoped you wouldn't send any soap, tooth-
paste, buttons or thread or other things which are obtainable here and
which are not quite so acceptable as smokes and candy. But please don't
let your feelings be hurt, for the cigts and candy more than make up

for the soap and toothpaste, which will be, of course, quite useful, and I really do appreciate my Christmas package very much. Well, I took some candy and cigts back down to the boys for the company dinner. And then I found that I was booked for provost (town) guard to go on at 7:30 and our big dinner was coming off at 7 o'clock. Well, I have been on duty for two Sundays past recently so I figured I ought not to be on, on Christmas so I saw the top-sergeant and got off. Then—I sat down and had my dinner altho I didn't eat much as I was saving my appetite for the evening. Some of the boys and an officer or two were lit up pretty well—I'll speak more about booze a little later.

Well, our next feature was a four-reel photo-play at seven o'clock. We first had some soup, then two dandy tender roasted chickens, peas, bread and butter, celery salad, rice pudding with jam, coffee, cottage cheese, oranges and nuts—so you see we had everything from soup to nuts. The Madame who cooked our meal has a mighty cute little girl about eight years old. I gave her an orange and some candy and had a lot of fun with her. She's full of mischief. Well, our party ended at 9:30 with candy and cigarettes and cigars and we went to our billets after a little chat. I hate to tell you what our meal cost us—about $3. a piece, but then, it was worth it—for a Christmas dinner. We had to pay $3. a piece for the chickens.

Saturday A.M. [Dec. 28, 1918]

Well, here I am just finishing up my letter—and in a nice bedroom which Tod and I have hired. We got thinking about it two or three days ago that we would enjoy sleeping in a bed so we found a nice little room with a good bed in it near my billet and we are now sleeping de luxe. There is no objection to our doing this as long as we are on the job for formations. Bill Jude and Scotty have a room nearby. It provides us with a good table to write on and hot water for us to wash with every morning. Distinct advantages, you see—all for the modest sum of one franc per night per man. As I sit here now, I am looking across the table and out thru the door into the other room where Madame and Monsieur are eating their dinner. Madame will cook us anything we bring in to her — more advantages. It hasn't been possible for us to do this before, but we have a <u>little</u> more liberty, now.

Well, in regard to liquor, I was going to say that the army has brought me many new experiences and associations with men whom I naturally wouldn't pick in civil life. However it's good experience and I value it very much. The boys and even some of the officers get drunk now and then. There is plenty of rum and cognac as well as red and white wine to be had and there are men in the army who want it. I believe it's a fine thing that prohibition is coming to the front at home for I've seen too much drunkenness among the boys — no more, understand, than at home probably, but I never had the opportunity to be in those environments at home — I never hung around saloons in Binghamton. Drinking by Americans and drinking by Frenchmen are two different things. Frenchmen have drunk always, more as water than as liquor, for good drinking water isn't very plentiful here. The French drink lots of light red and white wine — with every meal — and they do drink some cognac and rum but it is pretty rare to see a Frenchman drunk. But the Americans go at it for the sole purpose of getting drunk. That's why I hope to see the States dry. Well, I'm not going to tell you I don't drink over here — I do — but very mildly and sparingly. I occasionally drink a little white wine and very occasionally a little champagne — such as at our Christmas dinner, but very rarely and when I come home, I'll be "napoo-finis" — and I don't drink any cognac or rum or other strong liquors. So don't have any misgivings about me, Mother, for your little boy has seen more drinking and "high life" (really low life) over here than he ever saw before and he hasn't changed his opinions at all, thanks to his home environment. — Amen. (P.S. Couldn't drink much champagne if I wanted to, for it costs about $4 or $5 per quart bottle). And Tod thinks the same.

Thursday and yesterday we have sort of manouvers in the mornings and had our afternoons off. We are having all our afternoons off between Christmas and New Years. We are having lots of drill and inspections and I think we'll see home in another month. Things certainly point in that direction.

We had our regular Saturday morning inspection this A.M.

Last Monday we had a manouver and Tuesday, I've forgotten what we did do — so it can't be very important.

I have a list of our movements since our arrival in France and of my own such as to gas school and London, so we'll go all over them when I get home. Also a list of my letters to you, numbered, dated, and place where written.

Tod, as well as most all other fellows who have been to the hospital are short of money, so I have let him have some, to help him out. You see, when a private leaves the company, his service record is sent to a Central Records office and then on to wherever he is. Usually it is waylaid somewhere as in Tod's case and he comes back to the company, but his service record doesn't. So he can't get his pay, for his service record must be here, too. That is the reason for the paybooks — they take the place of a service record and each man carries his own, so wherever he is, he can get his pay. But we were just issued ours a short time ago and Tod can't get his pay book until his service record gets back.

Mail received as follows –

　　"Beaucoup" papers
　　Mother — Dec. 2
　　Father — Dec.2
　　Father — Dec 4
　　Myron Kipp — Dec 2
　　Marsh Williams — Dec 5

I have in front of me, the card Mother enclosed in my Christmas box. Just for a souvenir which has been across to me and back, I'll enclose it.

Marsh wrote that he is now supply sergeant and would have had a chance at a commission if the war had continued. He is in the occupation army, so he writes, and I expect by this time, is on his way to the Rhine. He has been down around Limoges and then to the St Mihiel sector.

Myron Kipp wrote a very nice and interesting letter and enclosed one of his store papers.

The seasons over here are more of a wet and dry variety than cold and hot. We had our first snow-fall on Christmas morning. It was a wet snow and melted almost as soon as it hit the ground. We are getting quite a lot of rain now, in fact our window is wide open here, now, as I write.

I forgot to mention that on Christmas eve, we had a band concert on the square from 8–9, then moving pictures from 9 till 11. Then the Catholic chaplain conducted a midnight mass at 12. We had all day Christmas off.

I am still enjoying my book of Christmas letters which Ede and Mother sent me. If you see any folks who wrote me, tell them I will thank them personally very soon.

While Tod and I were shopping on Christmas morning, getting together our dinner, we made a present to a little French girl and had a lot of fun. We took our chickens which we bought, live, into a butcher shop to get them dressed. The Madame had a cute little girl about four years old and so while the chickens were being dressed, Tod and I went out to the market and bought a doll and took it back in to her. She was tickled to death and the Madame and a nice young mademoiselle who was visiting her invited us to have a cup of coffee which invitation we accepted. You see we have our eyes out for these good-looking madamoselles.

Well, I can't think of another thing to write about.

With love from

Bob

Letter #35 written abroad and sent from the continent
Letter postmarked U.S. Army M.P.E.S., Jan. 10, 1919, 12 M
Envelope marked "Base Censor"
Received Jan. 30ᵗʰ 1919

Sunday Evening, Jan. 5, 1919
Connerre, France

Dear Folks,

"Beaucoup" mail the last week — as follows:

Father —	Dec 5
Mother —	" 8
Father —	" 9
" —	" 11
" —	" 12
" —	" 13
" —	" 13
" —	" 14
Edith —	" 11
Ed —	" 13
A.J. Parsons —	" 10 — Xmas card
Mr. and Mrs. Ralph Smith —	" 10 " "
Charlie Challice —	" 10 " "

forwarded by Mother

I received the oldest letter last and the latest, first. Rather mixed up. I don't know yet what the trouble is with Jim Nichols, but I'm sorry, whatever it is. And I never found out how Clarence Hotchkiss came out with his trouble.

Am mailing back my book of Christmas letters to you as I want to be sure of their getting home again for I value them very much and it is possible that we may have to turn our barrack bags back in again and come home with only our packs.

The pictures Mother sent me of the house and her in her letter of Dec. 8 are fine. You won't have to listen for the phone to ring and the postman to say there's a letter from me much longer for it looks now as if we would be starting for home "toute suit"—in fact I may beat this letter home. We expect to leave here for the port of embarkation this week Wednesday or Thursday.

I believe Ed Parsons' unit, the 51st Pioneers, is in the Army of Occupation altho I am not positive. You know it's a wonderful experience for a fellow if he goes into Germany—I kind of wish we had gone and yet—it's 50/50 for I want to come home "toute suit."

No, Father, I don't get a chance to get much reading material for it's all French around here and besides the war isn't over for me till I'm discharged—in other words—altho the fighting is over, there still remains drill, drill and reviews and inspections—honestly we've had so many inspections and reviews lately that I'm sick of them—company inspection, battalion reviews, regimental reviews, division reviews, corps reviews, all in anticipation and preparation for being mustered out, I expect. By the way, the 107th won the prize in a competition for the snappy and best conducted review and field inspection in the corps. It's awfully tiresome tho, to have to stand for 5 or 6 hours with a pack on and especially in the rain, a great deal of which we have had lately.

You judged correctly, Father, in that you figured Glisy is near Corbie. They are about five or six miles apart and our division H.Q. was at Corbie. I sometimes think you know more about our location and actions than I do.

Ede's letters were full of interesting things about her work and also she wrote she was losing a little weight which seems to tickle her immensely.

Ed wrote about his trip to Columbus to see Peg Harrington. Also that he was not sure whether he would be home for Christmas or not. Hope he made it.

Mr. and Mrs. A.J. Parsons and Mr. and Mrs. Ralph Smith sent me Xmas cards—also Mrs. Ralph is sending me "Life" for three months.

We get our December pay tomorrow. Hoorah!!!

Tod and I are enjoying our room and bed very much. It's a great treat.

Was on town (provost) guard New Years Day. Quite uneventful.

Am outfitted with a complete new uniform now. New uniform, new leggins, shoes and hat or rather cap.

You ask, Father, for my observations of country and people. It looks as tho we would be home so soon that I hope you'll pardon my asking if you will excuse me from writing about these things, and receive them by word of mouth very soon, instead.

Tod sends his best regards. It's 9:50 and the Madame is yawning, so I'll close.

See you soon. With love

Bob

Letter #35 included a copy of Bulletin No. 103, Headquarters 27th Division, dated October 21, 1918. The bulletin was a message from Major Gen. John F. O'Ryan, commanding officer of the 27th division. It is as follows:

BULLETIN)
No 103)

October 24, 1918.

Since the 25th of September — a period of nearly one month.— the division has been engaged almost continuously in fighting and marching. Some of this fighting involved a leading role in one of the fiercest battles of the war — the breaking of the great Hindenburg defense line. We have suffered the loss of some of our best officers and men, but unfortunately such losses are incidental to battles of such magnitude. Only divisions highly trained and disciplined, possessing the greatest confidence and morale and at the very top notch of their strength could have accomplished what this division and our comrades of the 30th accomplished in that great battle. Only such divisions could have met the sacrifices demanded, and with morale unimpaired have renewed the advance in the manner characterizing the operations of the past two weeks..

This is not the occasion to describe the Hindenburg defenses or the details of the battle for breaking them. That will doubtless be done after the war. The same comment applies to the details of the operations since that engagement. Nevertheless, the Division Commander cannot with-hold this expression of his admiration and respect for the valor and discipline as well as the endurance and spirit manifested by officers and men throughout this long period of fighting. These sentiments are stimulated by the events of the past week, when reduced in strength, the Division attacked the enemy, took the town of ST. SOUPLET, forced the crossing of the LE SELLE RIVER, and against strong opposition successfully assaulted the heights on the other side. Since that date the division has attacked daily taking by assault the town of ARBRE GUERNON and a number of strongly fortified farms and forcing a withdrawal of the enemy to the CANAL DE LA SAMBRE.

In this latter advance the division captured more than 1400 German officers and enlisted men, and a vast amount of military property including field guns, a great number of machine guns both light and heavy, anti-tank guns, trench mortars, dumps of ammunition and railroad rolling stock. In all this fighting the character of the enemy's resistance and the extent of his losses are indicated by the large number of enemy dead on the field.

The efforts of the past month constitute a record to be proud of, and their value is indicated in the commendatory letter from the Commanderin-Chief of the British Expeditionary Forces which has been published for the information of the division. Officers and men have justified the estimate made of the division, when after its arrival in France it was selected to hold the MT. KEMMEL sector against the expected great effort of the enemy to drive through to the sea. They have justified the opinions of their fighting qualities formed when that crisis, with the evacuation of MT. KEMMEL, had passed, and the division promptly attacked and took VIERSTAAT RIDGE, being, with the 30th Division on our left, the first American troops to fight on Belgian territory.

JOHN F. O'RYAN,
Major General.

Amiens, Imp. du Progrès.

Monday, Jan. 13, 1919
Connerre, France

Dear Folks,

It doesn't seem as tho a week has passed since I wrote you. Not a great deal has happened. Did I tell you that the Platoon was reorganized into new squads and that I am now in charge of the Reg'tal Message Center? I was in charge of a squad, doing squads right and left but now I am excused from all drill formations and just attend to the Message Center. Also I got permission from the Captain to sleep in a private house so I am enjoying a good bed. Tod and I are teaming up together.

We got our December pay yesterday after much delay. And it was American money except for a few francs. I don't know why we got U.S. money except that we must be booked to leave soon. We've got to go to the trouble of changing it into French money, now — at least some of it. When I was in London, someone stole my gas mask, helmet, bayonet and scabbard and sweater. As I had nothing to show for them (I didn't have time to get a notation of any kind as I didn't discover the loss till train time), out came $10 from my pay this month. "Ce ne fait rein."

We still have lots of rumors floating around that we will start for home soon and I still think it won't be long before we start, but nothing official has been given out so far. It's getting most tiresome to sit around just waiting. In last Friday's issue of the "Stars and Stripes" I saw a cartoon which is certainly quite to the point. A doughboy is sitting on a doorstep and at the top it reads "Waiting" — at the bottom "The hardest battle of the war."

The mails must have got stuck somewhere for we haven't had any for five or six days. I haven't had any since I wrote you last.

Today's "Daily Mail" should have some news of the first meeting of the Peace Conference, which will be of great interest, of course. I buy a "Daily Mail" and a Paris edition of either the "New York Herald" or the "Chicago Tribune," the Herald preferably, most every day and so keep in touch with what is going on. Can't get much other reading material except an occasional magazine or two such as American, Adventure or Literary Digest.

Absolutely nothing more to write about. With love from

Bob

Tuesday, Jan. 14

I had a "hunch" yesterday that we might get some mail last night. So I held this letter to see. We did. My share was eight letters and an armful of Presses and Republicans. In one of the latter I saw my name mentioned. Received a letter from Bill Hones, one from Joe Valentine, one from Frank and Ethel and five from you as follows:

Mother — Dec 15
Father —   "   16
    "   —   "   17
    "   —   "   18
    "   —   "   26

Mother acknowledges letters from London and Father in his Dec. 26 letter, mine from Rouen — on my return trip. The best news, as Father said, is that Ed arrived home for Christmas. Keep your uniform pressed up, Ed — I'll want to see how handsome you look when I get home. I surely did enjoy my Christmas book of letters — so much that I sent it home again to be sure to have it "après la guerre." Postage on it was "only" 7.85 francs.

It's wrong dope that the 27th is going to England to receive any decorations — just pure bunk — rumors. Glad Ede continues to enjoy her work. Frank and Ethel wrote a nice letter. Bill H. told of his doings and Joe V. wrote a fine letter telling about the business. I really get more information about the store from him than I do from you, Father. Tra-la-la, Father, so there!!

Must close. With love from

Bob

Letter #37 written abroad and sent from the continent
Letter received Feb. 4th 1919

Saturday, Jan. 18, 1919
Connerre, France

Dear Folks,

More mail since I wrote you last Monday — as follows —

    Mother — Dec. 22
    Father —   " 23
    Mother — " 29
    Father —   " 31
    Edith —   " 29
    Miss Hoag " 24 — Yonkers

I received the letters of the 29th and 31st before I did those of the earlier date. The mail seems all mixed up as usual. I received Father's letter of the 26th last week as I wrote you last Monday. It doesn't make the letters any less welcome, however.

We still await orders to move to the port of embarkation. And the rumors still fly. It looks now as tho we might move about Feb. 1st. It's enough to try the patience of Job — this everlasting, eternal waiting, waiting. One day our hopes are raised high, the next day they are dashed to the ground. If we don't move within a couple of months, I shall regret that the 27th wasn't included in the Army of Occupation, for I believe that the boys who are in Germany are seeing some worthwhile things, and having some valuable experiences.

Marsh Williams wrote me that he hoped I would be [home] by Christmas that I might meet his fiancée. Wish I could have, for more reasons than one.

So New & True coffee is now 32¢ wholesale — well of course that leads me to ask what you are selling Senate for? You may not realize how much I appreciate anything you write about business, Father, but now that I look forward to returning home soon, I am interested more than ever in anything you write.

I did not understand that we were entertained by the King in London. Due to the fact that we were attached to the British, we were afforded the privilege of a London leave, but now that we have been detached, no London leaves are given.

Father suggests I try for a week's leave to Paris. In the first place, it is impossible to get it. No leaves to Paris are given—that is, Paris is not a leave area for the American Army. When you go on leave, you go where they send you—not where you want to go. Of course there is a certain choice as there are at least a half dozen designated leave areas. Most of our boys go to the St. Malo leave area, near Nice, I believe. In the second place, I wouldn't ask for it, for I have had more than my share already. I had a furlough in the States, which many of the boys did not have, and I have had one leave over here already—to London—which, also, many of the men have not had. So I feel quite satisfied. If I didn't, I should. You mustn't forget, I'm still in the army. The old song runs—"You're in the army now, you're not behind the plow."

Sorry to hear of Porter Parsons' death. Hope Clarence Hotchkiss comes out all right.

Miss Hoag's letter was in answer to a postal I sent her from London. She wrote a very nice letter, enclosing a couple of clippings from NY papers, which gave great praise to the work of the 27th Division.

Edith wrote a most interesting letter about her Christmas Day. She was very busy and enjoyed her work immensely, she said. Received lots of nice presents. Also said she had been decorated for "gallantry in action." She was very much pleased with her "Croix de Guerre"—from Tiffany's and very handsome.

Last Wednesday night, Tod and I entertained Monsieur and Madame Cobin with a chicken supper—Grandmere, Madame's mother, was also present and Tod and I had a lot of fun. We bought two chickens at the market in the morning along with some lettuce and celery. Also got a can of peas. So we had quite a feed. French-fries, roast chicken, peas, celery, salad, bread and butter, coffee and cigars.

The Madame did the cooking besides furnishing the potatoes. We had planned to pay for everything, but the Madame refused to let us pay for what she did and furnished. By the way, I have learned to like salad with French dressing very much. I think I can vie with Ed now in the amount consumed as long as there is "par beaucoup d'huile" in it.

I haven't seen a match in a month except a few old-fashioned French sulphur matches. It is surprising to see how easily you can get along without them. I have a lighter for cigarettes and have to locate a stove when I want to light my pipe.

I just found out the other day that the Madame has a daughter aged 19 yrs. who is working in LaMans in a doctor's office and home. The Madame told me her daughter would be home in a few days — don't know for how long. Well, she arrived this afternoon and when I went up, I found "Monsieur" Ford "parlezing" — "Comment allez vous" and "Bon jour" etc. to her. She appears to be a very nice girl and this is one time when I find it most disconcerting not to be able to speak French fluently. Woe, me. However, I seem to have enough Jew blood in me so that I can carry on a limited conversation without saying much.

We had another review this past week and I think there's another next Monday. Fortunately, I don't have to stand any now as I am in charge of the Message Center.

General Pershing is in this area for several days stay and I expect we may see him here. Hope so, for I should like to catch a glimpse of the C. in C. of the A.E.F.

We are now directing nearly our entire energies toward the absolute extinction of the "toto" — as the French poilus call the cootie. They cling to a few of the fellows, yet mostly on account of the fact that until now, we never have had our blankets deloused. It is fairly easy to get rid of them by taking a hot bath and putting on clean underwear but if you go to bed at night in the same lousy old blankets, you're quite apt to have a few on you in the morning. We are taking extra care now as we expect an inspection by Embarkation Officers soon. If the regiment is in a good condition, we will entrain here and go direct to the port of embarkation.

Tod and I are feeling fine but naturally growing somewhat impa
tient at the delays. "Sacre" the delay.

When I started this letter, I thought it would be short, however
look it over—if you have a half hour of leisure.

Best regards to all my friends. Special best to Sally and Dorothy,
tell them. Love to all.

Corporal Robert Doan Truesdell (1212500)
Headquarters Company
Signal Platoon
107th U.S. Infantry
Amer. Forces
Corp. Truesdell
107 Message Center

Bob

1st ?—As this has been a great effort for me (ie—writing this novel-
ette)—if agreeable to you and the lieutenant, you might send it along
to Edie, the Red Cross Nurse, thereby saving me time, energy and
paper and still she would have the most complete news of my antics.
Yea, verily. Merci bien.

RDT

Letter #38 written abroad and sent from the continent
Envelope marked "Base Censor"
Received Feb. 17th 1919

Saturday, Jan. 25, 1919
Connerre, France
A.P.O. #748

Dear Folks,

Not much mail since I wrote you last Saturday—two letters as follows:

Father— Jan. 2
Mother— "   "

Sorry Father's eyes are bothering him. Hope he gets fixed up O.K. Wonder how I'll fare when I get home in regard to "civies," "mufti" or in other words, civilian clothes. So a suit costs $45 or $50, eh? How much for shirts, shoes, hats, etc? Think I'll try on my old clothes, if they're still around.

By the way, what's the matter with Ed? I haven't heard a word from him since he got home. For the love of Mike, slip me a letter, "Looey."

There certainly was quite a bunch of my old friends at Mrs. Williams' tea. I am very glad that Marsh's girl is so nice.

This week has been taken up mostly by a review by General Pershing and our Embarkation Inspection. Usually, we fellows like to duck every review and inspection we can, for it's the same old stuff over and over again, but this one, I wanted to go on. But as I am in charge of the Message Center, I had to stay behind. The C. in C.'s train arrived at Connerre station at 8 A.M. last Tuesday. On Wednesday P.M. the review of the eight regiments took place at the Belgium Camp about four kilometers the other side of LaMans. Some of the regiments had to hike it there, others were transported by auto trucks. Our third battalion had to hike, the rest of the regiment went by trucks. Tod left with the band on Monday night as they combined all the bands of the division for the review — the Massed Bands — the same as they had in the Camp Wadsworth concerts. He said the music was fine—in fact General Pershing remarked it was the best music he had heard in the A.E.F. The General inspected every company so all the boys had a look at him—sorry I couldn't go for I would like to have seen him. The weather was pretty cold but the sun shone. Well, I stayed back here. Tod came back Thursday.

On Thursday, the inspecting officer from the Embarkation Center arrived and inspected the company. Everything was O.K., I guess. It now looks as tho the division would begin to move about February seventh. I hope they don't postpone it again. This dope looks pretty good, but I'm getting most disgusted at all the rumors and postponements. When I see the Statue of Liberty, I'll <u>know</u> I'm near the States.

Tod and I are both feeling fine, and are enjoying our bed immensely. I got permission from the Captain to draw my rations from the mess sergeant so now we are eating at the Madame's house as well as sleeping. <u>No mess line for us</u>. It's almost too good to be true. We get along fine with the Madame, have a lot of fun and are learning just a bit of French. Wish we had a French-English grammar.

The only snow we have had was on Christmas Day and that was just a few flakes. The weather has been pretty warm and quite a lot of rain has fallen, but the past day or two has been pretty cool, in fact cold enough to freeze a half inch of ice, quite a change.

Today, this morning we are having the same old army-worn Saturday morning inspection. However I escape it on account of my job here. I sometimes think that I shall not be able to lose some of these army habits for some time after I get home. I've had over a year and a half of it now. I'll be falling in for mess, saluting everyone, looking for "cooties," etc.

As you will notice, I wrote the number of our Post Office at the head of this letter. It isn't necessary to put it on my letters—they are reaching me without it—but it would do no harm.

Received a lot of papers this week which were most welcome. By the way, when did Miss Ely take the place of Mrs. Bowers at the church?

Am watching the news of the Peace Conference with much interest. Try to get a paper every day, altho they sell out rapidly.

Will close with love from

Bob

Letter #39 written abroad and sent from the continent
Letter postmarked U.S. Army M.P.E.S., Feb. 3, 1919, 3 PM
Envelope marked "Base Censor"
Received Feb. 23rd 1919

Wed., Jan. 29, 1919
Connerre, (Sarthe) France

Dear Folks,

Just a year ago today, folks, I left Camp Wadsworth for an eight-day—or was it ten?—furlough home. And a year is a long time to be away from home. My best news to you one of these days will be that we have definite orders to move and I hope it won't be long. Things look encouraging but it will be ten days at least, I believe.

Everything is just about the same with both Tod and I. We are situated better than we ever have been, but the King's Palace in London wouldn't seem good to us as long as we are waiting to come home. We are both well.

Just after I had mailed my last Saturday letter to you, some mail arrived. My share was:

Mother—Jan 5
Ed— " 6
Father— " 6
" — " 8
" — " 10

Glad you liked the handkerchief, Mother. It was about time I heard from you, Ed, and don't rest on past performances, either—go right ahead and give me all the news often. I am always pleased to receive your letters. Oh, boy, that Binghamton Club writing-paper looked good. I was much interested to hear of Sgt. Jones' visit with Father. I'll sure be home for your birthday, Father. You didn't give me any particulars about what method you used when you sent the check to Tilley. Did you take it from my account as I asked? Please let me know about it.

Stock inventoried up pretty well, at that, didn't it? Hope to hear of more details soon.

Yes, Lt. Darling is at Tuffe which is about eight kilometers from here. The 1st and 2nd Battalions are billeted there.

You and the boys must have had an instructive and pleasant time in N.Y. at the convention.

Tod sends his best. Must close with love

Bob

Letter #40 written abroad and sent from the continent
Letter postmarked U.S. Army Postal Service, Feb. 8, 1919, 7 PM
Envelope marked "Passed by Base Censor" and signed "RH McIntyre"

Monday, Feb. 3, 1919
Connerre, France

Dear Folks,

No mail since that of a week ago yesterday, acknowledged in my letter of last Wednesday, the 29th of January. I was rather expecting to get some yesterday again, altho I have received your mail written up to Jan. 10th.

On the ninth of last month I wrote Marsh Williams a letter in answer to one I received from him in which he said he expected to be going up in the Army of Occupation. Yesterday my letter was returned to me marked "Return to writer"—and under an arrow pointing toward the address was written "Returned to U.S.A." I guess Marsh must have had the wrong dope. I hope they can soon write that on my mail, too. Well, Marsh deserves to get home for he has been over here for a year and a half, I think.

One manouver (?) (spelled incorrectly) this week to our credit and another inspection by the Chief of Staff, Embarkation Center, includes about all our activities for the week, other than our regular cut and dried duties.

We have had several light snowfalls the past week and the thermometer has been down to freezing. There is just about enough snow on the ground now to half cover it. Tod and I are very fortunate to have a warm place to sleep, for the billets are pretty cold for the men — they are mostly barns and without very good means of heating.

The latest rumors we hear now are that the 53rd Brigade starts moving the 6th and we follow soon after. The Division runner who was in this morning told us that [the] Division would move next Friday. It's a slow process, this getting back to the States but we're on our way, I know, by the appearance of things.

We expect to get paid in a few days, possibly Wednesday. Think of it, here we have been in this town for over two months and from our day of arrival, we have expected to start for home "tomorrow." It's been a waste of time. Last night I bought a French-English grammar and am looking it over some. Don't expect to accomplish much but will pick up a little. I tried to find someone in town who could speak English and who would give me some lessons in French but there aren't over two people in Connerre who can speak English, so there you are. If I had known on the start that we would be here for two months, I would have started studying sooner.

Tod and I are both well with the exception of slight colds, which seem to be quite prevalent among the fellows. It's the atmosphere, I think, for there's a good deal of moisture in the air, all the time. We're used to dry cold weather.

Well, it's just nine o'clock on Monday morning, the third of February. Oh, Lord, I wonder how many more Mondays we'll be hanging around this "dump." (Don't worry, my spirits will soon revive.)

My love to all of you.

Bob

Letter #41 written abroad and sent from the continent
Letter postmarked U.S. Army Postal Service, Feb. 12, 1919, 7 PM
Envelope marked "Passed as Censored" and signed "RH McIntyre"

Friday Evening, Feb. 7, 1919
Connerre, (Sarthe) France

Dear Folks,

Mail came in last Wednesday as follows:

Edith—	Jan, 13
Mother—	" "
Father—	" "
"Neudge"—	" 15
Father—	" 17
Mother—	" 19
Father—	" 20

Ede writes of her interesting work and also that Sid Farnsworth is home. She seems to be very busy. The picture of Helen Kellam and Reid jr., which Mother sent me was fine. Please give my kindest regards to Gladys McDane and best wishes for a speedy recovery. Of course, these will be a month late and probably she'll be all well by the time you get this, so on second thought, you better tell her I'm glad she's recovered so rapidly. (Tee-hee, Willie Jones.) Sorry to hear about Willie Banter breaking his arm. Hope he gets along O.K. — I'd like to have him along with all the boys at the convention. Have just received a bunch of papers and also am receiving "Life" regularly from Mrs. Agnes Weed Smith (Xmas present). I wrote and thanked her. Would you mind telling her I am receiving the copies each week and enjoy them very much? I have also read about Will Carver. He kept out of sight for quite a while, didn't he? To say that I am surprised is to put it mildly when I read in Father's letter that I received some votes for deacon in the church. It must have been a mistake. "Neudgey" wrote me a nice letter and I was very glad to hear from her.

I am sitting here at the Madame's table by the stove. She sits [on] the other side of the table darning socks and the "old man" is toasting his shins by the fire. Tod and I are both feeling O.K. and he sends his best to you. The only trouble with this place is the stone-floor. It's very cold on your feet. We are getting quite a little cold weather now. It is cold and clear tonight.

The Y.M. has changed locations here lately and we now have a much better and larger place, where we have movies and plenty of writing tables.

Well, we actually had our moving orders this week—to leave next Sunday—but, they were postponed. Honestly, I give up hope, almost. This everlasting, drawn-out waiting will drive us all "nutty"!! I don't know when we may leave, possibly in a week or so. I hope you continue to write, for letters were never more welcome than they are now.

Well, it's ten o'clock and I must turn in. Things worry along, the same way. Finis—news. With love from

Bob

The following letter is the last letter that Cpl. Truesdell wrote abroad.

Letter #42 written abroad and sent from the continent
Letter postmarked U.S. Army Postal Service, Feb. 21, 1919, 8 PM
Envelope marked "Passed as Censored" and signed "RH McIntyre"

Sunday A.M., Feb.16, 1919
Connerre

Dear Folks,

There doesn't seem to be a thing to write about to you today. Things run along in their accustomed course, each day our moving being postponed to the next. It is a most agreeable atmosphere to live in—we live in the future more than the present.

The 102nd Engineers and a detachment of officers from the Division were scheduled to leave on the Rochambeau tomorrow from LaHavre but that is postponed, I hear. The last I heard was that the first units of the division would start to move on the 18th, next Tuesday—but I suppose that will be postponed.

There is a great scarcity of reading material here. All we have is the "Daily Mail" and "New York Herald" Paris editions—no books or magazines and the time passes pretty slowly sometimes. I sent to Paris for a French grammar and am learning a little, but I really need an instructor to get all the conjugations etc. right. I get the pronunciation all right from the Madame and the Monsieur.

I got a little cold a couple of days ago and developed a cough but Madame has applied hot mustard plasters to my chest and I'm O.K. again.

I have two letters from Father received this past week dated Jan 23rd and Jan 25th. Not much news in either. Very sorry to hear of Henry's accident and hope both he and Dewitt are coming along O.K. Tod sends his regards.

With love from

Bob

The letter below refers to a letter written Sunday, March 23, 1919 from Camp Merritt. That letter is missing. The following letter is the last letter that, as a doughboy, Cpl. Truesdell wrote to his parents.

**Letter postmarked Brooklyn, N.Y., Upton Branch,
Mar. 28, 1919, 4 PM**

Camp Upton, N.Y.
Thursday A.M.
[Mar. 27, 1918]

Dear Folks,

I think my last letter to you was written Sunday. So I'll continue my tale from then on. Monday morning at eight-thirty we left Camp Merritt, hiked to Alpine Landing—about three miles—from there we took a ferry to 23rd Street and hiked up Fifth Avenue to the 7th Armory at 66th and Park Avenue. The new 7th NY Guard was out to welcome us and many civilians, too. Saw Tuttle and Bill Bloomer of the artillery but not to talk to them. We reached the Armory about 4 in the afternoon, threw off our packs and had a wash. Then I called up "Sam" Jenkins, went down to meet her and Vinton Stowell, and we had dinner together. Vint appears to be a very fine chap—I liked him very much. He has been sick with the "flu" so he didn't care about going to the theatre, but with his "kind permission," Sam accompanied me. We saw Ed Wynn in "Sometime" at the Casino. Sam is much interested in her work and told me quite a lot about it. I had a very pleasant evening with them. I went back to the Armory and slept as I figured it would be pretty hard to find a room at any of the hotels. Next morning—the day of the great parade—we were up at 5:30 making our packs and having our breakfasts. It was a beautiful day. We rode down to Houston Street on the 3rd Avenue "L," thank goodness we didn't have to walk down, and fell into our proper positions below Washington Square. It was eleven-thirty before we moved altho the head of the column moved off promptly, and we were not very far back. As I said, the

day was magnificent and, folks, you never have seen such a gigantic
crowd and decorations galore. I wish you could have seen it all without
the discomfort, but I would hate to have had you down here in those
tremendous crowds. There wouldn't have been anything left of you.
We couldn't march all the way up in platoon front—we had to break
up into [a] column of squads in order to get by, in a number of places.
The tops of the buildings and every window was crowded and the
noise was tremendous. It was wonderful but rather tiring as parades
usually are. I didn't see a person I knew altho I looked for "Sam" in
Sloanes and the Fords up near 70th St. We finished up near 116th Street
and took the "L" back down to the Armory. It was really a wonderful sight and something never to forget. Well, Tod was busy all this
time with his girl and so I busied myself with my friends as I figured
that "three is a crowd." I tried again to locate Pete Jenkins. I called
a friend of his at Flower Hospital and finally found that Pete was at
Hahnemann Hospital. So I proceeded to call him up at once. Somewhat
to my surprise I noticed that the address of the hospital was 67th and
Park Avenue and when I talked with Pete, I found he was right across
the street from me. So I ran over, stayed to dinner with him and then
we went down to see "Listen, Lester." Had a fine visit with him and it
was quite a coincident finding him so nearby. Early Wednesday morning we hiked down Park Avenue and to the 34th St. ferry where we
came across to Long Island City and took a train out here to Upton,
about two and a half hours ride. It is not nearly so pleasant a camp
as Merritt—don't expect it is supposed to be as it is a training camp,
proper, and Merritt is not. It is flat and sandy, like a desert and more
spread out—probably for drill purposes. Well, we won't have to be
here long, anyway. We (the 107th) are scheduled to get our discharges
a week from yesterday. Last night before we turned in, we had to sign
our discharges, turn in all ordnance property except our mess tins and
sign the payroll. So it's no more drill for [us].

I've changed my mind about going to see Marsh before I come
home, Father. I'm coming with the boys but I hope to get down and
see Marsh a couple of weeks later if I still have some money left. I

figured out that I would only save about five dollars by going to New Haven first and I believe I'd better come along home.

Someone told me that Roy Wilbur was in to see me at the Armory Tuesday. Sorry I wasn't there. I expect he must have come down to the parade of course—and I am wondering if he had a seat in any of the grandstands. If I had known there was someone coming, I would have sent my tickets home.

Tod and I are both O.K. Love to all.

Bob

At Camp Upton, the doughboys received their last army pay and discharge papers on April 2. Then they boarded trains back to New York where, "with final handshakes," they parted to return home.[48] Most of the men from Binghamton returned to their hometown together and then finally headed for home.[49]

Notes

1   Jacobson, *History of the 107th Infantry U.S.A.*, 61-63.

2   Seward, *Binghamton and Broome County, New York, A History*, 584-585.

3   Jacobson, *History of the 107th Infantry US.A.*, 63-64.

4   Matloff, *World War I: A Concise Military History of "The War to End All Wars" and The Road to the War*, 110.

5   Ibid., 112.

6   Persico, *Eleventh Month, Eleventh Day, Eleventh Hour*, 291.

7   Jacobson, *History of the 107th Infantry U.S.A.,* 64.

8   Persico, *Eleventh Month, Eleventh Day, Eleventh Hour*, 303.

9   Ibid., 304.

10   Van Ells, *America and WWI: A Traveler's Guide*, 57.

11   Keene, *World War I: The American Soldier Experience*, xiv.

12   Simkins, Jukes, and Hickey, *The First World War: The War to End All Wars*, 192.

13   O'Ryan, *The Story of the 27th Division*, 739.

14   Persico, *Eleventh Month, Eleventh Day, Eleventh Hour*, 307-308.

15   Keene, *World War I: The American Soldier Experience*, xv.

16   Simkins, Jukes, and Hickey, *The First World War: The War to End All Wars*, 193.

17   Jacobson, *History of the 107th Infantry U.S.A.*, 65.

18   Fussell, *The Great War and Modern Memory*, 64.

19   Ibid., 87.

20   Persico, *Eleventh Month, Eleventh Day, Eleventh Hour*, 361.

21   Jacobson, *History of the 107th Infantry U.S.A.*, 65.

22   Keene, *World War I: The American Soldier Experience*, xv.

23   MacMillan, *Paris 1919: Six Months That Changed the World*, 3.

24   Ibid., 15.

25   Ibid., 20.

26   Ibid.

27   Ibid., 63.

28   Ibid., 91.

29 Ibid., 95-96.

30 Jacobson, *History of the 107th Infantry U.S.A.*, 65-67.

31 Ibid., 67.

32 Ibid.

33 Hallas, *Doughboy War: The American Expeditionary Force in World War I*, 311.

34 Yorke, *The Trench: Life and Death on the Western Front 1914-1918*, 81.

35 Jacobson, *History of the 107th Infantry U.S.A.*, 68-9.

36 Ibid., photo caption opposite p. 56.

37 Ibid., 69.

38 Ibid., 70.

39 Harris, *Duty, Honor, Privilege: New York's Silk Stocking Regiment and the Breaking of the Hindenburg Line*, 334.

40 Jacobson, *History of the 107th Infantry U.S.A.*, 70.

41 In Cpl. Truesdell's hometown, the front page of the *Binghamton Press*, published on Wednesday, March 26, 1919, showed photographs of the parade: the 27th Division marching up Fifth Avenue lined by tremendous crowds; the 27th Division Headquarters Detachment, led by Capt. J. S. Wadsworth, approaching the Victory Arch on their way up Fifth Avenue; and the 27th Division starting up Fifth Avenue from Washington Square with the Washington Arch in the background.

42 Jacobson, *History of the 107th Infantry U.S.A.*, 71.

43 In *Lingo of No Man's Land: A World War I Slang Dictionary*, p. 8, Lorenzo Smith defines "blighty" as "the Briton's expression for home, England." It was also used for a wound which the soldier hoped for—a wound not permanently maiming but serious enough to get him sent back to England for treatment and recuperation. Soldiers apparently hoped for this kind of wound because it would get them out of the war.

44 Cpl. Truesdell again mentions his friend Tod. Since Tod is still in the hospital, it is possible that his illness is something more serious than swollen eyelids, perhaps some form of the influenza that was spreading quickly in the late fall.

45 Cpl. Truesdell's description of his visit to London sounds like he saw and did a great deal, but the visit probably would have been even more enjoyable if Bill Jude had also received a leave and been able to join him.

46 Cpl. Truesdell ends the letter with the idea that it seemed "almost too good to be true that we will be home around New Years." As it turned out, it was too good to be true. The soldiers of the 27th Division had a long wait ahead of them before they left France.

47 The article and photograph, shown at right, appeared in the *Binghamton Republican-Herald* on Thursday, November 28, 1918.

48 Jacobson, *History of the 107th Infantry U.S.A.*, 71.

49 Seward, *Binghamton and Broome County, New York, A History, Vol. I*, 585.

Serves with Old 'First' in France

CORP. ROBT. D. TRUESDELL.

The above photograph, taken in France, was forwarded to the corporal's father, Edwin S. Truesdell, arriving a few days ago with the word that the young man is now in a rest camp with his unit, the headquarters company of the 107th Infantry. Corporal Truesdell has written interesting letters concerning his experiences in France, extracts having been published in The Republican-Herald. He was with the former National Guard companies of this city when they went through their trying experiences on the Western Front. Mr. Truesdell is well known and extremely popular in the city and a host of friends are looking forward to his return with the other veterans of 'he did "First" soon after the holidays

EPILOGUE

Cpl. Truesdell was among the doughboys who not only survived the war but survived the war unscathed. Within his regiment, many were not so fortunate. The 107th Infantry Regiment total of those killed in action was 428. The number wounded was 1298 of whom 105 died of their wounds. In addition, 189 were gassed, 46 died of disease, and one drowned. The total number of 107th casualties was 1962.[1] Total casualties in the American Army, as of March 26, 1919, were 271,305, according to a short report in the *Binghamton Press* on that date.[2] Many, if not most, of those who died of disease had likely contracted influenza. In the A.E.F., of the more than two million Americans who served in France during World War I, about 116,000 soldiers died for the Allied cause, and, taking into account all the countries involved in the war, approximately 9,722,000 soldiers died through military action.[3]

Cpl. Truesdell was fortunate in another way. He knew he had employment at Newell and Truesdell Co. upon his return home. Veterans who would be looking for employment in Binghamton could take heart that "the employers of this city and vicinity are holding places for thousands of men who have been away...." Because the city anticipated a steady increase in the volume of business and manufacturing, employers were expecting to hire men "now beginning to stream back from camp and battlefield."[4] Bankers and lawyers were also ready to offer assistance to families of men who had been killed or who were otherwise on casualty lists. Services were to be offered without any compensation.[5]

Other ways that support was shown to Binghamton's doughboys included a new song called "Victory," with lyrics by Miss Fanny Lee McKinney and music by Miss Evelyn Jenkins Leighton, both local women. The song was scheduled to be performed at numerous organizational meetings and theaters by various choral ensembles.[6] In addition, pastors of local churches expected large turnouts at Thanksgiving Day services at which congregations would celebrate the newly won victory and hope for the early return of Binghamton's warriors.[7]

In the new year, Binghamton's citizens sought a return to the life they had enjoyed before the war. During the war years, train schedules had been reduced "as a measure of war time economy," but now, local businessmen wanted normal train service to be restored to increase business confidence and aid "in the return to peace time conditions of this locality." They were requesting the restoration of services on both the D. & H. railroad and the D., L. & W. railroad.[8] However, reminders of the war continued. On March 25, 1919, the *Binghamton Press* announced the names of 11 local men who had been killed in action, the date of their deaths, their place of burial, and the identification markings on their graves. Burial sites included Guillemont Farm, Bony, Tincourt, St. Souplet, and Montbrehain, all places in France where Binghamton men had fought.[9] Happier news was released the following day when the 27th Division announced the final discharge date of the 107th Infantry Regiment from Camp Upton: Wednesday, April 2, 1919.[10] That's the date when Cpl. Truesdell of the Signal Platoon of the Headquarters Company of the 107th Infantry Regiment of 27th Division would be going home.

While doughboys like Robert Truesdell began to re-enter civilian life, representatives of the various countries involved in the war continued to meet in Paris. After hundreds of formal and informal meetings, debates, arguments, and discussions that had begun in January, the peacemakers summoned the German delegation to a meeting on May 7, 1919, at the Trianon Palace Hotel in Versailles. There the Allies handed over the peace terms.[11] The treaty's various parts dealt with provisions including disarmament, demilitarization, Allied occupation of the Rhineland, loss of the Saar mines, loss of territory, and taking responsibility for its aggression (war guilt), which led to the establishment of reparations.[12] Back in Germany, political chaos became so widespread that the government had no leadership in the latter part of June, but the president, Friedrich Ebert, was urged to remain in office and finally managed to form a government on June 22 and to have a resolution accepting the terms passed in the National Assembly.[13]

The Treaty of Versailles, the most important of the treaties resulting from the Paris Peace Conference because it dealt with Germany, was duly signed in the Hall of Mirrors, setting of the proclamation of the German Empire in 1871. The treaty was signed on June 28, 1919, exactly five years after Franz Ferdinand and his wife had been assassinated in Sarajevo.[14] However, the U.S. Senate rejected the Versailles Treaty in November 1919 and again in March 1920; thus the peace treaty between the U.S. and Germany wasn't signed until August 25, 1921.[15]

The League of Nations, so important to President Wilson, was established by the Paris Peace Conference to be "an international organization designed to prevent wars through collective security and disarmament."[16] But despite Wilson's massive efforts, the United States did not join the League, and without the United States, the League of Nations was too weak to continue beyond the end of World War II.[17]

Robert Truesdell, who wrote so diligently to his parents and thus chronicled his experiences as a doughboy, returned to Binghamton, New York, and rejoined his family. His father, a highly regarded businessman in Binghamton, lived until 1939. Robert's beloved stepmother, whom he called Mother, died in 1938. He recalled how beautifully she played the piano when as a child he listened from his upstairs bedroom. His brother Ed returned to Binghamton, married, left a career in civil engineering, and ultimately joined the family wholesale grocery business. His sister Edith didn't marry until she was in her early 50s. She married a widower, Dr. E.R. Gillespie, a well-known dentist in Binghamton, and they enjoyed life together for more than 25 years.

Upon returning to Binghamton, Robert Truesdell resumed working at his father's company, Newell and Truesdell Co., Importers and

Wholesale Grocers. His entire career was at "New and True," where, after learning the various aspects of the business, he eventually became president of the company. Each year he got together with the men from Binghamton with whom he started his army service in 1917. They met for dinner on Armistice Day and no doubt talked about old times. A member of the American Legion, Mr. Truesdell was also active in business, civic, social service, and cultural arts circles in Binghamton, serving on several boards of directors. He studied voice for a number of years in a private studio and was tenor soloist for numerous performances of the Choral Society of the Triple Cities and also tenor soloist/section leader for 38 years in the choir of the First Presbyterian Church. He married in his mid-40s, and he and his wife, the former Adrienne Schmedel of Indianapolis, Indiana, had one daughter, Katherine Aline Truesdell.

In 1963, during a trip that Robert Truesdell and his wife made to England and France, they visited the home in Connerré, near LeMans, where he had been billeted after the Armistice before being shipped back to the United States in March 1919. The old French couple, who had been very good to him in those post-Armistice months and with whom he had corresponded for some years and to whom he had also sent checks from time to time, had died, but their son, who had served in the French army during World War I, lived in the family home at this point. Through correspondence in advance of the trip abroad, the son and his wife invited the Truesdells to visit them. With a hired car and chauffeur, who could act as interpreter, the journey from Paris was made, and the two couples met for the first and only time. One can only imagine the conversation between the two "old soldiers," who surely reminisced about the war years.

Robert Truesdell continued to live in Binghamton during his retirement years and died in 1973 at the age of 79.

Notes

1   Jacobson, *History of the 107th Infantry U.S.A.*, 146.

2   "Army Casualties Reported 271,305." *Binghamton Press,* 26 Mar. 1919: 23.

3   Hart, *The Great War: A Combat History of the First World War*, 468.

4   "Places are Held Open Here for Thousands of Workers Called into War Service." *Binghamton Republican-Herald,* 28 Nov. 1918: 3.

5   "Bankers Offer Services to Relatives of Boys Named in Casualties." *Binghamton Republican-Herald,* 28 Nov. 1918, 7.

6   "Victory Singers Render New Composition by Miss McKinney." *Binghamton Republican-Herald,* 28 Nov. 1918: 5.

7   "Real Spirit of Thanksgiving Is Evident in City." *Binghamton Republican-Herald,* 28 Nov. 1918: 7.

8   "Restore Normal Train Service." Editorial. *Binghamton Press,* 25 Mar. 1919: 6.

9   "Burial Places of 11 Co. H Men Announced." *Binghamton Press,* 25 Mar. 1919: 7.

10   "O'Ryan's Men Return to Camp for Discharges." *Binghamton Press,* 26 Mar. 1919: 20.

11   MacMillan, *Paris 1919: Six Months That Changed the World*, 463.

12   Meyer, *A World Undone: The Story of the Great War 1914-1918*, 710.

13   MacMillan, *Paris 1919: Six Months That Changed the World*, 473-474.

14   Ibid., 474.

15   Keene, *World War I: The American Soldier Experience*, xv.

16   Morgan, *The Concise History of World War I*, 121.

17   Ibid.

BIBLIOGRAPHY

Armstrong, Margery A. *Marblehead in World War I at Home and Overseas.* Charleston, SC: The History Press, 2011.

Audoin-Rouzeau, Stéphane and Annette Becker. *14-18: Understanding the Great War.* Trans. Catherine Temerson. New York: Hill and Wang, 2002.

Battlefields of France. The Northern and Eastern Railways of France, n.d.

Beatty, Jack. *The Lost History of 1914.* New York: Walker & Company, 2012.

Best, Nicholas. *The Greatest Day in History.* New York: BBS Public Affairs, 2008.

Binghamton Press, March 25, 1919.

Binghamton Press, March 26, 1919.

Binghamton Republican Herald, November 28, 1918.

Bonk, David. *St. Mihiel 1918.* Botley, Oxford: Osprey Publishing, 2011.

Bridger, Geoff. *The Great War Handbook: A Guide for Family Historians & Students of the Conflict.* Barnsley, South Yorkshire: Pen and Sword, 2013._

Bull, Stephen. *Trench: A History of Trench Warfare on the Western Front.* Oxford: Osprey Publishing, 2010.

Carroll, Andrew. *My Fellow Soldiers: General John Pershing and the Americans Who Helped Win the Great War.* New York: Penguin Press, 2017.

Carter, Miranda. *George, Nicholas and Wilhelm.* New York: Alfred A. Knopf, 2010.

Clark, Christopher. *The Sleepwalkers: How Europe Went to War in 1914.* New York: Harper Perennial, 2012.

Coffman, Edward M. *The War to End All Wars.* Madison: The University of Wisconsin Press, 1986.

Eisenhower, John S. D. *Yanks: The Epic Story of the American Army in World War I.* New York: The Free Press, 2001.

Englund, Peter. *The Beauty and the Sorrow: An Intimate History of the First World War.* Trans. Peter Graves. New York: Alfred A. Knopf, 2011.

Fitzpatrick, Kevin C. *World War I New York: A Guide to the City's Enduring Ties to the Great War.* Guilford, CT: Globe Pequot, 2017.

Fleming, Thomas. *The Illusion of Victory.* New York: Basic Books, 2003.

Fredericks, Pierce G. *The Great Adventure: America in the First World War.* New York: E.P. Dutton, 1960.

Fromkin, David. *A Peace to End All Peace*. New York: Henry Holt and Company, 1989.

Fussell, Paul. *The Great War and Modern Memory*. Oxford: Oxford University Press, 1975.

Gilbert, Martin. *Atlas of the First World War*. New York: Oxford University Press, 1994.

———. *The Routledge Atlas of the First World War*. New York: Routledge, 2008.

Grafton, Philippa, ed. *Defining Battles of the First World War*. Bournemouth, Dorset: Future Publishing Limited, 2018.

Grant, R. G. *World War I: The Definitive Visual History from Sarajevo to Versailles*. New York: DK Publishing, 2014.

Groom, Winston. *A Storm in Flanders: the Ypres Salient, 1914-1918*. New York: Atlantic Monthly Press, 2002.

Hallas, James H., ed. *Doughboy War: The American Expeditionary Force in WWI*. Mechanicsburg, PA: Stackpole Books, 2009.

Harris, Stephen L. *Duffy's War*. Washington, D.C.: Potomac Books, 2006.

———. *Duty, Honor, Privilege: New York's Silk Stocking Regiment and the Breaking of the Hindenburg Line*. Washington, D.C.: Brassey's, 2001.

Hart, Peter. *The Great War: A Combat History of the First World War*. Oxford: Oxford University Press, 2013.

——. *The Last Battle: Victory, Defeat, and the End of World War I*. Oxford: Oxford University Press, 2018.

——. *The Somme: The Darkest Hour on the Western Front*. New York: Pegasus Books, 2008.

History of Company "E", 107th Infantry, 54th Brigade, 27th Division U.S.A., (National Guard, New York), 1917-1919. New York: War Veterans' Association, 1920.

Hochschild, Adam. *To End All Wars: A Story of Loyalty and Rebellion, 1914-1918*. Boston: Houghton Mifflin Harcourt, 2011.

Holborn, Mark and Hilary Roberts. *The Great War: A Photographic Narrative*. New York: Alfred A. Knopf, 2013.

Holroyd, Jack. *Images of War: American Expeditionary Force: France 1917-1918.* Barnsley, South Yorkshire: Pen and Sword Military, 2012.

Holt, Tonie and Valmai. *Western Front—North*. Barnsley, South Yorkshire: Pen and Sword Military, 2014.

——. *Western Front—South*. Barnsley, South Yorkshire: Pen and Sword Military, 2005.

Jacobson, Gerald F. *History of the 107th Infantry U.S.A.* New York: Seventh Regiment Armory, 1920.

Jünger, Ernst. *Storm of Steel*. Trans. Michael Hoffman. New York: Penguin, 1961.

Keegan, John. *The First World War*. New York: Alfred A. Knopf, 1999.

Keene, Jennifer D. *World War I: The American Soldier Experience*.
    Lincoln: University of Nebraska Press, 2011.

Lacey, Jim. *Pershing*. New York: Palgrave Macmillan, 2008.

Lawson, Don. *The United States in World War I*. London: Abelard-
    Schuman, 1963.

Lebow, Richard Ned. *Archduke Franz Ferdinand Lives! A World Without
    World War I*. New York: Palgrave Macmillan, 2014.

Lengel, Edward G. "Meuse-Argonne." *American Heritage*. Summer 2010:
    31-39.

———. *To Conquer Hell: The Meuse-Argonne, 1918*. New York: Henry Holt,
    2008.

Lewis, Brenda and Rupert Matthews. *The Historical Atlas of the World at
    War*. New York: Chartwell, 2009.

Liddell Hart, B. H. *World War I*. Yardley, PA: Westholme, 1936.

Lloyd, Nick. *Hundred Days: The Campaign That Ended World War I*. Basic
    Books, 2014.

MacMillan, Margaret. *Paris 1919: Six Months That Changed the World*.
    New York: Random House Trade Paperbacks, 2003.

———. *The Road to 1914: The War That Ended Peace*. New York: Random
    House Trade Paperbacks, 2013.

Matloff, Maurice, ed. *A Concise Military History of "The War to End All
    Wars" and The Road to the War*. New York: David McKay Company,
    n.d.

Mead, Gary. *The Doughboys: America and the First World War*. New York: The Overlook Press, 2000.

Merriam Webster's Collegiate Dictionary. 10th ed. 1993.

Meyer, G. J. *A World Undone: The Story of the Great War 1914-1918*. New York: Bantam Dell, 2006.

Morgan, Pat. *The Concise History of World War I*. Woking, Surrey: Demand Media Limited, 2013.

Mosier, John. *The Myth of the Great War*. New York: Perennial, 2001.

Nelson, James Carl. *Five Lieutenants*. New York: St. Martin's Press, 2012.

O'Donnell, Patrick K. *The Unknowns*. New York: Atlantic Monthly Press, 2018.

O'Ryan, John F. *The Story of the 27th Division*. Vol. II. New York: Wynkoop Hallenbeck Crawford Co., 1921.

O'Ryan, Major General John F., Honorary Editor, Lt. Col. J. Leslie Kincaid, Directing Editor, Major Tristram Tupper, Editor. *The Gas Attack*. Homecoming Edition (a publication of the 27th Division). New York, March 1919.

Osborn, Patrick and Marc Romanych. *The Hindenburg Line*. Oxford: Osprey Publishing, 2016.

O'Shea, Stephen. *Back to the Front*. New York: Walker and Company, 1996.

Palmer, Alan. *The Salient: Ypres, 1914-1918*. London: Constable, 2007.

Palmer, Michael A. *The German Wars: A Concise History, 1859-1945*. Minneapolis: Zenith Press, 2010.

Paschall, Rod. *The Defeat of Imperial Germany 1917-1918*. Chapel Hill: Algonquin Books, 1989.

Paul, R. Eli. *The National WWI Museum and Memorial*. Marceline, MO: Donning Company Publishers, 2016.

Persico, Joseph E. *Eleventh Month, Eleventh Day, Eleventh Hour*. New York: Random House Trade Paperbacks, 2005.

Pitt, Barrie. *1918: The Last Act*. New York: W. W. Norton & Company, 1962.

Preston, Diana. *Lusitania: An Epic Tragedy*. New York: Bloomsbury, 2002.

Pritzker Military Museum & Library and Michael W. Robbins. *Lest We Forget: The Great War*. Chicago: Pritzker Military Museum & Library, 2018.

Remarque, Erich Maria. *All Quiet on the Western Front*. New York: Ballantine Books, 1985.

Roberts, Andrew. "Battle Scars." *Smithsonian,* July/August 2016: 56+.

Rubin, Richard. "In France, Artifacts of America's Role in World War I." *The New York Times*. 18 Sept. 2014: Travel.

——. "Where Americans Turned the Tide in World War I." *The New York Times*. 24 Oct. 2014: Travel.

———. "In France, Vestiges of the Great War's Bloody End." *The New York Times.* 24 Dec. 2014: Travel.

———. *The Last of the Doughboys: The Forgotten Generation and Their Forgotten War.* New York: Houghton Mifflin, 2013.

Seward, William Foote, ed. *Binghamton and Broome County, New York. A History. Vol. I.* New York and Chicago: Leurs Historial Publishing Company, Inc., 1924.

Schaeper, Thomas J. *Somewhere in France: The World War I Letters and Journal of Private Frederick A. Kittleman.* Albany, NY: Excelsior Editions, 2017.

Sheffield, Gary, ed. *War on the Western Front in the Trenches of World War I.* Botley, Oxford: Osprey Publishing, 2007.

Simkins, Peter, Geoffrey Jukes, and Micheal Hickey. *The First World War: The War to End All Wars.* Oxford: Osprey Publishing, 2003.

Smith, Lorenzo N. *Lingo of No Man's Land: A World War I Slang Dictionary.* London: The British Library, 2014.

Stallings, Laurence. *The Doughboys: The Story of the AEF, 1917-1918.* New York: Harper & Row, 1963.

Starlight, Alexander. *The Pictorial Record of the 27th Division.* New York: Harper and Brothers Publishers, 1919.

Stevens, Philip. *The Great War Explained.* Barnsley, South Yorkshire: Pen and Sword Military, 2014.

Stevenson, David. *1917: War, Peace, and Revolution.* Oxford: Oxford University Press, 2017.

Strachan, Hew. *The First World War.* New York: Penguin Books, 2003.

Stone, Norman. *World War One.* New York: Basic Books, 2009.

Todd, Col. Frederick P. and Maj. Kenneth C. Miller. *Pro Patria et Gloria.* Hartsdale, NY: Rampart House, 1956.

Tuchman, Barbara. *The Guns of August.* New York: Dell, 1962.

Van Ells, Mark D. *America and WWI: A Traveler's Guide.* Northampton, MA: Interlink Publishing Group, 2015.

Willmott, H. P. *World War I.* London: Dorling Kindersley Limited, 2009.

Woodward, David R. *The American Army and the First World War.* Cambridge: Cambridge University Press, 2014.

World War I: A Day-by-Day Chronology. Darien, CT: Ziga Media, 2013.

Yockelson, Mitchell A. *Borrowed Soldiers: Americans under British Command, 1918.* Norman: University of Oklahoma Press, 2008.

——. *Forty-Seven Days: How Pershing's Warriors Came of Age to Defeat the German Army in World War I.* New York: New American Library, 2016.

——. "Mom, the War's Going Great." *The New York Times.* 13 May 2018: Sunday Review.

Yorke, Trevor. *The Trench: Life and Death on the Western Front 1914-1918.* Newbury, Berkshire: Countryside Books, 2014.

INDEX